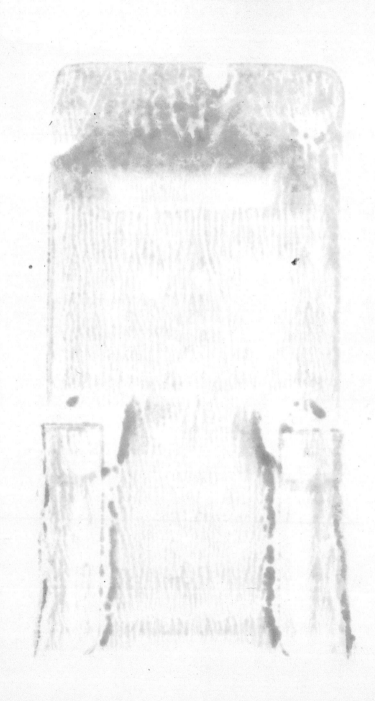

The Classical Drama
of the Orient

The Classical Drama of the Orient

HENRY W. WELLS

ASIA PUBLISHING HOUSE

BOMBAY . CALCUTTA . NEW DELHI . MADRAS
LUCKNOW . LONDON . NEW YORK

PJ
334
W4

PRINTED IN INDIA

By D. D. Karkaria at Leaders Press Private
Limited, Bombay and Published by P. S. Jayasinghe,
Asia Publishing House, Bombay 1.

To
Donald Richie

Prefatory Note

This book concludes an interpretation of the classical Asian drama commenced by my preceding volume, *The Classical Drama of India*. The object of these studies, considered collectively, is to describe basic similarities between the three great dramatic literatures, the Indian, Chinese, and Japanese, to examine their differences, and to consider their relevance to dramatic literature and theatrical practice of the present, both East and West. In this very considerable task, which I trust is a timely one, I have been profoundly indebted to too many friends and scholars to be mentioned here but I earnestly desire to express my gratitude for the assistance offered me by members of the relatively small community of scholars within these fields in the United States and also to friends from abroad. I wish in particular to mention a few of those who have either read my work in preliminary form or assisted in my researches : Dr. Kapila Vatsyayana of New Delhi, Professor H. H. A. Gowda of the University of Mysore and editor of *The Literary Half-Yearly*, Mr. Donald Richie of Tokyo, Professor J. I. Crump of the University of Michigan, Professors Ainslie T. Embree, Chih-Tsing Hsia and Royal W. Weiler of Columbia University. Finally, I wish also to make my grateful acknowledgment to *The Yearbook of Comparative and General Literature*, published by Indiana University, and to its editor, Professor Horst Frenz.

HENRY W. WELLS

February 1964

Contents

PART ONE

The Chinese Classical Drama

I / *Chinese Plays and their Translators*

CHINA HAS for centuries possessed a drama prized highly in its own land and comparatively neglected abroad. The West is thoroughly accustomed to the thought that good drama makes good literature, even the very best poetic literature, but also to the basically eccentric view that Chinese drama, regardless of its popularity and effectiveness in its own land, has comparatively small literary worth. This denigration is considerably more common in the West than in China itself, where the numerous editions of the plays indicate that they have, at least to some extent, been read as such and not regarded exclusively as prompting copies or cribs to the theatre. Performances of Chinese plays in other languages have been rare and when actually staged almost invariably seen in adaptations widely removed from the originals. There has thus been no more incentive for translations for use in the theatre than in the library. Whereas it is generally held that the Noh Plays of Japan and the formidable Sanskrit masterpieces are of marked literary merit, the Chinese drama has been more or less equated with the Kabuki and held to be exotic spectacle rather than drama, to represent, in other words, an art transferable neither to foreign words nor foreign stages. These views have been easily established and will be hard to eradicate. Yet especially insofar as literary merit is concerned, we seem at length to be learning that such sweeping opinions are injudicious. This book argues that whereas many of the plays are certainly undistinguished and many of the translations poor, several good and rewarding translations exist and that the field warmly invites a great deal more cultivation. Not

3

all translations into English will be mentioned but it is hoped
that enough will be discussed to give a useful analysis. The
translations are considered in terms of their merits as plays in
English and in terms of their fidelity to the spirit of their
originals, not as regards their literal or linguistic fidelity.
The theme lies in aesthetics, not in philology.

Why should there be translations ? To begin with, even a
cursory glance shows that Chinese plays have indirectly influenced the Western theatre to a much greater degree than
they have ornamented Western libraries. This has been so
from the beginning to the present. The first play to be translated into any Western language was *The Little Orphan of the
Family of Tchao,* rendered in an abridged form by the French
Jesuit, J. Prémare and included in a general history of China
edited and published by Du Halde in 1735. Two English
translations (1736 and 1741) of Du Halde's book contained
two anonymous versions of Prémare's translation. This play
provided the basis for Voltaire's *L'Orphelin de la Chine* (1755),
often celebrated as the first serious play to be presented on the
French stage in over a century without baroque costume and
with a compromise with historical decor. The Chinese play
was translated without abridgment by Stanislas Julien in
1834. It further inspired a sentimental English drama, *The
Chinese Orphan : an Historical Tragedy, Alter'd from a Specimen of Chinese Tragedy in Du Halde's History of China, Inter-
spers'd with Songs.* This was the work of William Hatchett
(London, 1741).

The regard for the spectacular set a precedent. In the
present century another play, *Intrigues of a Maid-Servant,*
was broadly adapted for English production by S. I. Hsiung,
under the title *Lady Precious Stream* (London, 1938). Thornton
Wilder, Bertolt Brecht and others of our times have been much
influenced by the Chinese stage. In all instances the theatrical
conventions, not the texts, have attracted the Westerners.
Intimate knowledge of the plays has escaped the general
public. It can safely be said that considerably less than a
hundred plays have been in any language translated or paraphrased and that in no case has a translation been widely
read. Although the books have not been easily procurable, the
explanation for this neglect lies even more in the outlooks of

possible readers than in any demerits of the plays themselves or even of their translators. Some translations are, indeed, conspicuously poor from every point of view but others, especially from the earliest and latest hands, have some merit as English works and can be read with considerable pleasure and assurance of their validity or at least as sincere and capable efforts in a task that should be eminently rewarding.

Although this chapter presents a roughly chronological view of the English translations, it is best prefaced by a few further summary comments on the Chinese plays themselves. For purposes of this study only the traditional Chinese theatre is considered. This restriction is practical because the Chinese theatre is for the most part one of the most profoundly and consistently traditional in the world. In China political revolutions have been much more frequent than theatrical. Although many types of plays and schools of theatrical music exist, all move, broadly speaking, to much the same effect. Conventions of the stage are the most obvious but those of playwriting are also binding. Thus Chinese drama calls for a narrative line drawn with a freedom close to that of fiction, blends naturalism with fantasy, insists on conventional morality, combines sung lyrics with chanted prose and speech, prefers pathos to tragedy and is in general clear in meaning and equable in spirit.

There is small doubt that the word "opera" frequently used in descriptions of the plays has assisted in our misconceptions of them. This encourages an unfounded inference that they exist primarily for the music and that their verbal element is subsidiary and inferior. In this regard almost all the Chinese theatre stands close to the Japanese Noh Plays, where an almost meticulous balance is maintained between poetry, instrumental music, singing, dancing and spectacle. No major element is sacrificed to another. Though some persons may at first be incredulous, this arrangement in no way prejudices the value of the words. Taste and imagination are sustained throughout.

That Chinese drama may in general be less poetic or at least less idealized than the Noh or the Sanskrit does not preclude considerable poetic and literary value. Highly aesthetic, it stands somewhere between pure poetry and a fiction that is frank entertainment. It is poetic in being throughout extremely artificial. Neither its moral nor emotional emphasis, any appearance to the contrary, weighs as heavily as might readily be supposed. The plays have the lightness of good Chinese food and the sophistication of the Chinese character. They obviously possess great value for the thoughtful historian, since they express the mind of the people with eloquence and breadth of reference. They vividly express both the Confucian and the Taoist philosophies. From the primary standpoint, the aesthetic, they are, naturally, of diverse value, some spirited and admirable, others, flat and commonplace. The theatrical style as a rule admittedly has more sophistication than the literary style. There have been more good companies than great playwrights. The always popular and frequently naive playwriting, arch and cultivated, paradoxically, as it often is, doubtless keeps the plays from the lofty heights of the masterpieces of Greek and English drama. Yet the total effect of many of the Chinese plays is deeply gratifying as art, as it is also happily unpretentious. Chinese art, more, perhaps, than that of any other people, can be classical without being pompous. The freedom from certain confinements of form common on the Western stage works to the special advantage of the Chinese plays today as the West itself moves farther and farther from its classical substructure. Although without the orchestral effects of the Sanskrit masterpieces, the Chinese plays have an even deeper humanity and more persuasive charm. The most widely admired of Japanese plays, Chikamatsu's *The Battles of Coxinga*, is virtually a Chinese heroic drama mulcted of several of its more poetic features. In neither poetry, essay nor fiction does China offer the world today a body of writing of higher potential worth. Such is the work to which translators have infrequently given their attention, often betraying inadequate skill and extreme amateurishness.

Regardless of the form of Chinese plays, whether verse or prose—and a play almost always moves freely between these media—at heart the writing is poetic. Too many artistic conventions are employed to have it otherwise. If not quite "the artifice of eternity," to quote Yeats, the Chinese drama is sufficiently poetic to be called the artifice of time. These conditions are written upon the surface and become the more impressive the more intimately they are examined. Comparisons between existing translations as well as theoretical considerations argue in favour of at least a considerable use of verse in translation. For the last hundred years approximately half the English translations have employed a very free verse in passages which in the original are couched in a strictly formal verse and, of course, have used prose for the prose passages. The earliest English translations are in formal prose, Augustan in spirit. This describes the two anonymous translations of *The Little Orphan of the Family of Tchao* and that of Thomas Percy, who rendered the same play (1762). These men and John Francis Davis, who rendered *An Heir in his Old Age* (1817), and *The Sorrows of Han* (1829), give the welcome impression of taking the Chinese playwrights more seriously than do their immediate English successors. The translators of *The Little Orphan of the Family of Tchao* see their original as an heroic drama, much as Voltaire apparently considered the French version by J. Prémare. Davis describes *The Sorrows of Han* as "a Chinese tragedy," and approaches his subject with a reverence that in turn begets the dignity of his own words. These versions reflect the neo-classical taste in England in the Augustan Age, for well across the border of the nineteenth century as Davis's work lies, it is essentially the product of a literary conservatism, of a hand trained in the formal schools of classical discipline. Neither the translators working in the eighteenth century nor John Francis Davis condescended to the Chinese, a point of view unhappily detectable in several of their successors. These serious-minded pioneers, the Marco Polos in English Orientalism, were impressed by the wonders of the new worlds they explored. Deeply a part of the traditions of the European Enlightenment, they went to the Chinese to learn, not to be entertained ; especially the Confucian emphasis upon conduct, morality and mankind's explicitly human condition appealed to them. They were cosmopolitans, with an equally sincere and pragmatic belief that all men are brothers. The disposition to find the Chinese quaint, foreign, or exotic entered Western thought with the Romantic Movement and with its subtle and insidious touch vitiated the translator's art and understanding. Yet it would be captious

7

to hold the first translations best. They omit considerable passages in their originals, being especially free with the Chinese passages in verse. They lacked the aids of more recent scholarship but they have a basic soundness of approach which later translators did ill to disregard. In some respects it would seem that the further we have advanced in knowledge of the letter of the Chinese, the farther we have diverged from its spirit. Still, Augustan smoothness and formality at times ill accord with the raciness of much in the Chinese plays. However ceremonious the Chinese may have been in daily life and above all on the stage, the gloss of Augustan decorum casts an unwelcome veneer over the surface of the Chinese words, sophisticated in their jade-like convolution, just as a high polish obscures the grain of fine, knotty wood.

The next translator, S. W. Williams, produced, in 1849, *The Compared Tunic,* basing his work on the French rendering by Bazin in his *Theatre chinois* (1838). This is a specimen of exceptionally fluent English prose, easy to speak and charged with considerable vitality. It is possibly the most fluent of all existing translations into English. Here again the translator makes us feel fully at home without gravely distorting the spirit of the Chinese or writing merely another English play. Even the plot puts a cultivated Westerner exceptionally at ease for it much resembles classical comedies based on recognition scenes in which stage devices are of importance. One of the closest parallels to Williams as translator is found in Donald Keene's versions of the "domestic tragedies" by Chikamatsu. Williams manages to be at once natural and artful. His original is more essentially poetic than Chikamatsu's "domestic" plays and his translation reflects this. Though without the gravity of the preceding translations, his work has a naturalness and charm at once convincing and beguiling. The play itself is not among the strongest but the translation follows a middle way that makes it appear one of the most attractive. It is a pity that it has not been reprinted in our own century.

The story of translations from Chinese drama neatly epitomizes the evolution of taste through three centuries. Taste in poetry reached what now appears to us to be a low-water-mark in the period epitomized by Tennyson and Longfellow, or, as might more accurately be said, in the second half of the nineteenth century. This condition is only too well reflected in the most unreadable of all English translations, three fine plays much abused by William Stanton. In a strenuous effort to make the plays poetic, he employs a diction and syntax known only to the pages of mid-Victorian verse. Whereas artifice in the Chinese theatre is always shrewdly calculated and significant, Stanton's excursions in style are literary affectations, reflecting the meretricious pseudo-elegance of a nouveau riche bourgeoisie. Dressing the downright Chinese words in Victorian plush, he can have created nothing but acute discomfort in the disembodied spirits of the old play-wrights. The pompous style is equally lacking in true dignity and validity. By stern exercise of the imagination the shrewd reader may possibly surmise the original values lying so well hidden beneath the entanglement of verbiage. But readers owe small gratitude to a translator so grotesquely unfitted for his task.

For over forty years following Stanton's dramatic mis-carriages only slight efforts and smatterings of scenes appeared in English. By the nineteen-thirties a revival of interest appears. First may be mentioned Ethel Van der Veer's ren-dering of *The Chalk Circle* (1933). That excellent dramatic romance, with its exceptionally well-delineated characters and unforgettable contrast between a corrupt and an honest judge, found a competent but not a brilliant English spokes-man. Her style admits troublesome archaisms : "It behooves us ;" "Let flow these rivulets of tears ;" in the midst of her agony the heroine speaks of her tormenters in the most un-emotional and stilted words : "Their sinewy arms rest not until I fall." Too often the words become flatly prosaic. A speaker dilates on "the facts appertaining to my case." (Othello's shade arises addressing the Venetian judges). On frequently encountering the un-English use of the participle, one imagines a sophomoric translation from Greek or Latin. So in a crucial passage we read : "Your husband being dead ;" "Death having taken my spouse ;" "Driven by natural per-versity." In such instances the style itself is indeed driven by unnatural perversity. For no visible reason, occasional out-croppings of biblical language occur. "It came to pass" that

9

the lady fell back upon the English scriptures. Biblical diction, of course, constitutes one of the rich resources of the English language, in certain instances useful to a translator, as in English versions of Sanskrit plays dealing with the sacred myths of the *Ramayana*. Much as the judgment of the righteous Pao-ch'eng resembles the decisions of Solomon, casual use of a biblical idiom in this translation becomes disturbing. And there are many clichés, as the phrase, "with crystalline purity."

Such quotations, to be sure, may in themselves give a distorted view of a rendering possessing at least some vigor. It shows the welcome advance in modern scholarship. But the translator may even err in an effort to give too full a rendering of the overtones or stylistic embellishments of her original. In this respect instructive contrasts are found when Van der Veer's translation is collated with that by Frances Hume, issued a score of years later.

This version, undated but issued in the nineteen-fifties, is offered as a translation from the French of the celebrated Chinese scholar, Stanislas Julien (1832). The English translator nevertheless on a few occasions utilizes a fresh examination of the Chinese. As English her version is livelier than Van der Veer's, even though it occasionally passes by a passage virtually untranslatable into a Western language. This is especially notable in the case of metaphors. Van der Veer in the prologue writes : "She knows the arts of writing and drawing, can play the flute most delicately and dance like the spirit of a white butterfly amongst the ethereal flowers of heaven." Frances Hume, who affects monosyllables, says only : "She can write, draw, dance, play the flute and she knows how to accompany herself while singing to the strains of a guitar." One translator prefers adjectives, the other verbs. The passage in the Van der Veer translation is obviously off key. To change the metaphor, it constitutes a purple passage. Whatever the Chinese play says, it is inconceivable that it presents the meaningless incongruities of Van der Veer's work.

Frances Hume's reliance on Stanislas Julien's version must partly account for her somewhat surprising stylistic conservatism, lending an oddly Augustan flavour to a comparatively recent publication. It is even a little difficult to realize the

Hume version as only a few years old, so strongly does it smack of the classic dignity of the first dramatic renderings from Chinese. Where the same passage is translated, the Hume version as a rule uses considerably fewer words. At its best it has masculine force and dramatic tang. It is generally dignified, rarely stilted. The verse and prose passages are at once distinguished from each other and harmonious with each other. The prose passages are less flatly colloquial, the verse passages less blighted by affected poeticisms than in the case of Van der Veer's. Frances Hume commands the surer ear for rhythm in both verse and prose. Her rendering has a somewhat austere, northern look. It is by no means inspired and its texture suffers from the condition of being twice removed from the Chinese. One might infer that its author had gone to school with Henry Fielding or Ben Jonson rather than with a master of the Yüan opera. Yet her version has competence and at least some measure of fidelity. The translator is wise in eschewing greater things than apparently lie in her capacity. Viewed in these terms, this constitutes a welcome and honest piece of work.

The Chalk Circle has exercised an influence on the Western theatre similar to that exercised in earlier years by *The Little Orphan of the Family of Tchao*. A very free rendering into German was made by Wollheim da Foncesca (Leipzig, 1876) and another version also taking considerable liberties with the original was made by Klabund (Berlin, 1925). Klabund's adaptation of the play was used in an English version by James Lavar in 1929, performed in London in 1929, 1931 and 1944. Bertolt Brecht's *Caucasian Chalk Circle*, essentially more Caucasian than Chinese, pays considerable deference to the Oriental stage practice but deliberately inverts much of the thought of the original and must be considered as a distinctly new work, in substance considerably further removed from the Chinese source than was the case with Voltaire's *L'Orphelin de la Chine*. A moral orthodoxy lies at the basis of all Chinese plays, as a moral heterodoxy lies at the basis of all of Brecht's.

In 1935 and 1936 respectively Yao Hsin-nung contributed to *The T'ien Hsia Monthly* able translations of *Madame Cassia* and *The Right to Kill*, the latter occasionally known as *A Fisherman Kills a Family*, *The Fisherman's Revenge*, and

The Lucky Pearl. The latter play, one of the raciest in the Chinese repertory, was at one time favored by the great Mei Lan-fang. Although a delight to read, its brisk lines read somewhat as a scenario and are clearly more distinguished for theatrical than literary values. These circumstances have made it one of the least embarrassing plays for its several translators. Two pairs of collaborators, Arlington and Acton and Yang Hsien-yi and Gladys Yang, have attempted it. These three versions are much alike and about equally successful. In the original many scenes are farce or extravaganza ; the leading motives, chiefly political, are perspicuous ; for a Chinese play, this is peculiarly lacking in nuance, philosophical depth or poetic sophistication. Yet it is eminently robust, human and artfully constructed and ˉsome of the verse passages show lively imagination. One is reminded of J. I. Crump's memorable observation that the closest Western analogy to the Yüan opera is in English *The Beggar's Opera*. There are better Chinese plays and their translators have risen to greater heights than in any versions of this, yet perhaps no Chinese play has been more adequately rendered or offers a readier opportunity for production on an English-speaking stage.

Madame Cassia is the title which Yao Hsin-nung gives to the play *Ch'i Shuang Hui*. Few translations of Chinese drama are as valuable to the English reader as this. As explained in his prefatory note, the translator was working not only from the book but from a theatrical experience which he has greatly enjoyed. His art conveys overtones in the text which would normally remain within the scope of the actors only. L. C. Arlington and Harold Acton's translation of the same play is much less illuminating. This is one of many Chinese dramas reaching a condition of high comedy, wholly escaping from the virtually inevitable offences against the aesthetic experience implicit in both satire and melodrama. The essence of the play lies in the humorous revelation of a discrepancy between what a character is imagined to think of himself and what social opinion, embodied in the audience, thinks of him. In *Madame Cassia* the angry jailor is a little foolish, the husband is exceedingly fatuous, the super-sensitive young wife a little absurd despite her wit, exhibited most of all when she suffers.

All are self-absorbed. Accordingly, there are at least two levels of meaning existing harmoniously. Pathos is reconciled with humor and humor with pathos. Although the audience is almost continuously laughing, it is also moved. The writing is much too sophisticated to be either sentimental or farcical. Hence high comedy. The reader of the Arlington and Acton version must work hard to detect in it these finer shades of humor so skillfuly captured in Yao Hsin-nung's more deft and pliant words. Besides, the latter, faced with what he is shrewd enough to recognize as an unusually grave problem, supplies a number of stage directions not in his Chinese text. Such insertions by an unskillful hand would be obtrusive. In this case they prove in good taste and possess quite extraordinary value. The extreme suppleness of Chinese humor has seldom been better revealed.

In the following year, 1936, appeared H. H. Hart's translation, *The West Chamber*. His version of this long work, especially in the earlier scenes, fails to escape a taint of the commonplace or of verbosity but as the dramatist's witty comment on the irrationality of the chief characters, a pair of young lovers, enhances both his humor and the emotional tension of his scenes, the translator fairly rises to the climax of one of China's dramatic masterpieces. Repeatedly the leisurely development in the earlier scenes of the novelistic type of Chinese play baffles translators, apparently impatient to arrive at the more high-pitched scenes in the later sections of the plays. In their movement the major Chinese plays are often closer to films than to Western drama, with its inheritance of the classical standard of compactness. Especially in Chinese and Sanskrit drama, the induction is likely to be long, artful, but relatively low-pitched, with more of charm than excitement. To one who is not himself a poet born, charm is more difficult to capture than force. Moreover, the Westerner must meet such playwriting as the Chinese half-way. The problem is not only one of language but of dramatic pace. Westerners are unaccustomed to plays as long as novels. To become at home with them, they do well to look for an element of lyric finality in the individual scenes, which these in the Chinese clearly possess. But this condition, in turn, places an even heavier burden on the translator's art, which must represent a lyrical drama not only with many sung passages but composed of scenes roughly comparable, shall we say, to Robert Browning's "Dramatic Lyrics", which are in reality lyrical dramas.

In the same year which saw the translation by H. H. Hart of *The West Chamber*, another translation appeared, that by S. I. Hsiung, contrasting with the former in some important respects. The most notable difference is that Hsiung's version contains the "Continuation," a series of four scenes carrying the story to a conventional happy ending. The earlier version merely assumes this solution of the plot ; the later brings it only too fatally before us. Scholars hold various views on the subject, though the general opinion is that the two Parts are by different hands and that the sequel is a materially later addition. Be this as it may, the sequel is even for a Chinese play almost shamelessly melodramatic. Part Two contains almost nothing of the wit or sophistication of poetry, psychology and character-delineation so conspicuous in Part One. The unfortunate suitor is a complete fool, a parody of aristocratic arrogance and a personification of stupid mendacity, who, on being roundly rejected, simply falls over dead. Surely, this is carrying the conventional happy ending too far ! It is a journeyman's work. In Oriental eyes the scene is doubtless the full consummation of the conventional conclusion, the absolute solution of the plot. One respects more highly the judgment of many Chinese scholars and producers themselves, who prefer to end the play as in the Hart translation. In some refinements, however, Hsiung's rendering may well be the better. Humor at the expense of monasticism and asceticism is much more in evidence in Hsiung's version of the play.

No single volume from the Chinese offers as broad or revealing a picture of the subject as L. C. Arlington and Harold Acton's *Famous Chinese Plays* (Peking, 1937). The book's flavor is largely explained by its genesis. It is one of the several fruits of years of playgoing in Peking by two sensitive and well-informed enthusiasts for the classical Chinese theatre. The book falls between a series of play-summaries aimed merely to acquaint theatre-goers with the stories of the plays and an anthology conscientiously compiled from the literary point of view. Nevertheless, it comes closer to the latter than to the former. Thirty-three plays are represented, all but nine with enough dialogue to constitute an English equivalent for the Chinese, theoretically, at least, inviting a production on a modern stage. Most of the plays are rendered from playbooks, a few are recorded by ear from the actual performances. Omissions are not fatally damaging and by no means invalidate the material that remains. The translators inspire confidence not only in their knowledge of the Chinese language but in their well-cultivated understanding of the spirit of the originals. The English is usually straightforward and at times vigorous. The work is much more valuable than a volume of synopses rather than translations, H. Y. Lowe's *Stories from Chinese Drama* (Peking, 1942).

The book's outstanding merit springs from the wide view and catholic taste of its makers. Almost all the chief types of Chinese drama are represented by Arlington and Acton : mythological plays, military plays, tragic or pathetic plays, romances, social comedies, dramatic satires and broad farces. It provides an inspring panorama. Within an equal space the view could not have been so extensive had a telescopic method in the translations not been used. This consideration should make the reader at least tolerant of the abridgments, which range from inconsiderable to drastic.

What the reader loses comes not so much from abridgment as from lack of attention to detail and above all from failure to convey the quality of the more emotional and more lyrical or poetic passages. It is to be remembered that the Chinese stage itself often produced scenes from plays or truncated versions. Except for a few incidental rhymes, the translations are entirely in prose, giving no conception of the several levels of presentation in the original or of the poetic elevation. We are actually in the vale of prose. Occasionally we are informed when a character passes from speaking to singing but the translation itself rarely reflects the change. In more tender or exalted passages the English at times becomes so inadequate as to be flat or positively banal. One receives an impression that the translators distrust the emotions. Thus the masculine harangues are handled admirably whereas the scenes of sentiment or pathos are likely to be extremely superficial. More than once the best that a tormented heroine can say is the deplorable cliché of the undergraduate translator from the classics : "Woe is me !" Woe indeed ! To conclude, in no book are the general intentions of Chinese drama so well disclosed. But the texture of the translations remains that most attractive to the translators themselves and very inadequately, if indeed at all, hints at the quality of a foreign literature or the refinements of a distinguished body of poetry in so many of its conventions and moods divergent from English literature. All the plays would appear to have been written by a single hand and that scarcely Chinese.

Although during the years immediately following Arlington and Acton's book there appeared in *The T'ein Hsia Monthly* a few translations of plays or scenes from the Chinese, for nearly two decades little or nothing introduced new elements into the picture. By far the most industrious translators since Arlington and Acton have been Yang Hsien-yi and Gladys Yang, who together have turned a dozen or more plays into English, published by The Foreign Language Press, Peking. Thus in 1955 appeared their translation of *The Palace of Eternal Youth*, in 1956, *The Fisherman's Revenge*, in 1957, *Fifteen Strings of Cash*, and *The White Snake*, and in 1958 a collection of eight plays by Kuan Han-ching : *Snow in Mid-summer, The Wife-Snatcher, The Butterfly Dream, Rescued by a Coquette, The Riverside Pavilion, The Jade Mirror-Stand, Lord Kuan Goes to the Feast*, and *The Death of the Winged-Tiger General*. These eight plays, though attributed to a single author, are of very unequal merit. Of this, more later. Also, *Fifteen Strings of Cash* has almost no pretensions to dramatic literature, being a naive story of detection of crime, addressed as low-grade melodrama to the most popular and superficially educated audience. It must be confessed that its translators render it as such. On the contrary, *The White Snake* is high-grade melodrama. The work has in recent times generally been presented as spectacle, with choreographic features uppermost. This treatment provides a fine specimen of dance-drama with its roots in folklore of universal significance and fascinating symbolism. The story, found over the length and breadth of the world, is best known in the West in Philos-tratus' *Life of Apollonius of Tyre*, and in John Keats' *Lamia*. A single spirit is incarnate successively as woman and snake. In its poetic symbolism the Chinese version possesses exceptional force and beauty. The myth, conceived from the masculine point of view, discovers in woman both a natural foe and ultimately life's sustaining and redeeming force. In the dramatic version of the myth the ideas are admirably worked out, especially with the introduction of a monk who embodies asceticism. The Chinese myth is far more profound than Keats' intellectualized allegory wherein reason demonstrates the beauty that is art to be the serpent of venomous illusion. The advantage is all with the Chinese. But as masters of the English tongue and of those aspects of poetry existing only through the medium of speech, Keats is incomparably more the artist than the recent collaborators in dramatic translation. Their words seem almost deliberately prosaic, the merest parody of the beauty of poetry or the eloquence of prose. Such dilution of the English language commits palpable offense against the myth's undying dignity. But for all this, the force of the symbolism shines through the dense veil of words.

Unquestionably the translators found more substantial literary material to deal with in *The Palace of Eternal Youth* than in the Mei Lan-fang scenario for *The White Snake*. The former is substantially a novel done in dramatic form, much as *The West Chamber*, so ably rendered into English by H. H. Hart and S. I. Hsiung. Chinese plays may be of any length, both very long and very short, and frequently a long play is known best not in its entirety but as short plays produced on different occasions and seldom in their right sequence. *The Palace of Eternal Youth* falls readily into several segments. The translators present it as a series of forty-nine scenes with prologue and epilogue. Their translations, like the scenes, are of unequal merit. In contradistinction with Arlington and Acton, the Yangs are comparatively weak in the more naturalistic passages and stronger in the more poetic. Here the love between the Emperor and his concubine is told in a style scarcely above prosaic commonplace. The poetry of the translation spreads its wings only in the Second Part, where the Emperor and others revere the relics of the departed martyr to love and where she herself materializes sufficiently to rejoin the Emperor in his dying vision and draw him back with her to their final union in the skies. These miracles are

effected with the aid of the most potent Chinese deities, the
Cowherd and the Spinning Maid, who meet once a year in
heaven after crossing the stream which we call the Milky
Way, lifted on the backs of birds. These starry deities much
enhance the dramatic legend. Its symbolism is aided by
images from art and magic. To unite the lovers aid is needed
from music and dance, especially the magic dance and song of
The Rainbow Garment Dance, or Mid-Autumn Festival.
(This, incidentally, is the root of one of the most justly celebrated of the Noh Plays, *Hagoromo*). Help is further received
from an aged minstrel, a necromancer, and the Goddess of the
Moon. The minstrel has made a rough notation of the dance-
music composed and first sung by the heroine, a minor deity
who assumed earthly form. Both the Emperor and his mistress
are part human and part divine, though her divinity is more
native to her own being than his divine property as monarch is
to him. There is much involved and moving symbolism here.
Far more than in their English play on the snake-woman, the
translators respond to the compelling force of this symbolism.
They were also working with a direct source much more
mature poetically. But they must themselves be credited with
rising to the height of their inspiring "argument" with at least
some success. The first half of the Yang play carries itself
along only as theatre. It has small literary merits. The second
half never sinks to banality and at times ascends to some
stylistic elevation. In Chinese drama are many such myths to
inspire future translators, conceivably better equipped than the
Yangs to appreciate them and clothe them in English words.

Earlier mention has been made of *The Fisherman's Revenge*,
successfully translated at least twice before the Yang work.
Inasmuch as the earlier versions were out of print and the
Yang play is by no means inferior to them, its appearance has
been a welcome gain. This spirited drama at least carries
itself without aid of peculiar literary refinements; the task of a
passable translation is relatively simple and also rewarding.
The translators have further rendered the Yüan drama,
A Slave to Money (in *Chinese Literature*, September, 1962,
pp. 53-92). The didactic element is uppermost. The rendering
is exceptionally smooth, perhaps indicating that considerable
experience has increased the facility of the translators.

The collection of eight plays, as previously observed, has serious inequalities. There is a sorry lack of imaginative phrasing. The style in the original may occasionally be plain but it can hardly be mean. Such is, unfortunately, the case in the following sentences : "Since I was a child I read a good deal, but I haven't yet taken the examinations". "It's an old woman, dad, nearly strangled to death". "If not for you and this young man, it would have been all up with me." "Wretchedness makes me weep, grief makes me frown." "You must think this over again. Take a grip on yourself, old man ! Don't give up so easily." "There was nothing wrong with the soup." All these are found in the first of the eight plays, which, its treatment of common life to the contrary, is certainly intended to be a serious work for which such threadbare diction falls amiss. In the second play we read : "I can't let him get away with that." "Lu Chai-lang was asking to be killed." A character in another play is repeatedly called "Aunty," giving a misplaced effect of low comedy. Where rhyme is used, words are dragged in to make the rhyme :

> A lonely, mountain in the rain,
> A mountain in the *snow*,
> Although they seem such simple things
> Are hard to paint, you *know*.

Occasionally the diction even approaches vulgarity, as in the phrase, "beauty spots." The style lacks focus. It rarely becomes succinct, often grows verbose. Some of the phrases just quoted might, to be sure, legitimately appear in the theatre of Bertolt Brecht—that is, conceding that his theatre is legitimate—but they are inconsistent with the intentions of the Chinese plays. The Yangs may further be criticised adversely for the intitial choice of their plays. One might have hoped that many Chinese works would have found their way into English before *Rescued by a Coquette*, with its vapid humor, at least to judge by the Yang version. Although some sophisticated humor occurs in the scenes depicting the aging lover in *The Jade Mirror-Stand*, clichés of romantic courtship have in English seldom been more brazenly flaunted. Finally, Acts Two to Four of *The Riverside Pavilion* are slight in any form.

19

Their deficiencies notwithstanding, the translations have merits and at times convey an impression of good theatre and even of superior playwriting. It is the middle ground of the Chinese bourgeois tragi-comedy that betrays the Yangs. They can rise to at least a perceptible poetic level, as witnessed in the second half of *The Palace of Eternal Youth*, and in the two slashing military dramas with which their selections from the works of Kuan Han-ching conclude. The second play in the book, *The Wife-Snatcher*, is light work of typical Chinese ingenuity, box fitted within box. Parents witness the eventful destiny of a loyal pair of young lovers. Artificiality becomes almost as marked as in Shakespeare's *Comedy of Errors*. Indeed, on this evidence it is easy to believe that some remote contact with Hellenistic or early Latin comedy had actually been established in China, much as Alexandrean drama unquestionably influenced *The Little Clay Cart*. The play calls for a fairly crisp, light dialogue, in good humor, which the Yangs provide. So one lays down their books with qualified feelings : gratitude that they have ventured so far and shown some appreciation of certain remarkable old plays but sadness that they have diluted and misrepresented so much that they have taken up and that they at times sink into such downright prosaicality. Earlier translators had more assurance, while at least one still more recent comer has far greater talent to show us wherein the power and charm of the typical Chinese play resides.

J. I. Crump's rendering of *Li K'uei Carries Thorns (Occasional Papers,* University of Michigan, 1962) is to the English reader a revelation of the unique quality of the Chinese stage. This is the more notable since the play itself is hardly one of the strongest of Chinese dramas. Yet all other Chinese plays in translation seem almost remote in comparison. Here is a translation that indicates the subtler aims of the old playwrights, what levels of language they employ and to what purpose. Here at last it is possible to discover through translation how inspired is the organic form of a classical Chinese play. Through superior grasp of the dramatist's technique he arrives at a correspondingly fuller appreciation of its spirit. He not only enjoys the story and the characters, as Arlington and Acton, Davis, and Williams undoubtedly did. He reveals the shading of the poetry and the structural scheme sustaining it. He does not pretend to give all that lies in the original, for he is too good a scholar to think that possible in any translation from any language, least of all from the Chinese. But by immersing himself devotedly in his original, he emerges with a version of poetic distinction.

It should by all means be noted that distinction on the part of a translator from Chinese is possibly more imperative where poetry and poetic drama are in question than is the case with almost any other language. Most imaginative Chinese writing appears at least externally to deal with the commonplaces of human nature and to deal with them with a pronounced directness of approach. A few basic situations have long precedent and are repeated interminably from play to play and poem to poem. An English rendering from Chinese of either a lyric or a dramatic poem is all too likely to seem commonplace where verbal nuance is not in evidence. Poem will repeat poem and play play unless the style itself has imaginative power. Little can be so dull or prosaic as a dull translation from Chinese, little so deeply and universally rewarding as a good one.

Although no single play can possibly represent the scope of the traditional Chinese theatre, so consistent are its general practices for a matter of centuries that a play of medieval origin exhibits a basic technique maintained in plays serious or light, in North or South China, virtually to the present time. The bold conjunction of song and speech, verse and prose, tragedy and comedy, symbolism and naturalism, remains constant. The established characters have been long-lived ; the scholarly lover, the noble bandit, the intriguing general, the wicked step-mother, the doting parent, the devoted child, the long-suffering heroine, the faithful servant, the cruel jailor, the clownish braggart and many others have changed remarkably little from century to century. Chinese drama persists as a singularly definite art-form. The culture itself has changed remarkably little. Hence the translator's solutions of his problems in one play, broadly speaking, hold good for virtually all. One accordingly turns to Crump's work with special interest, since he has clearly mastered the chief problems of rendering Chinese plays into English more fully than anyone thus far.

To begin with, wholly free from condescension, he regards the play seriously as poetry and as literature. He uses a comparatively large English vocabulary, preferring strong, colorful and figurative words, with metaphorical overtones. For the prose passages he employs for the most part a racy, colloquial idiom ; for the verse and lyrical passages, a considerably more imaginative and compacted style. Earlier translators dabbled in this method but none followed it with anything like Crump's consistency. He is first to distinguish between the sung, the "recited," and the spoken passages. Although his translation is nowhere distorted through efforts to suggest the basic sound-patterns of the Chinese, pains are taken to give something of the musical quality of the original. Rhymes, for example, are judiciously, though sparsely, used and an exceptionally large number of verse-forms employed, thus contrasting strongly with conventional English blank verse. No traces of stilted diction or antique finish can be found. The reader is aware that Crump's work does not resemble closely any English poem or play yet nowhere offends the spirit of the English tongue. The translator's outstanding quality is resourcefulness. He provides a dance of words, with rapid turns on every page.

This conjunction of admirable qualities may best be seen in the passage spoken by the hero, Li K'uei, on his first entrance. This is a soliloquy. Neatly as it serves its purpose by defining the character and sending the play merrily on its way, it constitutes virtually a poem in itself, after the manner of one of Browning's portraits in verse. Hence it lends itself well to quotation and requires little introduction. The outstanding feature is the sharp and dramatic contrast between the layers on which it is built up. It is a very fair representation both of the play itself and of Crump's artistry. It would take quotations from many briefer passages to add up to the clear impression given by this largely self-contained soliloquy. And no lesser fragment could show the all-important structural features so clearly.

"Drinking without getting drunk is worse than being sober. I am Li K'uei from Liang-shan P'o. Because of my dark skin men call me the Black Whirlwind. Brother Sung

Chiang has given us three days leave to enjoy ourselves and 'dance among the sprouts,' so of course I had to come down from the mountain to buy a few pots of old Wang Lin and get rotten drunk.

(*sings*) The spirit of drink is hard to lay,
And laid, the intemperate ghost rises again.
Seeking wine in the village I asked of Wang Lin—
(*speaks*) Said I to him can you find me some wine ?
But that rascal said nothing, only made a bee line from my hand. So I yelled to him, whoa !
· And I chased him and grabbed him so he couldn't go.
I lifted my hand just to tap him a bit,
then he splits his whiskers yelling, 'Daddy, don't hit !'
(*sings*) Said Wang Liu, they have some over there.
But this is the time of Ch'ing-ming.
The wind and rain are sadly tender with the flowers.
The soft breeze gently rises,
At evening the showers cease.
Yonder, half hid in willows, lies the tavern.
From the bright blaze of peach blossoms peeks
The fisherman's little boat. Blending with
Ripples in the green waters of spring,
Migrant swallows fly to and fro,
Sand gulls wheel far and near.
(*speaks*) Who says we have no scenery at Liang-shan P'o ?
I'll knock his teeth out.
(*sings*) For there green mountains stand in cloud-locked beauty,
And willow islands lie caught in nets of mists.
(*speaks*) There's a golden oriole peck, peck, pecking at a blossom on the peach tree and the petals are falling into the water. They're beautiful ! Where did I hear something of that sort ? Let me think —ah, it was brother Wu Hsueh-chiu who said it.
(*sings*) Light, impudent blossoms chasing the water's flow.

23

(*speaks*) Let me pick up a petal and look at it. How red it is !

(*laughing*) And how black the finger !

(*sings*) But how its make-up glows through a coat of white powder !

(*speaks*) Ah, I take pity on you, little petal, and toss you back to join the others. And I'll follow you, chase you, eager to run after blossoms.

(*sings*) And so I reach the shop at Meadowbridge hard by Willowford.

(*speaks*) This won't do ! I'll disobey Sung Chiang's orders. I'd better go back.

(*sings*) I want not to drink, but the waving of the wineshop flag has made my steps waver.
How it dances in the east wind atop its springy staff !

(*speaks*) Wang Liu, have you any wine ? And it won't be on the house, either. Look, gold chips, they're yours if you'll bring me a drink.''

In one respect this play lends itself more readily than most to the treatment that Crump accords it. The sorriest pitfalls for poetic diction are the clichés of romantic sentimentality and to these *Li K'uei Carries Thorns* offers scant temptation. The nearest passages to tenderness are the laments of the father for his stolen daughter. But the entire play is keyed to bravado and extravaganza. Its hero, as in a Noh Play, sets the dominant tone. This is neither downright farce nor senti-mental romance, the mock-heroic of burlesque nor the graver tone of tragi-comedy. Its particular bravura, peculiar to the East, has few even remote analogies in the West. One is suggested by the translator himself, who finds the Yüan opera in some ways parallel to John Gay's *The Beggar's Opera*. The latter is neither precisely farce nor satire, burlesque nor opera, light nor heavy. Like the Yüan opera, it combines in almost breathless succession song and speech, dance and naturalistic word and action. Another touchstone for its spirit might be Gay's delectable ''Ballad of Blackeyed Susan,'' one of the most archly witty of English lyrical poems. But by and large the Yüan opera is clearly more serious emotionally than Gay's intellectual spoofing. Its roots lie not in the cool-headed and sober calculations of an underground plot concocted by Chinese equivalents of John Gay, Jonathan Swift and Alexander Pope but in the mysteriously complex and eclectic world of myth and folklore. Especially in spirit, yet even in point of form as well, the most revealing English parallels are afforded by the lyrical dramas of William Butler Yeats.

There are some curious likenesses here that may or may not be held merely fortuitous. Wagers on severed heads strew the world of folklore and the poetry inspired by it as that medieval masterpiece, *Sir Gawain and the Green Knight*. The notion fascinated Yeats, all the more, perhaps, through his casual acquaintance with the Japanese stage. It is a prominent theme in *Li K'uei Carries Thorns*. The likeness between the author of "Lapis Lazuli" and the Yüan dramatist, however, goes much deeper than this, as Crump's translation shows. Yeats' Irish irrationality and resilience, his Dionysian freedom and exuberance, are scarcely to be matched save in such a Chinese play. Also, Yeats' conjunction of scrupulous aesthetic form with riotous fancy fully agrees with the Oriental work. Yeats' robust temper, impetuous gestures, large and highly figurative vocabulary and linguistic gusto suggest the vitality of Crump's translation. More clearly than any other English poet, Yeats shows the road by which English translators of Oriental plays may grope their difficult way to artistic ful-fillment. At the present time Crump's work is the latest and by far the best in the field of Chinese drama translations. It indicates an auspicious path which, it is to be earnestly hoped, he and others will follow with increasing rewards. It possesses the quality which, as Emily Dickinson declares, above all others defines any work of art—vitality. This distinguishes poetry from verse and Crump's translation of Chinese drama from virtually all others. Obviously, it is far rarer in translated verse than in fully creative verse. But the translator can possess it, as this work demonstrates. This quality alone can effectively redeem Chinese poetry and drama from an erroneous charge of the commonplace and the prosaic.

2 / *Narratives of Eros*

THE WORLD of Eros and his sea-born mother whose origin is celebrated with such magnificence by Botticelli is less pervasive a theme in Chinese art, poetry and drama than in Europe or even in the other great lands of the East. In China the family and the generations of men signify relatively more than the emotional life that clings to the meaning of generation itself. Nevertheless, mankind from land to land differs less than any superficial estimate supposes. The love-theme has seldom been more eloquently developed than in the minority of Chinese poems and plays devoted to it. Although the greater number of memorable pieces and of those selected as significant and representative for these studies dwell primarily on the values of the family, two of the longest and most famous plays are pre-eminently devoted to the love-theme. Outstanding works of dramatic poetry, they have special interest because of their narrative presentation, symbolical technique, and the texture of their style. They stand also in sharp and revealing contrast to each other. A general view of them offers a convenient introduction to the entire field of Chinese dramatic poetry. The love-theme will again become dominant only in the final chapter of these studies when, instead of being treated for itself, seen through the medium of a singularly entrancing myth the subject will be not so much love itself as the cosmic contention between sexual love and its opposite, not hate but asceticism—the conflict, in other words, between Eros and Anteros. The disposition to present love as a story of lovers, in form of a compelling narrative, proves one of the most striking features of dramatic writing in this domain.

Love becomes a story, an adventure, as, in Western terms, in the instance of Romeo and Juliet.

Chinese classical dramatists, being story-tellers of exceptional skill, no matter what may be their subject, possess an uncommon facility for projecting the spirit of narrative fiction onto the stage. To consider their methods from another angle, in their hands a story alters less in becoming a play than is generally the corresponding usage in the West. In some respects dramatic technique in Asia is more specialized than in the West, but as regards the story of the play the opposite proves the case. Western dramatic theory and practice presume a paring away of the material to meet the peculiar exigencies of the stage. As a rule Western plays are of well established and restricted dimensions in time. A Greek play is roughly 2,000 lines, an Elizabethan play, approximately twice this length. In Europe, the action of the play is likely to be enclosed or fenced in within a well-defined period of time, much as its scene is enclosed within a proscenium arch. But in the Chinese theatre freedom everywhere allowed to fiction prevails. Even Sanskrit and Japanese dramas are confined by more conventional limits. Although Chinese plays are given with the rigid prescriptions as to their style of acting and even their types of characters, no such prescriptions apply to their narrative. They almost invariably tell a story which may, from the Western point of view, be exceptionally long or short. It is true that the Chinese theatre in practice often appears episodic. In the case of long sagas on a single hero, the individual plays may well start *in medias res*. At least in recent times a day's program may also consist of scenes from plays rather than plays given in their entirety. This may well be a modern innovation, a blemish on the higher standards of the theatrical art and a regrettable concession to the actor's skill at the expense of the playwright's. Even in these cases, probably exceptions in the broad historical view of the art in China, the passages selected for presentation almost always have narrative value and come to well rounded conclusions. It is a good short story that comprises as well a part in a long story. Skill in narration is omnipresent.

The fluid or expansive character of the Chinese stage brings its aesthetics into alignment with the film as well as with

27

fiction. This likeness has considerable significance. From an historical point of view the film is the least "classical" of Western presentational arts. From the standpoint of its narrative movement comparatively few restrictions have been placed upon it. Much as minutes or years are equally at home on the screen, so are they on the Chinese stage. Even when Chinese plays first came to the attention of Europeans, Voltaire and his contemporaries observed their utter disregard for the conventions of time and place that wound protective arms around the neo-classical theatre. *The Orphan of the Family of Tchao,* which Voltaire refashioned as *L'Orphelin de la Chine,* told an excellent story of at least two generations. The Chinese theatre did not lack form in any respect. It merely observed a different form from that cultivated by Voltaire and other Europeans. In most of its phases Western drama as represented, for example, by the medieval stage, by Shakespeare and by Shaw, has indulged in digression and in a multiplicity of themes well beyond the customary practice in Asia. The narrative line in Chinese drama may be short or extended to great lengths but it will not be crisscrossed with matter arising from a variety of plots or ideas. The story proves forceful and attractive at the same time that it observes simplicity and forthrightness. Charming us by the directness of its flight, it has nothing of the interweavings of Celtic romance or of much of our more ambitious modern fiction. The dramatists unroll their ample scrolls before their audience as the painters offered their scrolls with a narrative content.

No one Chinese play, of course, covers the entire terrain of any long work of fiction. A collection of tales, as that concerning the evil statesman, Ts'ao Ts'ao, may be reproduced by a whole series of plays seldom, if ever, actually given in sequence or even collected as works of literature. The Chinese theatre seems not to have achieved the endurance of the week-long flights of theatrical effort occasionally occurring in Japan. Among the masterpieces of Chinese drama are pieces as long, say, as the longest theatrical journeys by Shaw or O'Neill but hardly more extensive. They require no such playing time as, say, Richard Wagner's *Ring des Niblungen.* Actually, no serious difficulty confronts the Western mind in accepting this feature of the Chinese works. The Western reader must not expect a play shaped according to his own conventions but the Oriental conventions are in this regard really more natural forms than artificial conventions and Western usage presumably brings the Oriental to a halt more often than his practices prove embarrassing to the Westerner. Today the latter knows the experience in his own film or fiction even though he has possibly not encountered it in his theatre. With only a slight effort of mental adjustment the road becomes open and clear.

The Chinese practices themselves altered considerably in the course of time, as well as in various parts of a large country. The Yüan drama, roughly coincident with our later Middle Ages, developed the convention of a play in four parts, usually in translation designated as acts. Certainly within these acts occur a large number of scenes, to use the familiar European terminology. The division into parts included some provisions for beginning, middle and end, and especially for musical regimentation, with the result that the four movements of the usual sonata form in Western music are suggested. In the later Ming Period much longer plays were frequently composed, with fifty or more scenes and no "act" divisions whatsoever. The differences between the schools, however, were by no means fundamental. A long Yüan play, such as *The Western Chamber*, hardly differs radically in its over-all form from a major work of a later period, as *The Palace of Eternal Youth*. These are two of the most remarkable plays with extensive narrative presentation. It becomes natural, then, to consider them in the forefront of these studies.

The Palace of Eternal Youth, one of the most powerful, beautiful and poetic of Chinese plays, written in 1688 by Hung Sheng, is a symbolical narrative drama in 49 scenes, without benefit of act divisions. The story which it presents at such length is actually the simplest. The Emperor, Ming Huang, falls in love with one of his ladies of the court, Lady Yang, and as time passes becomes increasingly attached to her, disregarding all other amorous relationships. He loses grip upon his government, favoring one of Lady Yang's cousins, the minister Yang Kuo-Chung, whose corruption in office rapidly undermines his regime. A rebel, the barbarous An Lu-shan, gains control, causing the death of Yang Kuo-Chung, the sisters of Lady Yang, and also the lady herself. Inasmuch as she is a demi-goddess, who in a previous incarnation was one of the fairies of the moon, her ghost is finally permitted to resume her celestial position. Yet she still longs for the Emperor, with whom bonds of undying loyalty and love have been pledged. Although he has reluctantly acceded to her death under pressure of the revolutionaries, he likewise remains faithful. Loyal supporters rescue the empire from the usurpers. The Emperor resigns in favor of his son. Those arch-patrons of true love, the Spinning Maid and the Cowherd, most revered of the celestial deities, take compassion on the lovers, on the Emperor's death reuniting them in heaven. Such is the story reduced to bare essentials. The rest, of which there is much, develops this universal theme. In its thought the play is metaphysical, presenting somewhat the same outlook as Petrarch's *Sonnets to Laura*. Its subject is the transcendence of true love, that is alleged to conquer age, infirmity, fate, and even death. There are some surprisingly platonic formulations of the idea. Thus, to quote from the translation by Yang Hsien-yi and Gladys Yang :

> . . . you, after faltering, kept your vow to the end.
> But all things are like the reflection of flowers in a mirror,
> You must shake off earthly dust to ascend to heaven together.

Chinese drama, like Chinese thought in general, swings between the two poles of Confucian reasoning and Taoist irrationality, between the factual and ethical mind on one side and the fantastic or mystical imagination on the other. *The Western Chamber* adheres to the former, though it is not so advanced in its Confucian attitude as such pre-eminently ethical plays as *The Orphan of the Family of Tchao*, *The Divided Tunic*, and *An Heir in His Old Age*. *The Palace of Eternal Youth* inclines strongly to the mythical and the spiritual. Though in this regard it is less mythological than the popular *White Snake*, it is even more in the idealistic philosophical tradition. It proves to be a play for the poetic dreamer rather than for the sober philosopher. Within its own category of the romantic and irrational it is difficult to surpass in any dramatic literature.

So conspicuous are some features of the apparatus of magic that its critic has small temptation to dwell on them. In culminating scenes, for example, a necromancer performs spells that become the occasion for much excellent pantomime and poetry. Since all Chinese plays are in a loose sense of the word operas, music frequently becomes itself a theme. One of the most celebrated of the plays is entitled *The Lute Song*. In this connection it may be noted that many famous Sanskrit and Noh dramas are built around legends of music : a vina or a flute becomes a leading property. Here the heroine, like any accomplished Asian courtesan, is a gifted musician and even composer. In her earlier phase, before the play's opening with her human manifestation, she has been one of the musical "fairies" of the moon, a sister to the angelic musicians of Persian mythology or to the musical dancers who illuminate the last act of Shelley's *Prometheus Unbound*. Lady Yang has sung and danced in heaven and at the end of her play is depicted as resuming these least rational of the presentational arts. Relatively little is said of her as a poet, though poet she is, but much as musician and dancer. Her inspiration is clearly depicted as more than earthly. In a vision during sleep a fairy brings her the music and choreography for "The Rainbow and Feathery Garment Dance." She is said to have improved upon the original dance as performed by the moon-spirits and to return after her human incarnation and death with this improved version. During the play's early scenes her version is composed ; just before the climax, it is performed on earth ; many scenes in the latter part of the play give warmly sympathetic portraits of the performers, especially the musicians. The work ends with a festive performance of the dance and music in heaven. This artistic creation is Lady Yang's highest accomplishment, the dance that finally secures the Emperor's wavering heart. During the earlier scenes his favorite dance has been "The Frightened Swan," composed by Lady Plum Blossom. But Lady Yang has "always wanted to compose a better tune." This in time she clearly does. Life is depicted as first and foremost a music-bearing tree. The thought obviously harmonizes with the more mystical philosophies. Although there remain in the play some strong ethical features, with sharp distinctions between the corrupt and incorrupt ministers, the accent falls chiefly on art. Hero and heroine prove by no means exceptionally just ; they are exceptionally aesthetic. It is an emphasis perhaps not often enough recalled by critics of Chinese thought who write outside China. Probably the greater part of the poetry of Li Po is inspired by essentially mystical experience. Po Chü-i is, of course, overwhelmingly ethical. But in Chinese art and thinking the odds are by no means always in favor of the more materialistic philosophy. It is of the opposite pole that *The Palace of Eternal Youth* chiefly reminds us. Here, if ever, is a moon-struck poem. The Emperor whose symbol is the sun holds our attention less strongly than his mistress, who is one of the goddesses of the moon. The atmosphere is pervaded almost to the degree of sentimentality by moonlight, by soft, ethereal music, by the tender sentiment of the landscape of early spring and by autumnal sadness. Insofar as it is simple, this is very literally a fairy-tale. Insofar as it is sophisticated, and this it is to the verge of decadence, it presents a delicate, long-drawn-out tissue of symbolism.

The most obvious of its symbols is the seasonal imagery which runs through the cycle of the year. The precise details may not at first be clear. The action covers a span of twelve years, though little is really made of this. As often happens in Asian plays, whether Sanskrit, Chinese or Japanese, the important action takes place on two years sharply contrasted with each other and separated by a considerable time-span. Behind this division is the dualism of earth and heaven, of the tormented world of social and political turbulence and the serene world in the palace of the stars, in other words, between the moral and the aesthetic phase of our existence. Its hero is a weak ruler but an accomplished dilettante, its heroine, the more idealized figure, is pure beauty. Even she as a ghost by discipline purges herself of her infatuation with the material world. But the heavens which revolve in serenity decree the conflicts that distress the created world beneath the sphere of the primum mobile and the Milky Way. Beside its river the Weaving Maid and the Celestial Cowherd live in love and peace ; those beneath their spheres are blighted by inconstancy. Hence the drama of the seasons, which even though revolving upon a well-poised wheel reflect the sad mutability

of all terrestrial matter, mind and feeling. The play opens with
a spring festival on earth and concludes with such a festival
in the skies. Divided by its subject-matter into two parts
(in this respect resembling the Petrarchan sonnet sequence)
the first year progresses from spring to winter, the second,
with an accelerated pace, from winter to spring. One is the
year of the Emperor's courtship, concluding with what virtually
constitutes a marriage vow ; the other, a year that begins
with death and mourning but ends in a triumph beyond death
and an idealistic proclamation of the immortality of the
spirit. The contrast is between a winter of discontent and a
vernal ecstasy. In the First Part the epicurean Emperor
enjoys with his people a spring-time holiday by the banks of a
delightful stream. He amuses himself in his pleasure garden.
When his romance with Lady Yang enters a stage of struggle
and intensity, the scene has advanced to the torrid temperature
of midsummer :

> The sun moves slowly
> Flaming on the sultry clouds
> Banked high above the palace. (*Scene XV*)

This heavy atmosphere makes the scene of the bath (*Scene XX*)
all the more ominous.

Twelve years pass. The severe seasons have set in. Scene
XXVIII occurs in dense autumnal gloom :

> Sorrow has dogged my step throughout my travels ;
> The far-off clouds that merge with the distant mountains
> Are like the tangle of my grief and cares ;
> In the autumn woods, that stretch to the horizon,
> The leaves are falling, falling,
> And in the sky a lone wild goose laments.

It will be noted that the scene also shifts from a luxurious and
fertile valley outside the walls of the capital city to exile among
the savage mountains. Lady Yang's death occurs in the
bleak season amid this austere mountain setting. The play's
landscape suggests a southern region where snow is seldom
seen but emphasis presently falls on the cold, winter rains in a

time of storm and tempest. One of the most inspired scenes, "Hearing the Bells," marries the meaning of music to that of the season. Bells suspended from the temple eaves give a melancholy sound as swung by the fierce gales which at the same time express and accentuate the Emperor's sorrow.

> Tinkling and jangling of bells
> And the dismal drip of rain
> Make me sick at heart.
> These melancholy sounds
> Carry across the hills and woods,
> Now high, now low, according to the wind,
> To mingle with my tears of bitter anguish.
> In this sad atmosphere,
> I think of the deserted grave
> Where the poplars rustle in the rain
> And her ghost is lonely now,
> With only the will-o'-the-wisp for company,
> And the glowworms in the wet grass.
> I am filled with remorse because in panic
> I did her a fearful wrong.
> Alone in the world, I have no desire to live on,
> But long to join her soon in the nether world.
> I cry, but the hills are silent ;
> Only the bells chime in tune with my sorrow :
> And the path is rugged and twisting,
> Like my tortured feelings.

Similar scenes are recapitulated toward the play's close but short of the ultimate happy ending. So in "A Rainy Night" (*Scene XLIV*), a musician sings a variant of the early song :

> The steep path winds across a thousand hills,
> And the way is rugged ;
> When a squall of rain sweeps over the treetops,
> The bells on the pack-horses start ringing ;
> The sound is like a lament
> Which echoes on and on in the lonely hills . . .
> And this I set down in music.

On overhearing this the Emperor remarks: "This is the tune I composed called 'Bells in the Rain.' When I was travelling through the mountains I heard bells ringing in the rain, and thought of her; so I expressed the sounds in music." But in the end bells ring out the gladness of a spring festival. The wheel has come full circle. Such an emphasis on the seasons is eminently appropriate in a play where several of the chief characters are literally astronomical.

The playwright's calculated study of contrasts, embellishing his essentially simple theme, is witnessed in much besides his study of the changing year. It produces dexterous interweaving in the scenes themselves. One would be hard put to find a parallel in Western drama, unless in Goethe's *Faust*. Throughout several scenes the stage is at least imagined to be crowded, as in the bustling scene of pageantry by the river (The Spring Festival: *Scene IV*). Here, as in the play as a whole, members of all social classes jostle one another. Crowding for elbow-room appear a "Country Gentleman," a "Country Woman," a "Plain Girl," as well as lords and duchesses. There are striking episodes dealing with peasants, blind folk-singers, stable grooms, char-women, and the common soldiery. During his flight from the capital, the Emperor is happy to receive from a loyal peasant a bowl of oatmeal. Scenes alternate between the gay, luxurious capital and the dingy poverty of the Mawei Station. They shift also from the hordes of barbarians, clad in rough wool and riding wild horses, to the effete life of eunuchs and court harems. They are at times eminently secular, at times purely religious.

Still other contrasts contribute to the play's vitality. The mere passage of time is less important than the changes which accompany it and which it may be imagined to effect. The time-span of the action, as we have seen, covers approximately a dozen years. More imaginatively considered, the story goes far deeper than its literal seeming. The Emperor is not merely a selfish monarch whose indulgence brings about the downfall of his regime. The entire episode of the temporary success and final defeat of the conspiracy against him amounts to little more than a device. Seriously considered, the Emperor is any man of normal sensuality who reaches full maturity and thereafter follows a declining path to old age and death.

The action, imaginatively understood, spans the lifetime of the average man. But by virtue of his superior imagination and spirituality the Emperor achieves a personal dedication and a grasp of the ideals of art and beauty that earn him entrance into the world of immortality. He reaches at least a lower order of Buddhahood, or enlightenment. This parallels the enlightenment which overtakes virtually all heroes of the Japanese Noh Plays. The Chinese play presents a secular facade but incloses within itself an altar lit with a sacred flame. The Emperor, paradoxically, is an aristocratic version of Everyman brought to salvation by beauty.

Conflict, contrast, irony are the essence of all true drama. Only on its surface is the play, if superficially examined, over-smooth or insipid. The first half is brightened with soft tints of hedonism, the second half shadowed through most of its scenes by romantic gloom and self-pity. The hero is in the first half self-indulgent, in the second, self-tormented. The first part has an abundance of sweetness, the second, at least a suspicion of exaggerated gall. Yet over and against these tones are modifying factors transforming possible monotony into liveliness. The second part abounds in Taostic magic. Much of the desired variety in the First Part springs from the somewhat conventional characterization of the unpredictable heroine. Far from being herself all of a piece, she exhibits the variety and contradiction of the eternally feminine. Her charm, as the Emperor insists, lies precisely in this sprightliness of temper. At one moment she appears to be wholly subservient, at the next, boldly assertive and even irate. In two episodes, the second much more violent than the first, she breaks away altogether from the pattern of the compliant court-concubine. On the day of the banquet by the river her vagaries grow violent. First she contrives to bring the Emperor and her older sister intimately together and then, fearing that she has gone too far, to the Emperor's disgust separates them again. At this the Emperor grows angry and for a day exiles Lady Yang from the Palace. The contrast between the two women defines the superiority of Lady Yang in the dramatist's eyes. Her sister proudly relies on her natural beauty, whereas Lady Yang enhances hers with generous use of cosmetics and other aids to beauty. When out of favor Lady

Yang discovers a way to win back the Emperor. She sends him a special lock of her hair, whereupon the quarrel ends.

The second and graver quarrel precedes the final reconciliation. Out of sheer restlessness the Emperor spends a night with Lady Yang's most formidable rival, Lady Peach Blossom. The heroine actually storms the door of that unfortunate lady's bedchamber and embarrasses the sheepish Emperor, who cannot conceal the evidence that he has not, as he pretends, slept alone. In short, Lady Yang is what Elizabethan playwrights describe as "a very woman." These appealing qualities successfully relieve the possible tedium of a platonic allegory. The felicitous ironies of the heroine's role extend also into the play's later part, where she appears first as ghost, or shade, and finally as a heavenly spirit. Gradually she outlives the sharpness of her grief but never the intensity of her love or the sadness at separation from the Emperor. By the decree of stronger deities than herself, she is confined to a narrow radius about her grave. In her first, futile efforts as ghost to follow her lover she is blown back by gusts of mountain winds. In the theatre itself the choreography would here be especially effective. Later, when more nearly serene, her shade is allowed wider excursions into surrounding territory. Finally, when, under Buddhistic instruction she recognizes the errors of her selfishness and carnality, she re-enters her ancient home in the moon. Her ghostly experience has been one of purgatory, not of hell, to whose deeper glooms only the villains of the play are condemned. Even in some of the latest scenes a delicate and highly moving irony appears, for happy as she is made by the blissful world of music and dance in the Palace of the Moon, she cannot overcome, as a true Bodhisattva should, the shadow of her personal affection for her lover. Angels, God's messengers, are properly without shadows. But in India and the Far East they become more sensuous than in the West and converge more nearly upon human nature, though never becoming identified with it. Lady Yang is of this description. She is a spirit who by her purity finally purges the Emperor of the last vestiges of his worldly dross. But insofar as the play is concerned we do not see her as a pure deity, for she is, more philosophically considered, the highest vision of deity accessible to the human mind. The Necromancer, or priest, enters into a trance, encountering reality beyond whatever can be postulated for the Emperor himself. Whether manifest as Lady Yang or as the spirit within the moon, the play's heroine is hybrid. Her ambivalence accounts for much of her force as an agent in true drama. In the highest heaven there can be no drama as commonly understood, for there can be no conflict. Drama springs, theologically considered, from the inconstant moon, not from the unchanging sun and stars. Virtually alone in the history of the stage, the Sanskrit playwrights rose beyond these familiar and all but universal limitations.

In its basic structure *The Palace of Eternal Youth* suggests the Noh Plays. In those marvelous fruits of Japanese culture the first half of the work commonly presents the embodiment of the chief figure in a minor or mundane manifestation, the second, in the true, heroic or celestial revelation. In each case the figure is in a sense a ghost but during the second appearance the more exalted and the closer to a superior reality. This is so with the heroine of the Chinese play. A dancer and musician of the cult of the Moon, she descends to the comparatively humble form of one of the Emperor's courtesans. It is in this guise that we first see her. In her final appearance she is again unmistakably the deity while her lover has himself been drawn into the sphere of a higher reality. The audience here, as in the typical Noh Play, is presumed to undergo a comparable enlightenment or discipline. But the Chinese play, in keeping with Chinese culture, is the more genial and humane. Emperor and heroine alike are much more fallible creatures, inhabiting a more recognizable world than the portentous figures of the Noh stage. The Chinese play is by far the more variegated and humorous. Witty, for example, is the picture of the dilemma of Lady Yang's sisters, at which the dramatist laughs up his ample sleeve. Though jealous of their more radiant sister, they cannot be too severe on her for they know well that only she and not they can hold the Emperor's heart and that their own promotion at court and that of their entire family springs from her power over the sovereign. Snipe at her they must but they cannot afford to attack her.

The Palace of Eternal Youth belongs to a distinct minority of

Chinese dramas in that it deals so little with family life and also so briefly with military life. Most Chinese plays lean strongly to one or the other side of this duality, unless, as occasionally happens, the two matters are combined. Here the afore-mentioned clannishness in Lady Yang's family gives best evidence of the foremost preoccupation of the dramatists, the family, while the brief scenes in the camp of the barbarians supply the chief element of military seasoning. This is seasoning and little more, contributing at least its increment to the panoramic scope of the work as a whole. Fundamentally, this is a love story given a metaphysical turn. Its true nature is elucidated by contrast with *The Western Chamber*, a love story given an unmistakably Confucian turn. The latter is a wry and rather unorthodox study of the daring of two women who defy parental surveillance and of a scholar who recalls that even Confucius tolerated love songs. This social setting of *The Western Chamber* has considerable importance. The catholic realism of *The Palace of Eternal Youth* may appear almost Chaucerian but at heart the play deals with the transmutation of the erotic impulse into aesthetic and contemplative vision. To repeat, it is first of all a metaphysical, not a moral, drama.

Its form calls for closer inspection than yet given for it excels in style and execution as well as in its superlative narrative line. The interweaving of certain symbols, as the moon imagery, the musical elements, the seasonal allusions, and the dances, has already been noted. Especially rewarding for study is the construction in the individual scenes, which range from soliloquy to elaborate polyphonic writing. The prevailing tone is, broadly speaking, lyrical. Each scene— and almost all are brief—has its emotional tone and unique structure. There is little or no witty prose dialogue but much antiphonal singing and strictly contrived stanzaic structure. The chief episode in the first scene, for example, is a passage of this description. Three stanzas occur, rendered in turn by the Emperor, the Lady, and the chorus of Maids. This provides an ascending pattern. After each stanza all persons present join in a refrain that is never varied : "May love reign as long as the earth endures !" This refrain may be taken as the motto for the play. Scene Four, "The Spring Festival," depicting the procession of carriages beside the river, is as much a model of grace as the relief processional sculptures that it so closely resembles. The episode, "The Writing on the Wall," Scene Nine, offers a model for use of foreboding or prophecy in the development of a dramatic plot. All hangs upon an epigram, or inscription. The episode, "Writing the Music," Scene Eleven, painted in a pale morning light, is one of the most delicate imaginable. The little drama, "The Lichee Fruit," Scene Fourteen, with its sequences of runners and horsemen, can hardly be surpassed as a contrived bit of naturalistic choreography. It is almost as much a dance as the dance scene which follows it. Military life is several times presented as a bright costume parade and scenic maneuver. Good examples are Scene Sixteen, "The Hunt," Scene Thirty, "Surpressing the Rebellion," and Scene Thirty-Four, "Recovering the Capital." A more lyrical passage than "Hearing the Bells," Scene Twenty-Eight, would be virtually unthinkable. In "The Rhapsody," Scene Thirty-Seven, we have a fascinating picture of a minstrel performing his recitation, in this instance, a recapitulation of the earlier action of the play. As its title suggests the very tender Scene Thirty-Eight, "Sacrifice at the Nunnery," is strictly ritualistic. The verses are in stanzaic form. All the leisurely scenes presenting the Necromancer are incantations, or Taoist hymns to forces governing the universe. The play appropriately ends with song and dance in heaven. An exceptionally large portion of it is sung in the manner of an Oriental "opera," which is not of course, even an approximation to any variety of opera known in the West but is still lyrical. The musical parts of *The Western Chamber* appear less specifically lyrical and more nearly in the manner of recitative. They are sung speeches. Although few speeches in *The Palace of Eternal Youth* extend to any great length, the entire dialogue and conduct of the play indicates a style of presentation where music and choreography play enormously important roles. This practice harmonizes the style with the content. It also contributes in important respects to the work's explicitly literary or poetic quality.

    The Palace of Eternal Youth is a sequence of lyrical scenes constituting agrand and virtually an epic design. Although the love story presents first of all, at least to Western eyes, an unmistakably romantic complexion and the smoothly running wheels of Oriental magic have an air of cheerful predestination, many scenes are hardened with an unmistakably earthy quality and majesty adheres to the mere scope of the conception. The play is Faustian in its breadth, though certainly not in its relaxed mood. The eye shifts with extraordinary rapidity between the highest and lowest ranges of society. There is an extremely large caste of characters. Vision seems aerial, all the more so because of the ever-changing clouds of magic enveloping it.

In all these respects the work proposed here as a companion piece for study, *The Western Chamber*, proves antithetical. Where one achieves grandeur, the other achieves intimacy; where one suggests a large orchestra, the other suggests a quartet. One, as its title declares, comes to its climax in the palace in the skies, the other, in the confines of an earthly chamber. The time-scheme of one encompasses many years, concluding with a vista into infinity; the other is contained within the compass of one change of the moon and even at its end reaches only a muted conclusion, since the marriage toward which the action tends is left in suspense, dependent for its full realization on the hero's success in his academic career and on his safety through many leagues of arduous travel. The action of one is in a sense everywhere. Some scenes are in the moon, in the higher heavens, on China's far-flung borders, in its capital city, in plain or country, during winter or summer. Not only is the landscape here smooth and there rugged; the hero and heroine travel, so that many of the most moving scenes are on the road; indeed, the climax of the action, the heroine's death, occurs almost casually as a calamity of the road at an impoverished temple among desolate hills. The playwright presents a cavalcade of scenes, shrewdly linked together but everywhere conspicuously on the move. In *The Western Chamber* the reverse of all these conditions obtains. With the exception of one or two extremely brief scenes of distinctly minor importance, all action takes place within a single city and, with the exception of an early scene, virtually a prologue, and the last scene, virtually an epilogue, all occurs inside the formidable walls of a Buddhist monastery.

The eye focuses on a central court or patio, with a few adjacent rooms, as a chapel, a guest-room, a library, and certain dormitories. The human spectacle itself is orderly and basically Confucian. The hero is a scholar, the son of a Minister of Ceremony, the heroine, daughter of the Prime Minister. During the period of the action she and her family are observing the ceremonies of mourning, more than ever restricting the freedom of her action. Two scenes of ceremonious meals hold conspicuous places. The action is the simplest insofar as the main contour of the plot is concerned. There is only one real happening or event : the bold act of the heroine to join the hero at night in his chamber. The point of the play is that all other actions are abortive. Basically, its thought is psychological: its depth, like that of any major work of art, is infinite but in this instance extends only within the interior spaces of the soul. The hero's role proves emotionally simple : he either grieves or rejoices. The heroine hinges on a calculated irony : she vacillates according to a strict rhythm, is reluctant to admit not only to others but to herself the depth of her commitment, stands forever wavering between bashfulness and boldness, sorrow and delight.

This extraordinary concentration of theme, without so much as the vestige of digression or subplot, is paradoxically exhibited in the one incident, necessary to give force to the story, which leads the eye outside the monastery walls. To save the desperate situation threatened by a bandit chief who plans the monastery's destruction and the heroine's rape, a most unconventional brother of the order appears. This clownish figure is the complete antithesis of the hero. Despite his membership in an ascetic fraternity, he is wholly epicurean a despiser of books, a recklessly bold giant of almost incredible physical strength. He hastens outside the holy walls to secure the aid of a faithful servant under the law. Shrewdly the playwright dips his brush in a totally new color to paint this one scene, itself too brief to constitute even a digression, necessary for the forcefulness of the story but in no way essential to its true connotation. Incidents that a less skilful playwright might have put upon the stage, the author wisely relegates to brief description. The ring is left unbroken ; the focus of attention remains secure.

In a manner worthy of a classical quartet we have a deft use of counterpoint. There are four principal parts : the two lovers, the witty maid, and the stern but ultimately reasonable mother. Other characters, as the abbot and his assistant, are obviously secondary and exist only in the role of background figures. A metaphor helps to explain the story. In American baseball idiom, the action hangs on the principle that three strikes would be out but a third and final effort may be crowned with success. Twice the hero loses courage and misses his opportunity but the third time he succeeds. Twice the heroine acts with duplicity on account of her instinctive coyness, leading the hero on while she seems to repudiate him and gathering increased force for her own passion. Fruition is measured by the difficulty of its attainment. Actually, the difficulty springs far more from the nature of love itself than from parental opposition. The greatest obstacles lie within. The mother likewise exhibits feminine duplicity or even sophistry. She promises her daughter to the man who liberates the entire company from the bandits and, after the liberation, repudiates her promise. But she, too, is only being coy. When she learns that, in defiance of her prohibition, the lovers have for a month been going to bed together, she bows to the inevitable. The plot, in short, is concentrated throughout, somewhat as a fugue, on the principal theme and its inversion.

The deliberateness and artfulness of this counterpoint is clear in the manner in which one scene mirrors another, either by duplication or by reversal. Thus it is twice through an exchange of letters or notes that the intrigue advances. On each occasion the dramatic surprise depends on the illiteracy of the clever but unbookish servant-girl. One delights in seeing—though on first acquaintance one may even remain unconscious of the artistry—that in Act One, when Ch'ang is away from Ying-Ying, he grows both boastful and bombastic and that in Act Eleven, when in her presence, he becomes completely tongue-tied. His bashfulness, derived from an excessive flow of emotion, is in fact only less conspicuous than hers. Ying-Ying is decidedly eloquent both before and after the play's climax, the first intimate meeting of the lovers. On this occasion Ch'ang does all the talking and, what is no less significant, all the singing. The playwright is swayed by the

43

convention that in one act only one character shall sing. This rule he does not observe scrupulously yet its force is pronounced. In this outstanding scene, to repeat, Ying-Ying neither speaks nor sings. Ch'ang as befits a scholar is exceedingly loquacious. But his loquacity depends on circumstance. Alone, among virtual strangers or in a state of emotional control, he commands great fluency. On suddenly finding himself in Ying-Ying's presence, he loses heart and with his loss of heart loses the normal command of his tongue. Embarrassment leads to silence. When, in Act Thirteen, he finally plucks up courage as circumstances turn in his favor, he releases this overload of singing, to which Ying-Ying's total silence provides the foil. Moreover, he is decidedly represented as the active party in the affair physically, though not ethically. It is she who has decided to come to his room, not he to hers. His visit to her room has been a miserable failure. But once safely in the Western Chamber, she is outwardly passive, he, outwardly active. No such contrast is, of course, intended in their emotional experience. Her silence is possibly more eloquent than his bird-like exuberance of speech, her restrained miming, more striking than his vigorous action. The scene is at the same time a study in dramatic technique and in both the psychology and the biology of sex.

In form and content, structure and meaning, the play attains great distinction. Its form, of course, becomes in itself an inseparable element in the feeling. The over-all simplicity and the inexhaustible intricacy of the poetic weave reflect the basic simplicity and intricate discernment of the poet's vision of life itself. All sound art is the embroidery of the commonplace, a manner of saying what is familiar with exceptional nuances. As with so many Oriental works, both dramatic and nondramatic, the poet seems to Western eyes to get under way slowly. The hero must arrive in the city, unpack his baggage, establish himself in his new rooms, and look about him before the vital parts of the action begin. Above all, it is of the very essence of the playwright's conception of the heroine that she should move slowly. The part of the antagonist, here the mother, must also be established before the true conflict itself can begin. We recognize in the mother the embodiment of organized society as a foil to the young lovers who are, however great may be his intellectual or her aesthetic refinements, basically forces in nature. Also, and much less obviously, the forces in conflict must be poised in spiritual fruition by the encompassing wisdom of a religious or spiritual philosophy, here appropriately Buddhistic, to balance the sterner and more firmly grounded doctrine of Confucian morality. The Head of the Monastery knows what is best, the mother, only what is proper, the lovers, only what they desire. The Monastery is thus much more than a merely formal setting or frame for the whole ; the background, too, becomes a vital part of the picture, a third necessity in its fundamental conception. Although the playwright shows no peculiar addiction to religion, among his moving scenes are the prayers offered in the greatest sincerity by the lovers for their union.

Ch'ang is shown as a scholar before he becomes a lover ; Ying-Ying as a gay young person of highly refined sentiment and taste before she, too, is swept away by withering though life-giving passion. In short, we are made to become interested in these people before we are asked to share their more violent and painful experiences. We observe Ch'ang as the travelling scholar, eager to inform his mind by his travels. On arriving at the city, he at once inquires as to its principal sights or places of cultural interest. He hears that there is but one worth mention, the monastery. When met by one of the lesser monks, he courteously accepts the invitation to inspect its art and shrines while reserving his chief thoughts to himself. On the following day he will meet the abbot, a member of his own class, an old and tried friend of his family, and hence his intellectual peer, if not even his superior. This is a civilized play presenting civilized persons as its characters.

The play's remarkable universality is evidenced in what may be regarded as points of momentous detail. Thus time becomes a poetic theme to be treated much as it is so memorably treated by Shakespeare. A lover, declares the English poet, is of impatience all compact. One of the most lyrical of his passages is Juliet's apostrophe to night to hasten its way, putting an end to the sun's tediousness. Such is, even to matters that approach the phrasing itself, Ch'ang's apostrophe at the conclusion of Act Ten. The passage calls for quotation :

45

Today, O unkind Heaven, why do you make it so hard for me to wait until the darkness comes? O Heaven, you have the whole universe at your command.

Why must you make just this day so bitter for me? Grant that the time pass swiftly. When one studies books and philosophy and engages in discussions, time speeds by, and soon the sun moves toward the west, and sets. But today, just because the pure peach-blossom has a rendezvous with me, time seems to drag, as though held back by most tenacious glue. Alas, it is only midday. Wait a bit. It seems most difficult for the sun to reach the western sky. In all the wide pure expanse of heaven there is no cloud. Gently comes the warm breeze. Where can I find the art of speeding time's slow pace? For then I could persuade the tardy sun to sink quickly in the west.

Ah, now it begins on its western course. Wait, wait yet a while. What seems to hold it back in the heavens? That lazy three-legged bird! Would that I had the bow of Hu I, to shoot an arrow at the sun and bring it tumbling down. Thanks to Heaven, thanks to earth, your light begins to wane. Ah, now the lamps begin to glow, and now the drum is beaten, and the bells boom out their call. I shall close the library door. When I arrive there, I shall gently grasp the swaying branches of the willow and lightly scale the wall. Then shall I hold my darling in my arms.

Inasmuch as a thematic manner governs the playwright's deeply conscious style, the reader cannot be surprised to note that similar imagery occurs in speeches by Ying-Ying later on.

Whereas *The Palace of Eternal Youth* is a long scroll unrolled before us, *The Western Chamber* is a diptych not impossibly designed for performance on two days. Part One ends with the mother's repudiation of her promise to give her daughter in marriage to the man who contrives the rescue of the monastery and its guests. There is a well contrived balance in this. The scene is a banquet, the table elaborately set. All have the right to expect the announcement of a marriage. But the mother prefers a previous commitment, a vague promise by her dead husband to marry their daughter to the son of the Minister Cheng. When lifting her glass in recognition of the dramatic moment, instead of announcing the marriage she bids the company drink to their friendship as that of brother and sister. In substance, she offers the young people a poisoned cup. The play's last scene also presents a banquet and a pledge with wine. Here, too, the cup is both ironical and sobering, a cup of parting and disunion rather than of marriage. But the second occasion differs radically from the first. It is in recognition, under the surveillance of the aging priest, that the social claim takes precedence over all personal claims and while by no means negating them, insists upon their subordination. Ch'ang must win his bride by first winning an official post through participation in the government examinations. In contradistinction from John Dryden's precept, only the scholar deserves the fair. The two scenes of ceremonious dramatic and symbolic drinking prove to be in important though unostentatious ways linked together as the two final episodes in the two contrasted sections of the play. The first part is in a sense merely a pedestal. On review it seems almost prefatory, so muted is its poetic tone, so completely commonplace is the story of the rescue from bandits. Yet it is really much more than a common pedestal. With many graceful carvings, it lifts the chief characters to an elevation from which they may be seen to perform their more significant actions.

Part One is sparse in humor and almost devoid of irony though the contrast between the timid scholar and his friend, the effectual general, must have had a piquancy even for the Chinese audience, thoroughly accustomed as it was to such civilized distinctions. The emotional intensity, irony and tempo reach a far different state in Part Two. As the action unfolds, the maid, Hung Niang, the most sympathetic character in the play, consistently rises in stature until in certain important scenes she commands an even more important position than the lovers, as even her singing role attests. This is partly, to be sure, because we see the lovers through her eyes, not through the mad and distorted caricatures which are the images their own passion throws on the screen of consciousness. If the lovers are the poetic souls who survive the storms of emotion, she is the shrewd pilot who takes them at length into port. She comes closer to embodying the main critical comment on the action than that worldly-wise mystic, the learned abbot. In broad, general terms she resembles the witty and useful maids of European classical comedy, best known, perhaps, in the works of Molière ; yet this woman has right to be considered as herself, not merely as a pawn in a large, though attractive, class. The part is by no means as simple as that in the run-of-the-mill plays in any literature. Not only is she the bright, intuitive mind, without aid of reading or of formal logic ; as events prove, she is fallible as well as witty and in several respects a sad as well as a glad spirit. It is true that she keeps her own spirit buoyant and sustains the spirits of the lovers. Yet her look of confidence is at times a mask or matter of face. Once or twice the playwright removes the mask and hints that she is herself vainly attracted to Ch'ang. Though devoted to her mistress, she is too human to be without at least a spark of envy. How moving is the picture of her in the cold outside the lovers' window, shivering and stamping her small feet on the dew-drenched moss !

The resolution of the entire action belongs to her and at no small cost to herself. According to the recognized relation of mistress and servant, Ying-Ying's irate mother has the maid actually beaten. Yet rising above her pain, she gives a succinct statement of the over-all situation that completely reverses the mother's judgment of the case and at length persuades her to accept the situation as inevitable. With much shrewdness, her chief appeal is directed to the character of the conventional person whom she addresses. She assures the mother that there will be more unfavorable gossip if Ch'ang's claim is denied than if it is accepted. In other words, society will be more disposed to blame the mother for insufficiently guarding her child than to blame the girl herself for following the path of nature. Hung Niang is, in fact, a shrewd and peculiarly lovable minor heroine. It should be further noted as a refinement of the plot that the first incriminating evidence of the habitual meetings of the lovers comes from Ying-Ying's really innocent and boyish young brother. The family, whether deliberately or not, is aligned against youth. Only Hung Niang is the true friend. The playwright's sympathies are largely, though not exclusively, with youth. This compromise the last scene, almost unexampled in Western drama and unusual even in Chinese, must attest. In the final judgment wisdom is crowned above either reckless passion or obstinate decorum and restraint. We are again specifically reminded that even Confucius viewed love songs in a kindly light.

The play is wise but to a far greater degree provides beautiful and moving theatre, stylized with the finest Oriental inspiration. The eloquent final stage-scene even suggests universality in stage business and technique. It resembles one of the most inspired conclusions found in Elizabethan or Jacobean drama, the last scene in the once enormously popular play, George Chapman's *Bussy D'Ambois*. Here is depicted a parting between an angry husband and his proud wife of small or at best dubious virtue. The playwright makes of the two doors that provided exits on the Elizabethan stage the vehicles for expressing his dramatic tension. In deep anger and sadness the two people part company, swearing an irrevocable oath that they shall never meet again. In the Elizabethan play, of course, the episode denotes moral conflict and strife, not merely the irony of a decision mutually accepted in good faith where passion temporarily bows to social obligation. Aesthetically, however, the two scenes are strictly comparable in their inspired symmetry. In the Chinese play are two imaginary wagons driven off in opposite directions, presumably not through doors but around the two ends of the stage. One road returns to the monastic city, the other leads on to the bureaucratic capital. Ying Ying takes one, her scholar-lover, the other. Her gestures in parting are delineated in words of great poignance. It is a surprising ending to a great play yet entirely in keeping with its pervasive use of counterpoint and employment of moving irony. The scene takes on the formality of a sculptural Chinese frieze. It carries one back to the purest art of the T'ang period, with profound mastery of sophistication and grace. Moreover, it is fitting that the drama should end so, for full of vitality and liveliness of wit and spirit as it is, it depicts love as no less an ordeal than a delight. All suffer, the mother from her broken pride, the daughter from her yearning, the distraught scholar, and the quixotically dutiful servant. As much is played in the minor as in the major mode, possibly even more. With classical moderation the Chinese playwright avoids both the banalities of pretentious tragedy and of shallow comedy. Neither is his play that monstrous hybrid, conventional tragicomedy. His tristful ending is the final nuance in his dramatic narrative. The last speeches give a fair specimen of the poetic and theatrical style :

(*Ch'ang*). Beloved, your words are gold and jade to me. One by one I shall engrave them on my heart. The time is not far distant when we shall behold each other once again. Do not allow your grief to overwhelm you. I go, bowing my head quickly, to hide the tears that start. I repress my sorrow, and seek to smooth my brow.

(*Ying Ying*). My soul is torn with anguish, I know not why. Would that I could follow you in my dreams ! (*Exit Ch'ang*)
The green hills have cut me off
From him to whom I bade farewell.
The beautiful forest has no charms for me.
The thin mists and vapors of the evening sky
Now hide us from each other.
On the old road at sunset
There is no one with whom to speak.
In the deserted fields the autumn wind mingles
With the whinnying of his horse.
Wearily I enter my cart
To return to my home alone.
When I came, ah, how fast !
When I depart, ah, how slowly !

(*Madame*). Hung Niang, help your little mistress into her cart. The shades of evening are already falling. Let us hasten back. Even though, after many twistings and windings, I have yielded to my daughter, I still believe that I have conducted myself as a righteous and strict mother should. (*Exit*).

(*Hung Niang*). Madame's cart is already far ahead of us on the road. Come, little miss, let us hasten and depart.

(*Ying Ying*). Hung Niang, look ! See if you can see where he is.
He is among the four mountains,

And spurs on his horse,
And all the while he watches
The setting of the sun.
At this moment the hearts of men
Are bowed down with grief.
How will this little cart
Ever bear the weight of mine ?

3

3 / *Oriental Tragedy*

ALTHOUGH THE exalted spiritual mood and emotionally depressed temper of Western tragedy are absent from the drama of the East, contrary to common opinion many outstanding features of tragedy as generally understood are present in the Oriental theatre. What rudiments of tragedy that theatre either lacks or possesses is a question first of all requiring an inspection of basic terms and ideas.

The extreme stylization in all Oriental theatre tends to diminish the violence of emotional impact present in the major serious dramas of the West. It is notable that an unqualified happy ending is most of all in requisition among the Sanskrit dramatists, largely, it would seem, because of the outlook of their religion. The Japanese Noh Plays often move in quite another direction, depicting a calamity followed long afterwards by the purgation of the soul tormented in a virtual purgatory, from which penance and Buddhistic prayers achieve redemption. This familiar formula at least approaches the Greek practice so shrewdly analyzed by Aristotle in his own works on purgation of pity and fear. According to this view, the theatre is a place for the cleansing of the most violent emotions through aesthetic inoculation. Because of the peculiarities of both Japanese stylized art and Buddhistic or mystical thinking the effect of Greek tragedy is never fully attained, yet there is an approach to it. The graver among the Noh Plays may be described as tragedy once removed. The shock treatment is more postulated than expressed. The audience itself may be purged but the hero's purgation resembles an offstage event in a Greek tragedy, something more assumed than depicted. Insofar as Japanese heroes and heroines are stronger willed than those in Sanskrit or Chinese drama, they also approximate the Western tragic norm. Leading figures in the most serious Chinese drama are less wilful and neither they nor the audience experience the shock treatment which Aristotle so memorably described. Chinese playwrights are unsurpassed masters of pathos, not of tragedy.

Yet the categorical statement that tragedy is non-existent or infrequently encountered on the Chinese stage proves misleading. A fair number of Chinese plays end unhappily. The answer, as usual, rests with the basic definitions. The dark grandeur of classical or baroque tragedy the East very possibly at no time attains. But China does with some frequency welcome plays of an eminently serious complexion depicting a leading character's death. For example, the universally fascinating theme of the accidental murder of a son by his father, old as *The Book of Genesis* and best known in the myth of Oedipus, occurs in the deeply moving Chinese play, *At the Bend of the Fen River*. Several sombre works of this nature not only refuse to be forgotten but invite close consideration. Although up to a certain point analogues helpful in a general interpretation exist in other literatures, Chinese plays of this type have a distinctive and an engaging flavor. In general they are not the greatest of Chinese dramas yet they express moods typical of Chinese thought in some of its important phases. Although they lack the impassioned abandon of European tragedy, they relieve the tendency to excessive artificiality vitiating so many overconventionalized and excessively repetitious Oriental works. If the human touch is itself one of the chief glories of the Chinese stage, this type, possessing it in amplest measure, should be valued highly. In China such plays are justly famous and stand among the Oriental dramas best known in foreign lands.

Snow in Midsummer, with a touch of Dionysian extravagance and fervor, affords a good example. The play virtually demands comparison with other pieces similar in the central theme yet differing in their temper and conclusions. *The Chalk Circle* is such a work, more vigorous in its temper and ending happily for its heroine. Here the happy ending is indicated from the first by the relative vigor of its heroine, passive but at least a little less passive a sufferer than customary in Chinese plays darkened by tragic fate. The tone is also highly moral and unmistakably Confucian. Attention is deployed among a considerable number of lively characters with widely divergent views of life. Thus the heroine's brother is petulant ; the first wife, as will later be observed in some detail, is a veritable Lady Macbeth ; an action very like a Shakespearean underplot introduces the theme of adultery. The play's fibre is made of sterner stuff than *Snow in Midsummer* and the type of work to which it belongs. In some respects, then, other plays come even closer to heroic drama if not to tragedy in the West, since they present more vigorous and affirmative attitudes. Chinese dramas that begin and continue in a pronounced pathetic mood are the more likely to conclude in death than those that are psychologically more animated. Yet it seems consistent that pathos should at its uttermost be consummated with death. At least the strong suspicion of moral evasiveness vitiating much Western romance seldom, if ever, contaminates the Chinese stage.

One of the chief preoccupations of the Chinese dramatists, lending seriousness and even tragic elevation to their work, is the suffering to which women are subjected by severities which the Chinese social system imposes on them. In innumerable plays the central figure is a long-suffering and unjustly accused woman. In two of the three works especially examined in this chapter such is the case. In the third play the central figure, to be sure, is a man, "the Winged-Tiger General," but of great importance are two women, his wife and his mother by an adoption, who sing the *planctus*, or lament, that constitutes the play's most impressive feature. Amidst a considerable number of ineffectual or despicable men, including the general-in-chief, these two women have by far the most active, discerning and sympathetic parts. It may well be much more than idle theorizing that Chinese playwrights and audiences compensated by the dramatic praise of women for the injustices suffered by them in real life. It is often seen that art's mirror of society far from being a faithful reflection of reality is actually its precise inversion, with the result that in criticism many hasty and groundless generalizations are propounded. The arts in a very real sense respond to life but serve ill as short cuts for impatient theorists.

A familiar formula in plays of various degrees of seriousness or tragic intensity provides that the hero or heroine shall die in the next to the last episode and that the final episode be devoted to the punishment of the guilty. It is thus more properly said of such plays that the climax or catastrophe is the death of the protagonist and that the actual conclusion presents the moral justification so much in demand in plays and in fiction throughout the world and in China the most conspicuously. In this regard the Chinese works are and are not similar to the conventional Occidental "tragedy." Insofar as the most important scene close to the play's end depicts the protagonist's death, one formula for tragedy is observed. But the emphasis on the punishment of the antagonist, or villain, is even more typical of Western melodrama or even high comedy than of tragedy. Poetic justice is singularly cherished by the Chinese, more consistently than by the Japanese or Sanskrit dramatists and even more devotedly than in Western usage. The Confucian devotion to morality largely accounts for this emphasis among the Chinese. The moral ending becomes virtually obligatory. So far is this true, that even in Oriental eyes and in those of the best playwrights one suspects it to have been a little perfunctory. At the play's end the theatre needed this pious fumigation in ethical terms. Such was the appropriate device for sending the audience home with the sense of edification and moral assurance. These plays terminate gracefully on a downbeat. No Chinese play ends with a bang. The emphasis on death is still paramount, although the fear and horror of death never dominate the Chinese mind as they dominate so many men and poems in the Christian Middle Ages. The ancient Mediterranean world made far more of death's horror than did the ancient Chinese, or for that matter, than the Indians or Japanese. The Tibetan mask of death is not typical of Chinese mentality. Siva, the Destroyer, is less potent an image in China than in South-East Asia. For the Chinese dramatists death is indeed a calamity but chiefly notable as the archway through which senior members of a family pass from a condition of honor to one of veneration, from parental dignity to the domain of ancestor worship.

The climax of these Chinese plays in question is still the death-scene. This, as in Japanese Noh Plays, is also frequently followed by the return of the protagonist as a ghost. Thus in both *Snow in Midsummer* and *The Sorrows of Han* the heroine appears in the last act in this supernatural guise. The play, then, does not end with the episode of death but with its consequence and shadow. Still, the scene of the ghost is invariably sad and deeply pathetic. It accentuates an already established mood of tragedy.

Chinese heroic plays are almost invariably tragicomedies. Chinese tragedy—if the name be allowed here—is seldom the story of the death of kings or heroes. It is, however, the story of the death of sympathetic figures, especially women. Insofar as these protagonists are often comparatively modest figures, without aggressive qualities or exceptional accomplishments, their fate accords more nearly with Western conceptions of the pathetic than of the tragic. But the seriousness of their situations, the depth of feeling and of grief, and the grim finality of their story surely entitle us to consider the telling of it as tragic in the Oriental manner. One recognizes a vital and primary distinction between such a dramatic romance as *The Palace of Eternal Youth* or *The Western Chamber* and the tragic *Snow in Midsummer* or *The Sorrows of Han*. In the more explicitly mental and less deeply emotional plays, where the mood turns to ethical indoctrination, as in *The Chalk Circle*, or to high comedy, as in *Madame Cassia*, the mood digresses still further from true tragedy. The truth, too often overlooked by Western critics, is that Chinese drama presents a wide and much variegated terrain, at times sharing considerably more with Western conceptions of tragedy than has commonly or perhaps at any time been acknowledged. Behind the often unpresuming words and the always intricate technique of performance lies a seriousness that may be all the more sincere because lacking in the inflated attitudinizing of much of the "high seriousness" of Western baroque "tragedy" or grand opera. As in other of their arts, the Chinese while presuming less achieve more. By shunning art's rhetoric they touch human nature more sensitively. Eschewing a violent attack they gain a deep tenderness of heart. They escape the sentimental by the old, direct road of simple statement where it is simplicity itself that casts its shadow of nuance. Behind the outward appearance of simplicity or even naivete lie much irony and sophistication. The closest approach in Western drama to this conjunction of qualities is found in the chief works of the always popular but never vulgar Lope de Vega. Or perhaps the music of Haydn conveys the idea still more directly.

As a favorite play in China itself in the tragic mode, the aforementioned *Snow in Midsummer* invites first attention. The core of this work is simplicity itself. A girl of seven is separated from her father and from this time to her death suffers almost every misfortune to which women in particular are exposed. After her execution on a false criminal charge, she appears before her father in her ghostly form. Their moving interview is the play's strongest scene. Her death in Act Three is also a memorable scene and with its supernatural elements shortly to be considered here constitutes the motive force of the myth. But the dramatist's special contribution to the story is the subsequent interview between man and ghost. This, too, is sound Oriental convention but in this instance a fruitful convention is brought to its most perfect consummation. The punishment of the wicked at the hands of the avenging parent amounts almost to an afterthought in comparison with the actual meeting of souls across the gulf that separates this world from the mystery that lies beyond.

Even in its bare outlines the story is sufficiently tragic. Still more so is it in its calculated and most consistent ramifications. The heroine has been a child of sorrow even before her separation from her father, when she was seven. At the age of three, when consciousness of the loss was already keen, she suffered the death of her mother. At seventeen she married only to lose her husband two years later. For a while she lived with her mother-in-law, a well-meaning but weak woman also a widow. Through circumstances attended with violence, the mother-in-law consents to a second marriage, an act almost always viewed with sour disfavor by Chinese playwrights. An odious boor attempts to blackmail the heroine into a similar marriage. Failing in this, he contrives a plot. This is aimed at the poisoning of the mother-in-law, but through an unexpected gesture of generosity on the mother-in-law's part the poisoned cup comes to the lips of the villain's father. (That a poisoned cup reaches the wrong lips reminds us first of all of *Hamlet*, but the incident became almost habitual on the Chinese stage.) The heroine is thereupon given the choice of being accused of murder or of accepting a hateful marriage. She stoutly refuses the marriage and trusts that a just court will free her. But an unscrupulous judge accepts the villain's account of the matter, aided by a bribe. The heroine is condemned to die. Among her final requests are petitions showing her affection for the timid mother-in-law. To the last she is admirable and pathetic, a stoical sufferer of the worst ills that flesh is heir to.

In the eyes of dramatist and audience she is even a nobler figure than a Western audience or reader may suppose. This lofty stature is attested by the miracles attending her death, the most sensational and memorable feature of her story. To recount this episode in other words than those of the playwright might seem superfluous, since the episode is so memorable, but in the present context it is of some value to stress the moving and deeply emotional properties of the scene, mounting to the elevation of true tragedy. Like all such tragedy, the scene evokes both exaltation and tears. Historically speaking, it has proved a climax not only in the play itself but in the Chinese drama as a whole. The heroine makes a triple prophecy : if she is innocent, she declares that on her decapitation her blood will spurn the ground and rise to stain a white banner high in air ; if she is innocent, though the season is summer, there will be a fall of snow burying the earth to the depth of three feet ; if she is innocent, the province where such injustice has been done will be without rain for three years. Needless to say, all these conditions become facts, though during the time no step is officially taken to redeem her reputation or to punish her evil accuser.

These scenes are clearly ceremonious as well as dramatic and folklore as well as fictional narrative. The sober stylization that is in substance ritual extends also into the conduct of Act Four. The father, never viewed by the playwright with disfavor, has placed his daughter when seven years old in the care of the well-to-do widow so that she may receive protection and he the money necessary for his trip to the capital, where he proposes to take the official examinations. He represents the highest ideal in the Chinese hierarchy of values, the mastery of Confucian scholarship and learning. He succeeds in the examinations and within the course of years rises to high position. With full powers to acquit or to condemn, he travels from county to county carrying the seal of the Emperor. At length he arrives at the city to which his daughter had moved and where she was executed. During her adoption her name was changed. Hence, though he receives the brief concerning her case, he does not at first recognize it as in any way concerning him personally. Weary from his travels, he sits at his table in the evening, a pile of official documents before him. The ghost enters, at first invisible. His eye skims the papers concerning her, which lie at the top of the pile. Judging this unhappy case to have been long ago decided, he transfers these papers to the bottom. The ghost dims the candle and restores them to the top without attracting her father's attention. This occurs three times, after which with terror he is convinced that a ghost lurks in the room. Finally, after the full dramatic suspense of the preliminaries has been extracted, the ghost manifests herself to him and the two engage in their tragically moving conversation, the unmistakable result of which for the audience is purgation of the emotions of pity and fear. The father's long soliloquy in this scene and the ghost's words demand quotation.

(*Tou*). Light the lamp for me. You have been working hard, and you may rest now. But come when I call you. (*The servant lights the lamp and leaves*).

(*Tou*). I shall go through a few cases. Here is one concerning Tou Ngo, who poisoned her father-in-law. Curious that the first culprit's surname should be the same as mine ! To murder one's father-in-law is one of the unpardonable crimes ; so it seems there are lawless elements among my clan. Since this case has been dealt with, I need not read it. I'll put it at the bottom of the pile and look at another. Wait, I suddenly feel drowsy. I suppose

I am growing old, and am tired after travelling. I will take a short nap on the desk. (*He sleeps. Enter Tou Ngo's ghost*).

(*Ghost*). *Day after day I weep in the underworld,*
Waiting impatiently for my revenge.
I pace on slowly in darkness,
Then am borne along by the whirlwind ;
Enveloped by mist I come swiftly in ghostly form.

(*She looks about her*). Now the door-gods will not let me pass. I am the daughter of Inspector Tou. Though I died unjustly, my father does not know it ; so I have come to visit him in his dreams. (*She enters the room and weeps*).

(*Tou, shedding tears*). Tuan-yun, my child ! Where have you been ? (*Tou Ngo's spirit leaves, and Tou wakes up.*) How odd ! I fell asleep and dreamed that I saw my daughter coming towards me ; but where is she now ? Let me go on with these cases. (*Tou Ngo's spirit enters and makes the lamp burn low*). Strange ! I was just going to read a case when the light flickered and dimmed. My servant is asleep ; I must trim the wick myself. (*As he trims the lamp, Tou Ngo's spirit re-arranges the file*). Now the light is brighter, I can read again. "This concerns the criminal Tou Ngo, who poisoned her father-in-law". Strange ! I read this case first, and put it under the others. How has it come to the top ? Since this case has already been dealt with, let me put it at the bottom again and study a different one. (*Once more Tou Ngo's spirit makes the lamp burn low*). Strange ! Why is the light flickering again ? I must trim it once more. (*As Tou trims the light, Tou Ngo's spirit once more turns over the file*). Now the lamp is brighter, I can read another case. "This concerns the criminal Tou Ngo, who poisoned her father-in-law". How extraordinary ! I definitely put this at the bottom of the pile just before I trimmed the lamp. Can there be ghosts in this office ?- Well, ghost or no ghost, an injustice must have been done. Let me put this underneath and read another. (*Tou Ngo's spirit makes the lamp burn low again*). Strange ! The lamp is flickering again. Can there actually be a ghost here tampering with it. I'll trim it once more. (*As he trims the*

*wick, Tou Ngo's spirit comes up to him and he sees her.
He strikes his sword on the desk).* Ah, there's the ghost !
I warn you, I am the emperor's inspector of justice. If
you come near, I'll cut you in two. Hey, boy ! How can
you sleep so soundly ? Get up at once ! Ghosts ! Ghosts !
This is terrifying ?

(*Ghost*). *Fear is making him lose his head ;
The sound of my weeping has frightened him more than ever.
Here, Tou Tien-chang, my old father,
Will you let your daughter, Tou Ngo, bow to you ?*

I venture to think this quite as moving a scene as the interview
between Prince Hamlet and his father. Clearly, even if the
play in a few respects fails to comply with the requirements
usually demanded for tragedy, it answers the chief of them in
ample measure.

The review or analysis has thus far considered in detail the
second and more impressive half of the play, namely, Acts
Three and Four. But no general appraisal of its quality can be
made without at least some attention to Acts One and Two.
It is true that on a rapid glance these earlier acts may appear
less as tragedy than as melodrama. Violent incidents occur
with considerable rapidity and with small benefit from a
poetic or an elevated language. The characters may seem in
some cases commonplace, in others, thoroughly contemptible.
The doctor who ineffectually plots the mother's murder, the
ruffian who foils his plan, and the still more bestial clown, his
son, presented with a half-animal mask and carrying the
depreciatory name of "Donkey," are all figures midway between
a crude melodrama and a sordid naturalism. The mother-in-
law contributes little to relieve this impression, though the
audience is evidently intended to have some compassion for
her in the unhappy alternative which she faces. At best, she
is an ironical figure. All these considerations notwithstanding,
the relatively low pitch of the play's first half is by no means
incompatible with scenes of exposition or emotional relief in
pure tragedy. The cynical doctor might be compared with the
Apothecary in *Romeo and Juliet,* the countryman and his
animalistic son with grotesque figures in many serious Elizabethan plays. Chinese plays often proceed in a leisurely

fashion, as a rule introducing an abrupt though strictly preliminary action that nevertheless is considerably removed from the heart of their story. This is often presented as a prelude before Act One. One sorrow must tread upon another's heels until we begin to envisage the full extent of the burden to be carried by the unfortunate heroine.

The Chinese attitude toward the unhappy father needs to be carefully noted, for whereas his actions are likely to appear heartless in Western eyes, the thought that a true scholar can do no wrong and that one's duty to the state is even more compelling than that to the family must be clearly understood. In the last act his heightened rank gives him increased dignity but does not essentially alter the role that he plays. He is intended as a thoroughly sympathetic character. Thus his parting from his daughter in Act One is only less tender a scene than his return and his interview with her disembodied spirit in Act Four. In both parts of the play these two figures rise above the sordid generality of mankind and move the body of the play along the axis of tragedy.

Man's overshadowing fate is sometimes presented in Western criticism as the surest criterion of tragedy, even more significant than its presentation of mortality and its purgation of the destructive emotions. From the heroine's first appearance as Tou Ngo in Act One it should be realized that she is a foredoomed character, one against whom destiny has aimed its irresistible and deeply poisoned arrows. Even the first speech describing her history shows the worst ills of life accumulated and still accumulating on her head. She is at once the symbol of suffering womankind and of the slings and arrows of ill fortune. So strong is this symbolic aspect of the dramatic idea that it even approaches allegory. The play is thus a fable of the soul. The philosophy emerging without undue didacticism from it is virtually that already observed in *The Palace of Eternal Youth*. To cite the concluding aphorism of a typical English Morality Play of the sixteenth century, virtue is victimized in this world and triumphant only in the eternal world beyond the manifestations of mortality. Insofar as there is a triumph of justice and truth beyond the grave, the philosophy diverges from the conception of tragedy and constitutes a species of divine comedy. But, after all, the present play makes few statements, if any, concerning a transcendental world. The ghost is herself all-too-human. Unlike *The Palace of Eternal Youth*, this is not a metaphysical poem. The conclusion, which stresses the restitution of the sufferer's earthly fame and the corporeal punishment of her accusers, smacks of a thoroughly down-to-earth philosophy. The ritualistic elements are aesthetic rather than explicitly religious, belonging to folklore rather than to theology. The play's sentiment clearly owes much more to Confucianism than to Buddhism. It is true that in some respects the heroine resembles Sita in the great Sanskrit religious dramas, but in the end the one remains a woman and the other truly a goddess, even though an Earth Goddess of fertility and motherhood. These qualities in the Chinese work bring it the closer to tragedy and dissociate it from a religious or symbolical pageantry. Although a much humbler work than Bhavabhuti's great musical drama in praise of Sita, it actually comes much nearer to the coordinates of tragedy as commonly understood in Western criticism.

Snow in Midsummer, though comparatively brief, is an ironic drama of considerable complexity. In contrast, another almost equally famous play, *The Sorrows of Han*, is still briefer, more explicitly tragic, and in quality suggests such a powerful and succinct lyrical tragedy as the celebrated *Ballad of Sir Patrick Spens*. Nothing for the theatre can be simpler or more direct than this eminently tragic tale, whose somberness is indicated even in its title. The story can be quickly retold. For many generations an understanding has existed between the Han Emperor and the ruler of the Tartar kingdom that peace shall be maintained between them as long as the Emperor gives to the Khan one among the favorite women in his household. For a while, it seems, the Han monarchs had discontinued the erotic institution of a harem of favorites, though meanwhile the agreement between the two powers had been duly observed. The Emperor who occupies the throne during the time of the play decides at the advice of a minister to reconstitute the harem. That all may be fittingly done, he allows his minister to survey his empire in order that he may bring to court a hundred of the most beautiful young women procurable in his kingdom. This with much bribery and corruption the minister does. Portraits of the beauties are painted by way of an index. But since the family of the most beautiful of all the girls is poor and can pay no bribe, the minister has her portrait defaced and succeeds for a while in keeping her out of the sight and knowledge of the Emperor. One day, however, he hears her playing her lute and so comes to meet her. At once realizing that he has been cheated, he selects the girl for his favorite queen and falls fervently in love. The minister he condemns to death but this singularly wiley man escapes to the Tartars. To their king he carries a true portrait of the lady. On seeing this the barbarian monarch naturally demands her as his prize from the Emperor. The Emperor at first refuses the disturbing request but realizing his power weak and that of the Tartars strong and with his own will bent beneath the pressure of his ignoble nobles, he finally yields. Moreover, the queen insists on giving herself up as a sacrifice for the peace and prosperity of the realm. She deeply loves the Emperor, despite what seem his failings in Western eyes. The Emperor accompanies her to the bank of the river dividing the two realms, where she is handed over to the embassy from the Khan. But before she can be delivered to him as his prize she drowns herself in the stream. This deed, like the death of Tou Ngo, occurs in Act Three. Act Four, as in *Snow in Midsummer*, depicts a vision and a ghost, though in *The Sorrows of Han* the conception is more subjective. Thought focuses on the Emperor's grief. In a dream he fancies his wife returning to him but abruptly snatched away by a Tartar soldier. It is a nightmare. In the end the Khan is sympathetic and remains at peace with the Empire. He is even revolted on hearing of the duplicity of the escaped minister, whom he returns to the Han realm, where he is tortured and killed as sacrifice to the spirit of the dead queen. Though the fatal river runs through the desert, eternal green springs from the garden beside her tomb.

As a tragedy this work is much less equivocal than *Snow in Midsummer*. In structure it shuns the discursive, fictional manner of such works as *Snow in Midsummer* or *The Chalk Circle* and approaches the short story. It altogether dispenses with the psychological subtleties and ironies that enlarge the economical narrative of *The Western Chamber* into virtually a slow-moving psychological novel shaped for the stage. The cast of characters is small. The whole is brief ; there are relatively few scenes, few long harangues and certainly no complexities. One might almost suppose it to be a scenario or truncated version and the latter suggestion may possibly be true. The few words spoken by the heroine on the occasion of her suicide are not easy to conceive as the actuality of the scene. Miming may do much yet here it may well be that in some productions of the play a considerable passage occurred missing in the best-known printed versions. Be this as it may, the work as a whole is strikingly of a piece and strikingly effective. It is naked tragedy, in some ways more powerful for having so few embellishments, ornaments or digressions of any kind. The ballad-like forthrightness of the style gives it dignity. There are no grotesque or half-humorous episodes, as in the other plays so far discussed in this book.

In important respects *The Sorrows of Han* stands apart from the majority of classical Chinese plays that have descended to the present time, though in no way can it be called in the least unorthodox. Its dramatic technique has what may be described as a primitive appearance. Relatively little real dialogue occurs, in other words, the characters engage in remarkably little actual exchange of words. About half the lines, whether spoken or sung, are directed to the audience. This convention appears, of course, in all Chinese plays but here to a much more marked degree than usual. It presumably bears witness to the Oriental drama's obligation in its origins to animated recitation. The present play is, accordingly, suggestive of a canto in an epic poem presented half as recitational poetry and half as a truly dramatic text. This primitivism from a technical point of view far from vitiating the work in respect to its art form gives it the peculiar charm of a style to some extent archaic. It smiles at us with something of the look, half naive, half sophisticated, of a sixth-century Greek statue. Although by no means as technically mature art as *The Western Chamber* or *The Chalk Circle*, it has not only a peculiar charm but a peculiar tension and energy, as half-opened leaves in April. Here is a refreshing elegance in the season of the dramatic year for which the critic should be truly grateful and by no means apologetic.

Such a piece might be commonplace were it not for its great structural and emotional integrity. All stands in the most perfect balance. The last act is even decidedly unusual, for it presents as the play's major scene a vision enacted as a play within the play. Possibly the brevity of the scene with the heroine's suicide is a calculated stroke of art to retain emphasis upon the Emperor, the only character who sings. The play's title in itself indicates that he, not his mistress, is the main focus of attention. It is his infatuation with her, his indignation at his feeble supporters, and his grief at his great loss that the playwright seeks primarily to depict. True, the heroine's part abounds in pathos and especially to a Western audience may appear dominant. But to the Chinese the Emperor's feelings carried the greater weight. Hence the last act belongs to him, not to the ghost of his mistress, who, after all, appears to him only in his dream. Although his fate is interwoven with hers, it is for him that the dramatist chiefly cares.

The play is the stronger as both a work of art and a tragedy in that it has no direct political bias or propaganda. The minister is a rogue and is duly punished. There is merely an attractive contrast between the barbaric court of the Khan and the elegant and even effete court of the Emperor. One nation is in no decisive way favored above the other. The Khan is no villain for insisting on his hereditary rights. His generosity and high-mindedness in abstaining from grievance against the Emperor and in returning the deceitful minister to his doom place him in a strongly favorable light. Both monarchs are in a sense redeemed through the heroine's death. The Khan no longer contemplates a war of invasion, rapine and destruction. The Emperor is no longer suspected of being merely selfishly indulgent. The depth of his love and affection is at last revealed. The moral dignity commonly associated with the Western conception of tragedy is achieved. Indeed, the sobriety of this play comes closer to the seriousness of the major works of Sanskrit or Japanese drama than to the typical Chinese play whose moods are more mercurial, pliant or Shakespearean.

Plain and divested of ornament as this play is, it has many nuances that belong to a refined art. One, that follows a well-established Oriental tradition, may be selected for attention, namely, the use of pictures as stage properties. This virtually constitutes a leit-motif. A lying picture of the heroine is shown the Emperor in Act One ; a true picture is shown the Khan in Act Two. The subject is repeatedly recalled. This type of incident is, of course, common to both folklore and romance. It has a considerable place in Sanskrit drama, where it is used by the greatest masters, as Bhasa, Kalidasa, and Sudraka. There can be small doubt of its theatrical effectiveness.

The Sorrows of Han also provides for calculated use of music and choreography. It is through overhearing the singing and lute-playing of the heroine that the Emperor first becomes aware of her. The bellicose manoeuvers of the Tartars evidently entail scenes of dazzling spectacle, choreography, acrobatics and military music. The dramatist has much more in mind than contained in the bare words. Having such firm control in the execution of his artistic purpose, he achieves a goal more closely akin to Western poetic tragedy than to the lighter forms of theatrical entertainment. In point of artistic sophistication this work stands midway between *Snow in Midsummer* and a play more overtly tragic but also more akin to a folk or popular art, *The Death of the Winged-Tiger General.*

This is a drama of intrigue ending in death and lamentation. Although no actual fighting occurs, it further belongs in the category of military plays, since it celebrates in particular the military prowess of its hero, who appears in his warrior's elaborate paraphernalia. Yet it proves in several respects an exception to the rule, most notably in its tragic conclusion. Its picture of official life is dark indeed. Except for the naive but valiant hero, there are few, if any, honest or capable men at court. Hamlet himself was in a similar company. The general-in-chief is an habitual drunkard, utterly irresponsible. For his advisers he selects chiefly two favorites who confess that they have no ability whatsoever and love only the pleasures of debauchery. Omitting the hero, the only sympathetic characters are two women, his wife and his mother by adoption. It is these who take the principal part in the scenes of grief at the conviction and the funeral of the hero. The plot is extremely simple, indeed elementary to such a degree that it discourages summary. The spirit more concerns us here. The theme becomes virtually that so much favored by the

Renaissance masters of drama, the unequal, fatal and tragic struggle between the lion and the fox, the noble innocent and the intriguing villain. It provides the Oriental equivalent to the plot of *Othello*. The Chinese play is less decorous or exalted yet moves with like inevitability to its denouement. The simplicity and directness of treatment suggests epic writing of considerably more force than complexity, such, for example, as may be found in *Beowulf*. In the broad or psychological sense in which the word "tragedy" is employed in these pages mood means more than form. It is in the purgative force of tragic calamity and the grave outlook prompted thereby that *The Death of the Winged-Tiger General* most nearly accords with the Western formulation of the idea. Almost instinctively on assimilating this work we set it down as tragedy in its essential meanings, whatever the detailed features of its execution may be. From as early as Aeschylus weeping women gathered beside the corpse of a hero have provided the simplest condition for the tragic scene. Women mourn also at the tomb of Hector and at the tomb of Christ. Here we have tragedy, pure, simple and moving. There is even something of the lyrical or Aeschylean in this stark Chinese drama, for it contains many lyric passages repeating heroic formulations of praise for the doomed protagonist, much in the manner of classical strophic verse. The formula for the whole is utterly simple. The hero occupies the center of a highly contrived design, with the weeping women at one side of him and a host of buffoons ingloriously at the other side who by malignant fate and superiority of numbers bring him to his death. The play is thus a prolonged dramatic song joining paeons of praise with a heavy burden of lament. The tragic idea could hardly be expressed in a form more essential to itself.

Although the translation leaves as English poetry something to be desired, formal laments by the two women have the spirit of poetic tragedy. The mother exclaims :

Cruel Keh-yung ! You believed two lying scoundrels and had Tsun-hsiao killed so unjustly.
Five carts pulled in five directions—
Even a man of iron would utter a cry,
Bone and flesh were torn apart,

His blood stained the yellow sand.
Never again shall I see my son—
The thought of it breaks my heart.
I am bowed with sorrow,
And Tsun-hsiao has gone to the shades.
(*Weeps*). Ah, Tsun-hsiao, my son, your mother will die of grief!
The wife laments :
Ah, Tsun-hsiao, my heart is broken.
I wave the pennant from side to side—
Your spirit must not lose its way!
My tears stream unceasingly,
My heart is burning with anguish.
No matter how long the road,
I shall reach my goal in the end.
I wave the pennant,
I carry the box with your ashes on my back.
Your spirit flies on high—where is it now?
Surely this is Winged-Tiger Valley?
You must not miss the place and pass us by.
I cannot stop sobbing with anguish,
Faint with sorrow . . . .
His father has admited wronging him,
His comrades-in-arms are wailing bitterly ;
Recalling his mighty deeds and immortal fame,
They have put on mourning for him
And are kneeling before the shrine.
Alas, your achievements were vain—
Quiet hang the two iron maces,
The bright embroidered flag flutters in the wind,
The painted drum sounds and the bugle.
In tiger-skin turban
On bay charger,
Bearing steel-tipped arrows
And bow with painted tassels,
You stayed in frosty tents in ice-bound country
Where battles raged and enemy forces swarmed.
Seeing these relics now,
My heart bleeds for you, Tsun-hsiao.
The tiger-skin robe hangs limp before your tent,

In vain you risked death to restore the house of Tang,
Or galloped across the bridge with lance in hand—
This is the end !
In vain you routed Huang Chao with eighteen horsemen.

In the face of such a passage all tragic dirges seem molded into one.

4 / *Tragicomedy*

THE THEORY and practice of "tragicomedy" as evolved under
the auspices of Italian scholars in the sixteenth century offers
a useful introduction to one of the leading aspects of the
classical Chinese theatre. Although in this, as in most theatrical matters, the Chinese dramatists themselves, unlike their
Sanskrit predecessors, appear to have been more pragmatic
than philosophical, their favorite practices point strongly in
the direction of tragicomedy. Notwithstanding a few important
exceptions to the general rule, tragedy in the sense of a serious
play with an unhappy ending and an aspiration to sublimity
remains a rarity. The Chinese do not like extremes. Only a
minor proportion of their best plays are in the strictest sense
of the word comic, that is, frankly light and laughter-provoking.
Fun in the classical Chinese theatre is more likely to be trans-
fused with elegance and sophistication than to be slapstick
or farce. Their major plays evoke many smiles but few guffaws.
Perhaps their favorite and most notable general feature is the
conjunction known but on the whole not generally popular
in the West of the formal happy ending following scenes of
much seriousness. Western traditions for some two or three
centuries acknowledged tragicomedy but, except for opera,
strongly tended to favor pure comedy or pure tragedy. Comedy
might descend to the low or farcical or rise to the intellectual
and refined. But there was long an apparent suspicion that
in the instance of strictly serious writing the formal happy
ending signifies a dilution or diminution of the serious effect.
Serious critics have insisted that life is serious and even tragic
and should so be presented in the interests of realism, if from

no other consideration. The graver the main scenes of the play, the more strongly the unhappy conclusion, or formal ending for tragedy, is in request. These views appear frequently in Shakespeare criticism. The most admired and often produced plays are frankly tragedies or comedies, as *Hamlet* or *Twelfth Night*. The very nature of Shakespeare's historical plays precludes the artificially contrived ending for either tragedy or comedy. Each of the historical plays, of course, concludes with something of a resolution of the moral and political problems raised in the course of its action but none, not even *Richard the Second*, quite answers the demands of tragedy. For this their moods are too complex. Nor is any of them, not even the Falstaff plays, a true comedy. To see Falstaff in pure comedy we must turn to *The Merry Wives of Windsor*.

It is of critical interest that the graver plays with happy endings written during the great dramatist's mid-career, as *Measure for Measure*, and *All's Well That Ends Well*, have often been described as "problem plays," but seldom as tragicomedies. No more is the latter term used in the instance of such semi-serious plays as *The Merchant of Venice*, or *Much Ado About Nothing*, the plots for both of them having their roots in medieval fiction. Tragicomedy as defined by Renaissance critics signified not a hybrid form of humor and pathos but the truly serious play almost, if not entirely, indistinguishable from tragedy until its very last scenes. Considerations of rank and class, though to modern eyes comparatively superficial, were among the pragmatic points at issue. Comedy dealt with the more modest orders of society, with gentlemen, with citizens, or, if farcical, with the peasantry, unlike the graver plays having their commerce with kings and princes, especially as these were shown in their official roles. Tragicomedy moved on a socially and morally exalted plane. The happy ending was in no way taken to reduce the level of its high seriousness. This species of drama as a distinct type was, in fact, unknown in English until Beaumont and Fletcher and their school, taking themselves quite seriously, brought it to sudden perfection. Shakespeare, promptly aware of this development, at once responded with his own tragicomedies, *The Winter's Tale*, *Cymbeline*, and *Pericles*. (*The Tempest* more nearly resembles a masque). With singular sensitivity to the times, he responded to the new type of satirical tragedy introduced by Ben Jonson, contributing his own *Coriolanus* to it. Western practice habitually agreed with the Chinese only in the field of baroque opera. The story of Mozart's *Idomeneo*, with its serious tone and happy ending, offers one of the closest approximations among major works in the West to one of the prevalent phases of dramatic story-telling in China.

These retrospections are not actually digressions in an investigation of the classical Chinese stage. Of course the considerations of social rank, so important in the West, signify little or nothing for Chinese drama, which is essentially one of the least restricted of all great dramatic literatures in its address to or treatment of any single class. Written for an intensely class-conscious society, it is itself without class bias, being addressed to the gratification of society as a whole. Even for Western drama, this consideration remains subordinate in any really serious appraisal. The obvious fact is that tragicomedy, viewed in the long run with suspicion by the West, offers an analogy to the type of drama viewed with special approval by Asian playwrights. Both Sanskrit and Chinese dramatists strongly favor it. In the East only the Japanese habitually and intimately coincide in their views and practices with Western distinctions between tragedy and comedy. The Athenians varied a day's dramatic offering with two types, presenting a trilogy of tragedies followed by a satyr-play. The Japanese, with even more virtuosity, interjected farces, or *kyogen*, between the presentation of their eminently serious and often tragic Noh Plays.

Emphasis in Chinese thought on morality and on the poise between the basic forces in the universe assisted in dissuading them from the emotional extremes favored by their island neighbors. The Chinese, even more than the Indians, revere poise of mind. The theological Hindus favor a view of the universe obtruding more openly upon their view of human life. This is to say that they are at heart a more religious and less ethical people than the Chinese. Siva is both creator and destroyer. But the Chinese are the most optimistic of Eastern peoples. Despite all life's bitterness and contradictions, they

73

prefer to think of it as somehow resolving itself in the end for the best. The iniquities of one generation will be corrected in the next. The over-all view is cheerful. Hence many of their gravest and most deeply moving plays come at length to a happy resolution. This is not owing to the romantic sentimentality that beset the generation of Charles Dickens but rather to the basic character of a great and thoughtful people. Tragicomedy, as already observed, achieved only a moderate success in the West. Its measure may roughly be taken when the achievements of Shakespeare in tragedy and Ben Jonson in comedy are compared with those of Beaumont and Fletcher. From causes deep-seated in the outlook of the two halves of the world, the Chinese in the analogous domain achieved more favorable results. Even the Westerner on considering their works is unlikely to raise the objections brought against the inconsistency of the grave contents and cheerful conclusions of the Beaumont and Fletcher plays or in the long line of romantic melodramas succeeding them. The Chinese works are very much of a piece. Chinese dramatists are an integral part of their civilization as a whole whereas Beaumont and Fletcher were primarily spokesmen not for English culture as a whole but for the courts of King James and King Charles.

This does not mean that the Oriental playwrights were themselves entirely unconscious of a problem and especially of the suspicion of a sentimental optimism. On many occasions their humor is alone able to carry them across a perilous bridge to safe landing on the opposite shore. Where the Westerner finds the objections of logic and improbability difficult to overcome, the Easterner dismisses the difficulty with reference to his faith in magic. Thus the ending of an extremely popular play translated under the title, *Madame Cassia*, has a jaunty air of sophisticated parody. A group of characters speaks as follows :

(*Li Ch'i*). T'ien Wang is like a bird caught in a snare ; Yang Shih is like a fish caught in a net. Their flesh will be sliced into a thousand slivers. My heart feels satisfied.
—You may deceive man, but you cannot deceive heaven.
(*Kuei-Chih*). Good and evil fortune depend on the turning of a wheel.

(*Chao Ch'ung*). Whoever injures others is bound to receive retribution.

(*Li Pao*). Who shall Heaven spare ? Surely not the wicked !

(*Exeunt omnes, chuckling joyfully*).

Although this play is rich in the most highly calculated emotional ambivalence, in part tragedy, in part high comedy, there can be no doubt as to the studied levity of the conclusion. The playwright not only knows his optimism to pertain to the theatre, not to real life, but presumes the same awareness on the part of his educated audience.

Again, in *The Shephers's Pen*, a play translated, with considerable omissions, by Arlington and Acton, an intensely serious action contains a fillip of high comedy at its conclusion. The wicked mother-in-law brazenly swears that she is innocent. 'If I am truly guilty of what I am accused of, I hope that a dragon will bear me away on its claws." The stage direction follows promptly : "Immediately an actor impersonating a dragon drags her off." The philosophical levity becomes unmistakable. The felicitous ending in no way vitiates the force of the whole. On the contrary, it assists the play with use of a contrasting frame and even a Western reader or spectator will in all probability gain considerable pleasure from it. The spiritual energy is simply not depressed by a want of a tragic conclusion. Ending the business of a serious play in an optimistic vein is no more injurious to its success than is the conclusion of a piece of classical music with use of the dominant chord. Wisdom, poise, and contentment are valued more highly than shock therapy or naturalistic truth. Moreover, the studied artificiality of all Chinese drama is agreeable to an ending conspicuously contrived in the cheerful vein. The production is clearly in no way intended to mimic or duplicate life ; it is designed, as Aristotle declared tragedy should be, to operate favorably for the welfare of the soul.

One of the most celebrated and brilliant of Chinese plays, *The Chalk Circle*, illustrates these conditions most clearly. Poetic justice is here measured out most effectively. The very essence of the play's meaning hangs on the belief that real life all too seldom exhibits these happy solutions. The play's story contrasts the crude, cruel and corrupt judge, appearing

in Act Two, with the intelligent, merciful and honest judge
appearing in Act Four, which is the last. There is a strong
inference that in real life there are more dishonest than honest
judges. The playwright does not propose to represent what is
typical, or life as it is. Being an idealist, he proposes to show
what life should be. But the case is not as simple as this
statement implies. Far from representing life as pleasant,
much the larger part of the work exhibits it as unpleasant.
Until the last tenth of the play, all goes badly. There is no
hero. The heroine suffers the most cruel and unusual torture.
Romantic sentimentality cannot vitiate so satirical a view of
existence. The ending is a pure convention, acknowledged as
such. In a formal harangue Hai-tang summarizes the entire
action from the point of view of accepted morality. Her
speech has a lyrical spirit and a stanzaic form. In other words
the happy ending constitutes virtually a ritual. A more
formalistic conclusion would be unthinkable yet aesthetically
and psychologically it proves eminently gratifying. In no
way does it betray a serious view of the play's general content.

> Neighbors ! said you not
> That before the judge
> You laid bare your hearts,
> That your words were of
> The very essence of truth ?
> Old women ! said you not
> That after so many years
> It was impossible for you
> To recall your memories ?
> Clerk of the Court ! said you not
> That the magistrate was true and honest,
> That he applied the law faithfully ?
> Dame Ma ! said you not
> That by your prudence and wisdom
> You held first place ?
> But finally the Supreme Judge
> Of Kai-feng-fu has unravelled
> The threads of their odious weft.
> These people over there
> Are to be sent into exile

Upon the frontier
In a barren and uninhabited land.
Those two most guilty ones
To be punished in the main square.
It is worthy, Lord, that this
Story of the Circle of Chalk
Should be made known
Even unto the four seas,
And be brought to the knowledge
Of the whole Empire.

This work is itself much more serious and less ambivalent than another typical variety of Chinese drama that may be termed Chinese high comedy, perfectly exemplified in *Madame Cassia*. Its general tone, dark, sinister spirit, and brutally naturalistic and harsh characterizations relate *The Chalk Circle* to much Western drama. It is a little as though the mordant *Troilus and Cressida* had been given an ending as idealized and optimistic as that of *A Midsummer-Night's Dream*.

Much of the strength of *The Chalk Circle* lies in the exceptional scope of its qualities, for though comparatively simple as a dramatic narrative, it is complex in its characterizations. One uses the word comparatively; while in plot it is less complex than, say, *The Divided Tunic*, it is much more so than *The Western Chamber*. The striking contrast lies between its forthright story and the ironic characters who appear in it. The heroine, Hai-tang, has been a woman of pleasure until, well along in Act One, she becomes a devoted wife and mother. Her own mother is typical of the ambivalent roles frequently found in Chinese drama, being half sympathetic, half distasteful. She loves her children but is too demanding of them and in the instance of Hai-tang takes the questionable course of encouraging her practice of courtesanship in order to relieve the poverty occasioned by her own widowhood. Hai-tang's brother is a still more questionable character, madly antagonistic to his sister not because of her prostitution as such but because her profession casts aspersions upon himself. He cannot bear to be sneered at on the ground that his sister is a woman of pleasure. In Act Three their position becomes

77

reversed. On learning the full circumstances of his sister's life in Lord Ma's household, he withdraws his antagonism. He is pictured as a selfish young man, given to his own pleasures and singularly obstinate in his opinions, until hardship teaches him to follow a more commendable course, to apply himself with steadier discipline and finally to become a responsible member of his family and servant of the state. He is the prodigal son, neglecting his mother and quarrelling with his sister. In time he reforms his character as he enters into a delayed maturity. This is an unusually involved and, especially from Western standards, unusually interesting part.

Lord Ma, like the mother, is an ambiguous character, selfish in pursuit of his own pleasures, incapable of managing the personal problems of his own household, and of maintaining an equitable relationship so far as his two wives are concerned. He is represented as weak and over-emotional, especially in the scene in which he rashly rebukes Hai-tang and completely loses control of his feelings. We have lost faith in him before he dies from poison.

The lesser characters are virtually caricatures of cupidity, all venial. The evil judge is a portrait of judicial corruption that would have delighted Daumier. Similarly, the bribed witnesses and servants of the court personify social or judicial degeneracy. The drawing is memorable. Evil as these persons are, one is not led to consider them as monstrous. Rather, there is a comprehensive indictment of society. There are, however, two truly prodigious figures, Lord Ma's first wife, and her lover, the unscrupulous clerk of the court, Chao. She is a veritable Lady Macbeth, he, an outrageous self-seeker, as arrogant as Diomedes and as corrupt as Iago. Yet it is typical of Chinese drama, didactic as it often becomes, that even these figures are not conventional stage villains. In pursuit of her own desires at the expense of all morality, the woman becomes a truly magnificent embodiment of evil. Her audacity makes her virtually superhuman, her jealousy, almost heroic. Beside her, her lover seems weak and pale. She not only murders her husband but causes the torture and conviction of her rival, the second wife, and brazenly appropriates the child, with unexampled arrogance and insolence pretending that she is the child's mother. The barren woman

outfaces the fruitful woman. Her whole conduct is the quintessence of falsehood. In pretending to favor her rival she actually
intrigues to have her destroyed. Her assumed generosity in
the matter of the gifts to the impoverished brother of Hai-tang
results in the latter's undoing. Her assumed affection for
the child conceals her harsh and relentless cupidity. She
seeks wealth at the expense of other peoples' lives. She is a
fascinating and arresting stage figure, the ideal hypocrite, far
more noteworthy, for example, than any other of the innumerable wicked step-mothers who literally crowd the scenes
of the Chinese theatre. One is reminded of the great figures of
Renaissance melodrama, as John Webster's "White Devil."
Her last words suggest to an English reader the memorable
closing lines in the part of Christopher Marlowe's Piers Gaves-
ton, who scorns the world and goes "to discover countries
yet unknown." Defiant to the end, she mocks her judges and
scorns her cowardly lover: "You craven-hearted coward,
you! Make haste and confess. What do you wish me to say?
It was I, I who did everything. Anyway, is death so great a
misfortune? When we have lost life, shall we not rejoice in
being reunited in a better world like a devoted wedded couple?"
This is bare-faced irony. She despises Chao as a man yet
accepts him as an accomplice in both love and crime. His
own servile attempts to crawl out of his predicament and
place all blame upon her mark the final distortion in his
detestable character. Both are justly condemned to the
bitterest punishment and most ignominious death. As dramatic
figures they reach imposing stature. Moreover, they are seen
in strong contrasting colors both between themselves and
against the other figures, especially the passive heroine and
her mercurial brother. They are the active forces that set the
plot in motion. She is by far the most vigorous figure in the
play, dominating all its characters, as he is the ruling figure in
the corrupt courtroom, overshadowing the weak and sensual
judge. The delineation is exceptionally strong. Largely because
of this intensity, the play approaches the height of tragedy.

Less need be said of the heroine primarily because here the
conception is so much the simpler. If there is any complexity,
this lies in an ambiguity unhappily not untypical in Chinese
literature. The emphasis upon torture strongly suggests

masochism. As already remarked in connection with *Snow in Midsummer* and *The Sorrows of Han*, the Chinese fondness for exalting women in the fictional and theatrical worlds and praising them for their long suffering suggests a compensation for the subjection frequently meted out to women in real life. Be this as it may, the part is a very striking one. Excellent contrasts are achieved between the image of Hai-tang as the youthful courtesan, reluctant in the practice of her profession, and her extreme fidelity as wife and mother. The play's graph is unusually clear and gratifying. Lady Ma is the moving force while Hai-tang is the passive center about which all revolves. The basic conception itself has tragic dignity. It is also thoroughly Oriental.

The dignity becomes further enforced by the beauty of the composition and the imagery. The long first act abounds in dramatic business. The second act, set in the court of the corrupt judge, though hardly extraordinary, proceeds with moving force and directness. The mounting waves of false witnesses prove especially effective. This is obviously good theatre and serious in its intent. Act Three changes and advances the imagery. It contains much extremely effective pantomime, especially in the motions of the characters to combat the fierceness of sleet, snow and gale. The innkeeper in the rugged mountain pass affords a striking interlude cast in the manner of the grotesque. One is reminded of vivid images in Chinese painting. The painful journey of the convicted woman, staggering under the blows of her captors and those of the elements, provides ideal stage action. The corruption of the ceremonious court and its attorneys descends even to the lowest orders in the social classes. Effective in heightening both the action and the emotion is the entrance of the impatient conspirators in crime, Lady Ma and Chao. Fearing that the court servants may neglect their instructions to murder Hai-tang before delivering her to the high court in the capital city, the two follow along the wintry track as wolves in melodrama following blood-stains in the snow. The act further presents the moving reconciliation of brother and sister, an episode artfully reversing earlier positions. Once the sister was fortunate, the brother unfortunate. But at long last he becomes a powerful judge, she a miserable person condemned to death. In his youthful days he reviled her, whereas now he recognizes his error and gives her protection. The act ends indecisively, as any episode in the course of a well-constructed play must end up to though not including the last. Lady Ma and Chao escape in the course of a scuffle. The entire act is exquisitely molded into the play's over-all composition.

Act Four is, of course, the counterpart of Act Two, one depicting a just, the other an unjust court at law. The play's forthrightness of design is sustained in spirit by the folkloristic episode of the chalk circle, a judgment much in the biblical style, associated with the wise King Solomon. Once more admirable in composition is the abrupt reversal in the action. At first the righteous judge appears at the point of condemning Hai-tang. The circle itself initially seems a device working against her. Happily, through her own explanation of the case—which it is now assumed was already clear to the judge— the tables are turned in her favor. Every line in this act falls with precise calculation into its place and contributes to the forceful and accumulative effect. The happy ending is in no sense a betrayal of the foregoing grim contents. Rather, it is the logical conclusion that has been long and devoutly desired. A tragic ending for a tragic story would in this instance have resulted in sheer monotony and repetition. The playwright's scheme provides for a diptych, with one courtroom in bold contrast to the other. Neighboring the two courtroom episodes are the two acts of free-moving dramatic narrative, the first furnished with a degree of urbane elegance, the second, with harsh and brutal scenes of lawless life amidst rugged mountains on a snowy winter evening. One is a picture of civil life, the other of mere barbarism. So the play marches steadily to its reasoned destination, intense as all true tragedy but relieved at length by a humane and well calculated ending. In a typical Japanese Noh Play the tragic mood or tension is sustained to the last. The breath is always held taut. The more genial Chinese theatre in the end releases the tension not only with a sigh of relief but with ultimate contentment. Surely, an unprejudiced reader will find no cause for complaint at the dramatist's decision, which sacrifices little or nothing of the play's tragic power. The heroine experiences a virtual resurrection from her misery. And resurrection is no trifling matter.

The Chalk Circle undeniably suffers somewhat in its poetic power not from its happy ending but from its obvious didacticism and its climax in the domain of anecdote and parable. The circle itself is an instance of witty Oriental trickery, an eminently intellectual device, somewhat short of the dignity of a high tragic action. The three preceding acts may be less striking than the last but possibly stand upon a higher plane of poetic imagination. Still, *The Chalk Circle* is obviously purer poetry and tragedy than Bertolt Brecht's witty reversal of the tables of orthodox morality in his *Caucasian Chalk Circle*, a direct reply in what Brecht conceives as modern terms to the art and morality of the Chinese masterpiece. His work is palpably far more didactic and considerably less tragic or poetic than the Chinese play. How the two shall be measured as to their merit no doubt depends on the temperament or the philosophy of the individual appraiser, although it is, I believe, difficult to deny that Brecht's virtuosity impinges upon vulgarity and egotistical exhibitionism, in sad contrast to the dignity and humanity of the Chinese work on which it is based. As already observed, *The Chalk Circle* stands among the most notable and widely produced of Chinese classical dramas. One of the most tragic or exalted it is not. These ideals are better exhibited in works with less a didactic and satirical purpose, with richer pathos and a more explicitly poetic tone. Such is a play which at least occasionally passes under the title of *The Shepherd's Pen*, where the Chinese formula for tragicomedy is even less equivocally exhibited. The passions are even deeper, the denouement more spiritually exhilarating.

The work as translated by Arlington and Acton may be regarded as a relatively short play or as part of a long one. Early scenes in the play depict the sufferings of mother and daughter-in-law in their beggarly life among impoverished herdsmen. This segment takes up the action at a moment near its climax.

Together with a large number of justly famous Chinese dramas, this has for its subject the reunion between two generations in a family. Sanskrit plays frequently deal with the separation and reunion of a man and a woman. But the Chinese theatre also in comparison with that of the West is less erotic and more social, dealing specifically with the institution of the family, strictly as conceived in the Confucian ethical system. Approximately half the plays examined in detail in this book accord with this description. Sons or daughters recover lost parents, or parents recover their lost children. Brother and sister are reunited. The prodigal returns, as in *An Heir in His Old Age*, or the daughter recovers her lost father, as in *Madame Cassia*. Specially gay formulas of music are used to accompany these scenes of recovery, as though their magic had to be attended with some enchanted melody. In separation lies the deepest and most tragic pain ; in reunion, the purest and most exalted joy of which human beings are capable. The plays may well end with an embrace but it is an embrace conceived in other than the familiar erotic terms. It is the symbol for family stability, continuity and unification. Such plays are marked throughout with a rare sincerity and emotional warmth. Beside them many of the more formal of Western classical tragedies actually appear formalistic and cold. Chinese playwrights are masters of a spiritual naturalism. In their themes they play with fire but, as all true artists, so play with fire that the spectators are warmed and not consumed. Pathos is sincere, controlled and of maximum force.

A brief recapitulation of the main action of *The Shepherd's Pen* sufficiently illustrates this. A son has been sent to the wars on the far-flung frontiers of the Empire, leaving behind him his mother and wife. The wicked mother of the hero's nephew, jealous of the better branch of the family, conspires against the unprotected women, driving them into the countryside, where they languish at the point of starvation. Furthermore, she intercepts letters from the hero to his home. On hearing the threatening news of his return as a victorious general, she erects mock tombs and circulates the report of their deaths. But the good women are not dead. The hero returns, visits the supposed graves, and dissolves in sorrow. As part of the ritual of grief, he establishes a station where for a given number of days the poor shall be fed. To this come the two women, his mother very old and almost totally blind, his wife, in only less miserable a plight. They stagger onto the scene late, after breakfast has been served and before dinner. The wife pleads with the soldiers, declaring that the old woman is in danger of imminent death. Can they not find something for her ? It is discovered that the general has been so distraught that he has left his own bowl of rice unconsumed. The mother may have that ; but she is cautioned to take great care of the general's bowl so that it may not be broken. The mother catches a glimpse of the hero. In her resulting doubt and confusion, she stumbles and breaks the bowl. The worst punishment is threatened by the heartless soldiers. But the hero is predisposed to pardon. After one of the many scenes of protracted pantomime and delay characterizing this drama, the persons come to recognize their true relationship. At first they hesitate, since each supposes the other dead. Moreover, in the course of years and fate their conditions have radically changed their appearance. The final recognition is tender and joyous in the extreme. The evil woman and the stupid nephew are confronted with this new and unforeseen situation. How a demon conveniently carries off the woman has already been revealed in these pages. The nephew is left to shift for himself, inasmuch as he has been duped and is merely dull, not wicked. Poetic justice is strictly observed as the play ends with the virtual ecstasy of its chief honorable characters. Directness is, both aesthetically and morally, its salvation. The portraits of all the chief characters, especially in whatever concerns their emotions, which constitute the core of the playwright's theme, are drawn with extraordinary skill and delicacy of feeling and perception. If this is not tragedy, it is almost more than tragedy. The depth of pathos here may well be more valuable than the excitement and shock characterizing the Western masterpieces. Refined in its means and profound in its ends, the Chinese play equally stirs the heart and imagination. This is not tragedy in the academic sense of the word nor is it strictly optimistic tragicomedy of the neoclassical Renaissance and the doctrinaire Humanists. The Chinese usage is happily without a name, safely beyond the sharp arrows of pedantic marksmanship. It is what it is, providing a deeply moving human and aesthetic experience. *The Shepherd's Pen* is but one of many works fully answering this description.

5 / *The Comic Touch*

CHINESE DRAMA abounds in comedy presenting many varieties of humorous theatre readily accessible for enjoyment by the world at large, no doubt with some dialects of the comic spirit virtually untranslatable to foreign minds and stages. There is apparently a good deal sly and oblique in the age-old traditions of China that remains untransportable. The theatre of the Far East itself is an institution singularly well built into a culture in many ways peculiar to itself. Everywhere comedy has the habit of local allusions, of glances at the peculiar customs, folkways, and legends of a people. No effort will be made in these pages to explore the darker chapters of this story in China or to illumine obscure corners. None need be, for enough of virtually universal significance remains which needs only to be seen to be appreciated. It is sufficient as a preliminary gesture to bow to the more mysterious or exotic thickets of Oriental humor and to pass unto a plain potentially open to all, unique and refreshing in its aromas as well as stimulating and exhilarating.

The general theme of humor on the Chinese stage would be much too broad for these studies, since any inclusive description would require an ample volume in itself. Here humor ranges from farce to philosophy. Of the former a typical example would be *Thrashing the God*, a skit about three rascals who attempt to evade a draft into the army by impersonating three statues in a temple. Even here there may be a faint element of the serious, as this always exists where profanation is present, but such thought is in this instance left well beneath the level of consciousness. This one-act play affords really inspired though thoroughly orthodox stage-business that rises to considerable heights in mimicry and miming. It may be recalled that a similar scene appears in the Sanskrit master-piece, *The Little Clay Cart*. Another brief play, *The Five Flower Grotto*, beginning with sheer nonsense ends with a surprising touch of philosophical allegory. It presents a troupe of dwarfs whose acrobatic antics plunge them deeper and deeper into trouble. They are summoned before a court as fantastic as they themselves. The action concludes as the pompous judge steps down from his grave throne of justice only to discover that, his official dignity set aside, he is himself merely a dwarf like all the rest. The moral of this eminently theatrical tale is simply that all men are brothers. It is an ideal allegory to express the very essence of the Chinese huma-nist philosophy of life. The first of these plays reveals the unsurpassed artfulness of Chinese pantomime, the second, the wit and wisdom of the Chinese masters of genial, graceful and winning aphorism. Both plays are unusually accomplished but by no means essentially rare in their general orientation to art or thought. Such works, though delightful, will bear little exegesis and any critic does well to shun the redundancy that might arise from extended commentary on them.

Satirical comedy, as known in Europe, or a witty critique of manners with considerable acerbity, does not flourish in the more genial Chinese soil. One of the closest approaches to it, perhaps, is the popular and ancient play, *The Butterfly Dream*, based on a story, as old as Petronius, of a clever husband who feigns death, thereby revealing how lightly his wife esteems him. She gladly mutilates what she supposes to be his corpse in an effort to please her new lover. The Chinese play is by no means as cynical as the same theme when treated by writers as dissimilar as Petronius, George Chapman, and Christopher Fry, yet satirical in some measure it undeniably is. Considering what indefatigable moralists the Chinese can be, the reticence of their playwrights in this regard is truly remarkable.

Subtler and more elusive fields than downright satire or clowning as a rule invite the Chinese playwright. Many of the problems of Chinese theatrical humor at its best may be explored by attention to a single play and in the interests of fruitful economy such will be the present course. The play chosen here is well known in China and enjoys the advantage of being translated by Yao Hsin-nung in the pages of *The T'ien Hsia Monthly*, volume one, 1935, pages 540-584, under the somewhat questionable title, *Madame Cassia*.

This translation is brilliant and in spirit almost unique. Clearly, it is a work of rare insight and enthusiasm. The English is fluent and impeccable, the stage directions are unusually full and revealing, and the Introduction provides one of the most illuminating of all essays on the general subject of Chinese comic acting. A comparison between this rendering and the relatively prosaic and unhappily abridged version by Arlington and Acton reveals the gap between the inspired and the merely competent. It is evident from the prefatory remarks that the translator has been induced to undertake his task by his keen relish and attentive observation of a live production. He declares that in his considerable experience with the Chinese stage this play has given him the greatest pleasure. His obvious intimacy with a work full of the most delicate nuances enables him to contribute a version of singularly revealing quality. One hears the inflections of the voices and vividly sees the gestures and expressions of the actors. What may possibly be missing in the words is incorporated in the stage directions that constitute a peculiarly intimate and animated commentary. A few of these directions are worth quoting. Thus : "His eyes blink like those of a fox as he chatters into Li Chi's ear." "He holds out his long beard and looks at it regretfully." "He stops short and hesitates, with the timidity of a villager meeting an official." "He prolongs the sound to a musical length and, humming it like the murmur of a distant kite-bow, smells the petition". "Chao Chung stares straight before himself and totters like a marionette in the hand of an amateur". With these welcome and never obtrusive signs before him, the reader of Yao Hsin-nung's version enjoys an unusual opportunity to reconstruct a superior performance of the play and to gain some intimacy himself with the more delicate shadings of its intention. It is, of course, possible that the play has in China itself been given with a variety of interpretations and possibly that represented here merits no peculiar priority. The work is evidently one of those many-faceted things that can be seen

in many different lights and from many angles. It can, for
example, be understood either as sentimental melodrama or as
pure parody, although these views would presumably be
extreme. The translator goes to neither of these extremes,
although he leans considerably more in the direction of high
comedy. His ambivalent position is summarized in his stage
direction describing the play's "hero" on his first entrance.
"Magistrate Chao belongs to the conventional 'young scholar'
type—moody, obstinate, femininely handsome, and so much
'book-poisoned' that he is helplessly stupid and dumbfounded
when confused or faced with unexpected difficulties but
unusually sensitive and even witty when untroubled and
happy."

The dominating feature of the play is simply this : that each
character is a conventional figure on the Chinese stage delineated
here with an exaggeration of his or her known qualities until
they impinge on the ridiculous or the absurd. There is a
continual ambiguity. At one moment an invitation to take the
character as seriously as he takes himself prevails and at the
next, to view him with a smile. Unquestionably much freedom
is left to the actor or possibly the director as to the course to
pursue. On the whole Yao Hsin-nung inclines to the more
humorous view, following the actual production that he has
seen. He has been especially delighted by the man playing the
part of the heroine and interpreting her feminine wiles in the
most arch manner possible.

This condition characterizes much that in all civilized lands
can be described as high comedy, the formula for which is
that none of the persons in the play sees himself as the audience
sees him. To be more explicit, none realizes that he is to a
considerable degree ridiculous ; each takes himself altogether
in earnest. The unimportance of being earnest or, conversely,
the importance of not taking one's self too seriously, is the
prime theme in such comedy. No one is as absurd as a thorough-
going clown yet none without pronounced eccentricities.
Here the heroine is all the more feminine for being a palpable
exaggeration of well-known feminine characteristics. She is
and is not a coquette, being at the same time under the dominance of her capricious emotions but through this very cause
holding control over her pompous husband, who is utterly

unable to predict her multifarious whims. Repeatedly she breaks into tears, promises that she will on no account yield to them again, and the next moment weeps more violently than ever. The audience has genuine sympathy for her sincere feelings and even her sincere promises but over and above this is amused at her delectable illogicality. The woman falls into an exaggerated condition by following her heart at the expense of consistency or logic, the man, by following his egotistical pride and imagined dignity that renders him equally the butt of the comic spirit.

If any exception be taken as to Yao Hsin-nung's interpretation of the play, this must be to his over-emphasis of the role of the heroine, with whom, it seems, he is almost romantically in love and at least as infatuated as the scholar-husband himself. All the characters are fascinating and none is more conspicuously so than the husband. He is an honest man with many good qualities and is, in fact, a flower of an extremely ripe civilization. The truth remains that in a charming way the civilization itself is over-ripe. He is a veritable parody of punctilious officialdom that nevertheless escapes philistinism because it is based on aesthetic as well as moral standards and is the full blossoming of the Confucian conception of the complete gentleman. He looks toward an emperor who is symbol of enlightenment as well as the focus of power. His attainments in scholarship notwithstanding, he is wholly subservient to his wife. That he assumes a dignified and majestic mein and she assiduously affects the role of the frail and yielding woman, the moon to his sun, completely contradicts the realities of the case. It is she who controls his emotional tides. He officiously requests her to grind the ink for him—a menial task unbecoming in a gentleman—while in fact he is the putty in her hands. Towards the end of Act Two he embarrasses her by his sensuous enunciation of her pet name, whereas at the act's end in the game of playful rivalries she checkmates him by impersonating the Emperor's Inquisitor whom he has presently to face. The last episode has special significance inasmuch as it proves prophetical of the actual situation in Act Four, when her husband, the petty official, will cower in terror before the august majesty of her brother, the Inspector General.

The audience at the same time sympathizes with her husband's jealousy yet realizes it to be utterly unfounded and ridiculous. It seldom if ever questions his standard of values yet continuously finds his attitudes mildly absurd. He is in all things supersensitive, exaggerated in joy and sorrow, pride and humiliation. Very literally, like all Chinese dramatic characters, he wears his heart upon his sleeve but he in the most pronounced manner possible. This is a supersensitive portrait of a super-sophisticated man. A more delectable role in high comedy would be virtually unthinkable. The part is actually much more complex than that of his wife; he himself has many feminine characteristics, visible in all sections of his role. Thus his wife pleads : "He is a man with a dove's heart. Please do not scare him." Conversely, of a specially piquant flavor is the heroine's disguise as a man and her embarrassment in having her disguise abruptly uncovered. Of all persons she would seem the last to succeed in a mask of masculinity. These inversions of sex play a major part in the Chinese conception of comedy. They are of the nature of the Chinese theatre itself, where the male actors who play the women's roles exaggerate the feminine qualities and in many instances the men acting as men show a perverse skill in making the men whom they represent as feminine as possible. Chinese comedy becomes all the more natural by circumventing nature, for nature herself is a woman and therefore perverse. Mother Nature we know well, but whoever has heard of a Mr. Nature ? Judging from the Chinese stage, Nature is a mammal, man, a book.

The brother who has at a tender age become an imperial legate also shows amusing inconsistencies, though these are less pronounced, partly because the role itself is of relatively less importance. The sharpest distinction is drawn between his dignity when presiding over the court as the high judge and his plain humanity when, in the inner room or retiring chamber, he declines into being merely a junior member of his family. A similarly diverting distinction is made between his high position and his youth. Almost gratuitously, it would seem, he warns those about him not to laugh at him because of his extreme youthfulness so incongruous with his exalted position. He has not quite as dove-like a heart as his brother-in-law, but, all the terror that surrounds his throne notwith-standing, he displays the modesty amounting almost to timidity characterizing Chinese gentlemen-scholars as tra-ditionally depicted on the stage.

The father stands much closer to frank caricature. It is true that he represents the acme of tragic grief possible as con-ceived by the Chinese mind. He is a venerable parent, guilty of no crime, who has been unjustly accused, imprisoned, put, even before the eyes of the audience, to the severest torment, and condemned shortly to be beheaded. His cries of agony are carried by a messenger from heaven itself through stout walls to the miraculously sharpened ears of his devoted daugh-ter. His worst torment of all is to have been separated from his two children, both lost even before his conviction for murder. His situation could hardly be worse. Little or nothing occurs during his appearances in the earlier parts of the play to detract from the gravity of the scene. As long as his salva-tion is unforeseen, his condition is treated with a fair degree of sobriety, though virtually all the characters around him are subject to the gentle ridicule or raillery so familiar to the Chinese theatre. But once this tragic tension is removed, even this role is swept perforce into the comic complex of the general scene, indeed the old man is drowned deepest of all under the waves of laughter. On the one hand he is given the official title of "grand lord patriarch," on the other, he becomes the obvious butt of the playwright's mirth, a ridiculous old man whose eccentricities prove far greater than his venera-bility. Quite naturally, he breaks out into violent bitterness against the scoundrels who have betrayed him. The episode requires quotation :

> *Mme. Cassia.*⎫
> *Chao Chung.* ⎬(*Together*). This is no dream.
> *Li Pao-tung.*⎭
> *Li Chi.* Ah ! No dream ?
> *Mme. Cassia.*⎫
> *Chao Chung.* ⎬(*Together*). No, not in the least.
> *Li Pao-tung.*⎭
> *Li Chi.* If so, my children, there is really such a thing as the Heavenly Way ?

Mme. Cassia and Li Pao-tung (*Together*). There is a Heavenly Way.

Li Chi (*To Chao Chung*). And, my good son-in-law, there is really such a thing as the Rewards of Nature, that gives the good and the wicked what they deserve ?

Chao Chung. Most certainly, there is.

Li Chi (*Realising that it is after all no dream, he bursts into a peal of most hearty laughter*). Ha – ha – ha . . . .

Mme. Cassia.

Chao Chung. (*Fearing that this wild rapture will cost him a disjointed jaw, they support him and remind him of the danger*).

Li Pao-tung. Look out, father !

Li Chi. It's all right, it's all right. (*He suddenly recalls the injustice he has incurred and drops into a frenzy of grief as if he has become insane*). Ough ! Now, the scoundrel, T'ien Wang, is like a decoy bird. And that woman from the House of Yang shall be caught like a fish in the net. When these two malefactors are put under arrest— (*He breaks off and stamps his feet with hatred*).

Mme. Cassia. ⎫
Chao Chung. ⎬ (*Together*). Take care of your health, father !
Li Pao-tung. ⎭

A few moments afterwards, when the conviction of the malefactor and his second wife is assured, he is again laughing with such uncontrolled glee that his family thinks he is once more endangering his jaw. No doubt the audience is equally uncontrollable in its laughter. King Lear has changed back to Polonius. The part has again shifted from the tragic to the comic key. All this makes its comment upon real life but in itself remains the artifice of the stage. Life itself may well be at the same time tragic and ridiculous though hardly in the drastic extremes realized in the presentational arts. This complex role must evidently be played with intimations of the comic even in its earlier parts and without the excesses of sheer farce even in the hilarious conclusion. This conclusion, moreover, clearly means more than a commentary on personality or even on old age. The exaggerated acclaim for belief in Heaven's Way, with social justice for all, becomes in actuality an oblique aspersion cast not only on the conventional happy ending but on optimistic assumptions regarding life itself. In the play's conclusion, the literal meaning to the contrary, there is, in fact, more of Taoist anarchy than of Confucian order. Throughout its scenes we have been indeed subjected to an insinuating doubt regarding the validity of officialdom and the cultural system on which it rests. The doubt remains rather the aesthetic suspension of belief than any calculated or satirical attack on an accepted social, moral, and political order. The play is art, not even propaganda levelled against propaganda. Above all, it expresses sheer delight in human inconsistency. This is high comedy because of the elevation from which human life is observed.

Further light concerning the father's role can be had from the role of the Warden, or Jailor, a thoroughly conventional figure in the Chinese theatre. (We meet his like in the Christian saints legends.) This role, like figures in the circle of the Malebranche in Dante's *Inferno*, makes evil ridiculous. One also suspects that the vision passes through the ridiculous to a further comment, namely, that evil is an absurd distortion of human nature, whose norm may be taken as good. Cruelty is depicted as absurd. To those who suffer it, it is indeed infinitely real and terrifying, but to those who practice it, a footless folly. The villain or liar thinks of himself as the clever man who deceives others when in fact he is a stupid man who deceives only himself. Such is the idealistic assumption behind the part. Its result in artistic form is caricature extended into the grotesque. These roles in Chinese drama—and there are many—are expedited with clownish costume, make-up, gesture, and elocution. The general impression is that familiar to Westerners in the art of Peter Breughel, though Breughel can at times be more satirical and bitter than the Chinese masters, whose basis in philosophy is actually more serene than that of thinkers in the most restless and transitional period of Western civilization, the fifteenth and sixteenth centuries. The jailer is a liar, a hypocrite, and a brute, whose one quality even greater than his cruelty is his cupidity. But in a single respect, most important of all for the aesthetic analysis of the play, he is like all the other characters: the audience sees through him while he does not see through himself. No character in this play remotely attains the Socratic ideal of self-knowledge. Here is the essence of its comic spirit. The audience is not only above the emotional storm; it is above, or considers itself temporarily above, the delusions, great or small, which the characters are heir to. Such is the aesthetic heaven of high and pure comedy, an illusion effected by the playwright causing the audience to smile at delusions in others while temporarily, at least, undisturbed by their own. In theory it is, of course, quite possible that the delusions depicted on the stage, as vanity, affectation, cruelty, inordinate joy or despair, are also lodged in the breasts of the spectators. If so, the play may conceivably have an educational value, easing the victims of delusions by laughter when they are often themselves among the last to be aware that their faults are being amended. They are unconsciously relieved of their folly by recognizing faults in others which their pride will not allow them to acknowledge in themselves. It may well be that more has been accomplished by inducing persons to laugh than by inducing them to think rationally. A whole catechism of virtue may be less efficacious than the comic stage and Confucius no more effectual in behalf of civilization than Molière. The blemishes in human nature depicted in this play are both the lighter distortions of personality, as vanity in the hero and timidity in the heroine, and the graver crimes against society, as the sins of the evil wife and the vicious jailor. All are subjected to the same comic mirth, as a rule gentle in its spirit but recuperative in its power. Such comedy is a medicine for human ills; it works while the judicial consciousness sleeps. We are aware of a delightful savor but unaware of the nutritious elements which the food contains. This is a refined comedy, beside which the satirical art of an Ibsen or a Shaw seems prosaic or flat-footed. It is impalpable as pure sunlight, as refreshing as a cool breeze from the sea. Possibly Yao Hsin-nung is right; the Chinese drama may have nothing better to give us. Even more than this; it is possible that no drama is more mature.

All peoples experience passion and violent emotion. All are potentially capable of tragedy. Only advanced civilizations possess the requisites for a refined comedy. This the Chinese achieved, as manifest in many products of their culture, as their sculpture, painting, poetry, drama and prose. Here is one of their rarest and most precious contributions to the spiritual treasury of mankind.

As there is a forescene to the play, *Madame Cassia,* so there must be a postscript to this chapter. The thinking implicit in all its varied scenes confers a gentle ridicule on the most sacred concepts in Chinese thought ; the studious scholar, the venerable parent, the guardians of the law, the mistress of the family are all depicted as faintly absurd. Although little is spoken that, one presumes, might not be language heard hourly in the streets of an old Chinese city, the spirit is everywhere colored with a wilful contradiction of the orthodox, with a tincture of the fantastic and preposterous. The whole is lifted bodily out of the every-day world by a species of humorous levitation. We are actually in a cloud-land as extravagantly unreal as that of Aristophanes' *Clouds,* or *Birds.* Establishing this atmosphere for this airy, fantastic world, the playwright literally sets his forescene among the clouds. The deity of the Planet Venus appears, attended by four young "cloud-cherubs". He despatches his celestial messenger, a Taoist angel versed in acoustics, to arrange for a magic diffusion of sound, so that the groans of a tortured old man in prison shall pierce massive walls to reach the ear of his daughter, at the time wholly unaware as to where he is or even as to whether he still lives. The father's words and groans are actually repeated, as an echo or a refrain. The scene radios sound without benefit of mechanism. There is a likeness to the airborne music that Ariel projects in *The Tempest.* A key is set for the imaginative license of all that follows. Where such supernatural events not only occur but are blandly taken for granted, virtually anything may readily be said of human life, no matter how far it diverges from orthodox opinion. The body of the play may still remain comparatively mundane while the soul is that of art and beauty unfettered by any conventions other than art and beauty themselves. The bias towards naturalism which to some degree almost all men feel will be suspended in this world of palpable magic. For the main section of the play at least a few assumptions of reality are coolly maintained. Toward the conclusion, however, the unmistakably poetic view of aesthetic

95

convention and unreality breaks out once more. Speech again becomes conspicuously lyrical. The three younger members of the family repeatedly address their honored parent in chorus. The clouds of fantasy have again appeared over the horizon, comedy proclaiming anew the best of all possible worlds. A rosy smile of cosmic optimism surrounds and in part defines a world that proves equally absurd and delectable. An arch critique of society and of the personal life is sustained on the airy wings of an essentially poetic imagination. The key lies somewhere between raw laughter and a smile, never as raucous as the one nor as tame as the other. It is the finest temper of man caught in his most civilized hour, amused at the inevitability of his own ridiculousness.

6 / *The Ethical Theatre*

THE CHINESE theatre achieves an extraordinary blending of the ethical and the aesthetic. To the amazement of Western eyes, at least, it resembles a valentine and often reads somewhat like a catechism. The most superficial acquaintance with the actual stage discloses elaborate embroidery, fantastic headdresses, pheasant plumes, birdlike movements, and mincing steps. There is a world of porcelain delicacy almost as unlike the everyday world as possible. To superficial thinking its relevance seems slight. The abrupt passage from street to theatre resembles the entrance into a world of dreams. Yet the plays were traditionally acted in the most open and public manner possible, on scaffolds erected in parks and public squares or at the intersections of highways and obviously belong in an intimate way to the people. On closer inspection it must appear that they are not the opium of the people but that they contain within themselves the most revealing expressions of the ideals on which traditional Chinese society rests. They ornament society, it is true, but they also successfully delineate its foundations. The rational Western mind views such a paradoxical conjunction of elements with much suspicion. Especially the Protestant mind distrusts a sensuous rhetoric alleged to express serious feelings or ideas. Similarly, it is feared that religious exercises that are spectacular cannot also be sincere. One must severely dispense with these suppositions if one is even to begin an understanding of the Chinese stage. Fortunately for the mere reader, the difficulty here is not great, for the ornaments of the Chinese theatre are almost exclusively in the productions, not in the words themselves, which are often wholly bare of rhetorical pretensions.

Although China is the land of the dragon and phoenix, it is also the land whose citizens have been most devoted to practical and pragmatic matters, expressed through their singular addiction to endless treatises on history and ethics. It is a land of both poetry and prose, of delectable dancing and interminable indoctrination, of the wine cup and Confucius, of poets as drunken as Li Po and as sober as Po Chü-i. Strange to say, these opposed elements do not result in the violent conflicts and dissonances that might be supposed. Entirely contrary to what might be presumed, the art is rarely trivial and the ethics seldom deadly. Instead of contradicting each other, they prove complementary. The sober man does not strike the drunkard but lends him his hand for his support. The drunkard does not scorn the moralist but may even concede some plausibility to his views. Between the two extremes lies a sociable interval, brightened frequently by instinctive awareness of the humorous incongruity. One hears relatively little of deadly sins and still less of the evils of frivolity. The cultural climate is much too sophisticated for the boorishness that too often accompanies Western fanaticism and Christian morality. Chinese indoctrination of the old school is by no means incompatible with either art or charm. When the Chinese dramatist is didactic, his manner accords more with the urbane humor of a Geoffrey Chaucer than with the unrestrained belligerence of a Luther or a Savonarola. Marco Polo, the humorist, delighted in China but there is small reason to suppose that John Milton would have done so.

It is in this cultural climate of China that the explanation lies for the comparative artistic success of so many moralizing plays. These works seemingly lie adjacent to the heavy-handed moralizing of much Western bourgeois drama yet never closely resemble it. The Chinese works are preserved as flourishing art because they are serious without being solemn. Their artifice maintains an aesthetic distance while their subject-matter insures a moral and emotional relevance. The elements are delicately blended. The villains usually have some alleviating good features and the heroes and heroines are not without some mitigating frailties. The soggy and sentimental morality of Dickensian society is unknown.

Although their greatest plays are by no means the most strongly ethical, even their most ethical plays frequently have considerable attraction. The important problem of art and ethics, so peculiarly pertinent to a broad view of Chinese drama, can most conveniently be considered by reference to only a few plays. This problem is actually not alone the relation of good and evil to art but of the pleasant and the unpleasant, of optimistic illusion as opposed to honest confrontation of reality.

Something has already been said in these pages of the happy ending, a fictional convention as optimistic as it is widely prevalent. In such endings morality and happiness are as a rule closely joined, since happiness is presumed to derive in so large a measure from the triumph of the good. Happiness is the cake that the justice of fate gives us for being good. Yet it is to be remarked that the good man in Chinese drama is seldom if ever goody-goody and the wicked seldom so far removed from the audience's conception of itself as to be essentially alien. Thus the monstrosity of Western melodrama is avoided. This does not mean that evil is shunned by the Chinese dramatist. He is actually more the realist than the masters of the Western melodramatic stage. Since he wields a less lugubrious scourge of vice than the Westerners and escapes their relatively barbarous conception of sin, he escapes also the heavy-handedness making so much Western didacticism distasteful both as manners and as art. The Chinese are also less heavyhanded in their morality than the Japanese. This contrast appears conveniently as the famous *Orphan of the Family of Tchao* is compared with the most celebrated of Japanese romantic dramas and that closest to the Chinese play in its theme, Chikamatsu's *Battles of Coxinga*. Morality in the Chinese plays is much more aristocratic and less strident, that in the Japanese, more bourgeois and blatant. The distinction is not easily defined but is strongly felt. Coxinga's enemies are no more evil than Tching yng's but are considerably more denigrated in the eyes of the audience. Coxinga is almost absurdly arrogant and self-satisfied, while Tching yng simply does quietly what he is called upon to do. The plain truth of the matter is that the Chinese play is the more civilized.

A similar contrast is invited by the Chinese *Chalk Circle* and Bertolt Brecht's deliberate reply to it, *The Caucasian Chalk Circle*. In one play the moral emphasis is quiet and assured, in the other, blatant and banal. The Chinese theatre orchestra is often loud and raucous as heard by Western ears but not so the Chinese moral indoctrination.

The happy ending is palpably an aesthetic device, remarkable as a rule not so much because it is happy as because it ties together in harmonious polyphony so many strands scattered throughout the play's course. The artifice proves even more important than the mood. From the formal point of view a similar ending would be appropriate even in tragedy. The fault of a rude didacticism is that it offers a false simplification to principles of both art and life. The whole becomes too perspicuous ; the imagination has been inadequately exerted, so that the work in turn insufficiently exercises the imagination of the audience. The Chinese works, or at least the better of them, escape mediocrity because they achieve a degree of subtlety, even when expressing familiar ideas through the medium of stories in themselves sufficiently perspicuous. They are popular but not vulgar. Nuance is not buried beneath overemphasis. It is hardly arguing in a circle to observe further that they are not vulgar because of the aesthetic sophistication of the audiences which they served. Here, too, are various adjustments and degrees. *The Orphan of the Family of Tchao* is apparently addressed to a more decorous audience than *The Divided Tunic*, yet whatever *The Divided Tunic* lacks in texture and style is to a large extent made up by a greater complexity of design, or, in other words, by a complexity of incident and plot. Chinese masterpieces are not commonplace for the sufficiently clear reason that their art is intricately spun. This will at once appear when a critic undertakes a detailed exposition of the art. The study of art is always the study of nuances. (In Bertolt Brecht are no nuances.) Crude didacticism or banal optimism is without nuance, but the Chinese drama is richly endowed with it. In exploration of this proposition a review of three famous plays is invited, with special reference to a quality conspicuous in all three : the force of a moral or ethical content. The first of these works, *The Orphan of the Family of Tchao*, is courtly, feudal, heroic, the second, *The Divided Tunic*, at least in its setting, middle-class, bourgeois, commercial. The third, *An Heir in His Old Age*, stands between the two, in form closer to the first, in social reference closer to the second. It stands central in the area of the explicitly didactic Chinese play and, moreover, offers an outstanding specimen.

The Orphan of the Family of Tchao is in essence a story of clan loyalty based on hereditary obligation. It proves no accident that it was, during the mid-eighteenth century, the first Chinese play to be translated into a European language, attractive in part as a document in behalf of personal loyalty flattering to the ears of the Bourbon throne and the other well-established monarchies of Europe. The hereditary nature of the obligation appears in the plot's concentration upon an infant, the sole heir of a noble household. All focuses upon him. The relatively brief passages before his birth and after his maturity mean little. When the play opens, his mother is pregnant with him ; much the greater part of the last act is actually a narrative recapitulation of the events occurring in his infancy. A faithful retainer substitutes his own child for the heir with the expectation, actually fulfilled, that the humble child shall be killed under the misconception that he is the heir. Another follower of the venerable House dies with torture rather than reveal the location and identity of the noble child. The mother commits suicide, aesthetically considered, so that the focus of our attention may on no account shift from her offspring to her. The entire play is a study in fanatical devotion. Action is extremely simple, scenes are few in number but present one admirably contrived climax after another. The action as we understand it could not begin otherwise than where it does nor end at any point except its conclusion. Treatment of the "antecedent action" is masterful. The play is an unsurpassed realization of the classical spirit in art which is substantially the same wherever it may be found. The simplicity of the theme is matched only by the delicacy of its development, the significance of the idea by the richness of its execution. Incidentally, when Voltaire derived from this play one of his own most successful dramas and indeed one of the landmarks of neo-classical drama in Europe, he was strongly fascinated both by the theme and the manner. In the Chinese play he recognized a masterpiece at least comparable as art to the best of Raçine and wholly intelligible in its basic idea to long-established currents in Western thinking. Voltaire's own observations that the Chinese playwright was innocent of the classical canons of form and in a single play presented a character first as an infant and later as a man of eighteen years detracts little or nothing from his admiration for virtually all the play's essential features. The play's relation to Japanese thought presents quite a different aspect. Chikamatsu borrowed the idea but not the form, for his own derivative play is in the loose, serial style of the typical "chronicle history". The Chinese play is also a sequence of "big" scenes but a sequence whose parts fall in place with complete inevitability and without the shadow of digression.

Translations of this play, as already observed, exist in both French and English. Much more scholarly and complete renderings will in time doubtless be made but one wonders if any will be more nearly adequate. It is clear that the Chinese work is profoundly classical and presumably in an essentially classical age deeply sensitive to dignity and decorum alone can its spirit be most fully captured.

The Orphan of the Family of Tchao solves the problem of fusing art and morality because of the deep-seated conviction and utter sincerity of the motive which in turn leads to the virtually undeviating perfection of the expression. The two become one and, so far as the work itself is concerned, inseparable. Much didacticism produces artlessness because the thought to be expressed is an abstraction, not an emotional experience or conviction. The product fails to reach the area of art because the thought fails to advance to the condition of a social, psychological or personal reality. We are left with a vapid generalization which, if pompously insisted upon, becomes first banal and last hypocritical. The experience does not warrant the weight alleged to be attached to it. Tales of personal loyalty are, of course, known the world over. The tale of the Forty-Seven Ronin, the epics on Roland, Siegfried or Lancelot, and the far older passages dealing with clan warfare in the *Mahabharata* all belong in this category. But it would be hard indeed to discover a single and succinct expression of this ideal more adequate as art or moving as a moral exemplum than this Yüan drama. More serious than most tragedies, it will always touch the heart and arouse the gratification of achieved beauty. It is also a tale based on one of the most elemental of passions, revenge. But here the theme of jealousy converges with that of loyalty. This vengeance is ethical in being, as the cliché has it, a "primitive justice." The passion, however, is held subordinate to the ethical conception. The basic factor is not the hero's hatred of his enemy but his devotion to his clan. Happily, the play escapes the melodramatic emphasis on hatred and jealousy which vulgarizes so many specimens of Italian grand opera. The Chinese play is made of nobler stuff. In consequence, the conclusion depicts a sacrifice to the soul of an ancestor and not a further crime.

The extreme awkwardness of didacticism as Westerners too frequently know it is better understood as a provincialism than as a defect extending throughout the world's literature. Inherited from Christian preaching, it reached its apex with the middle-class morality of the eighteenth and nineteenth centuries. No intrinsic reason exists to render art useless. The satirical Aristophanes is a greater poet than the romantic Menander. On the contrary, all major works of literature or the stage are bearers of rich social and spiritual values and should be so appraised. The strictly formalistic or the strictly emotional criteria for art are both inadequate, one resulting in aridity, the other, in a sentimental romanticism. The human story read with any degree of fulness insists upon a humanistic appraisal of art valued in relation to spiritual content. The ethical factor in the theatre should be cherished, not feared, though undeniably it is wise to exercise continual solicitude that the ethical content, enjoying the sentimental ambush of a debased art, does not become decadent and accordingly equally destructive to the end of art and morality. The profound conviction in China of the value of family life accounts for much of the sincerity and validity of the art itself.

Faced with such a work as *The Orphan of the Family of Tchao* one returns repeatedly to the thought of its universality, demonstrated, perhaps, no more in its basic ideas than in its specific manifestations. The development of the play's theme leads to a biblical primitivism and an alliance with the world-wide elements of folklore. Any Westerner considering the play is almost sure to note in Tou Nago Cou's slaughter of three hundred innocent infants up to the age of six months, undertaken to insure the death of a particular heir, an analogue to the biblical legend of Herod's slaughter of the Innocents. The incidents are similar, as are the principles of art implicit in the two works. There are, of course, "cheap" villains in Western films and on the television screen. No one would rightly level this charge against the wicked characters in the New Testament or in the Yüan play.

The Divided Tunic presents work of a very different complexion, less elegant as art than the foregoing but none the less successful and noteworthy. It employs a far larger cast of characters and range of incidents and scenes. Though in each case a score of years is covered by the story, the effect of succinctness, so highly cherished by the author of *The Orphan of the Family of Tchao*, is far from the thought of the author of *The Divided Tunic*. The latter frankly seeks the effect of scope and license which the former eschews. When summarized, the plot sounds positively moralistic, in some respects resembling the vulgarized tales of honest and wicked apprentices in the educational literature of the eighteenth century. A couple at least middle-aged has considerable wealth and a romantic and foolish son, doomed to suffer for his own generous errors. The family sits in an upstairs gallery overlooking the street, on which snow falls with its accustomed beauty. The imagery is sufficiently striking to warrant quotation. The symbolical significance of the snowstorm appears later in the play as the scene of luxury, ease and delight is exchanged for one of extreme hardship and misery :

> (*Chang*). Winter is just setting in, the snow falls in large flakes and everywhere drifts and covers the ground. My son is in a room above, adjoining the window, and has prepared a table, and says I and my wife must go up and enjoy with him the sight of the falling snow, and take some cups of wine. (*He and his wife go up*).
>
> (*Chau*). The lustrous whiteness of this snow is the emblem

of purity. I cannot doubt but that it is a presage of happiness for the state.

(*Hiauyu, perceiving his father*). My father, my mother, see here ; the azure tint of this snow is well worth looking at. While looking up and down the street from this verandah, I have prepared a cup. Come, my parents, enjoy this charming sight. Bring the wine, Hing.

(*Hing*). Here it is.

(*Hiauyu, presenting a stoup of wine*). My father, I beg you to take a cup of wine.

(*Chang*). These thick snowflakes, my son, are truly very beautiful. The clouds, like ruddy vapors, extend and group themselves on all sides ; large flakes whirl about in the air ; the north wind blows violently ; the sight loses itself in the silvery horizon. Who would be able, at such a time, to meditate calmly when on his horse, as Ming Haujin did ?

(*Hiauyu*). This snow, which comes so opportunely, is a happy presage ; it affords us a pleasant prospect for winter.

(*Chang*). We are now just at the commencement of the cold weather, and so you say the winter is here ; well, on my part, I maintain it is spring.

(*Hiauyu*). But, father, it is autumn now. How can you take this to be spring ?

(*Chang*). If it were otherwise, how could the blossoms of the pear, petal after petal, fall as they do ? How could the flowers of the willow fly about so in eddies ? The pear blossoms heap themselves up and form a silvery ground ; the willow flowers rain themselves to heaven like a waving tiara, and fall again to the earth. I have before my eyes a delightful prospect, it is the most fortunate moment of my life ; draperies of embroidered silk are suspended for me, a rich carpet of flowers is spread beneath my feet ; I am served to the full of delicious wine. Though in reality, I am only a plebeian, a simple citizen of the Phoenix City, yet for all that, I seem to swim in luxury, and my robe to be ornamented with dragons.

The family's aesthetic joy is abruptly broken when an

impoverished wanderer falls prone upon their doorstep. On bringing him into the house, the son is at once attracted personally to the pathetic visitor. So far does this attraction extend, that he induces his parents to accept this specious-looking visitor as his adopted brother. The strange young man makes a parade of being virtuous. In fact, he devises a plot, using superstitions to which the older people are wisely hostile, to lure the son and his wife from the parental home, even without consultation with the parents, an act that in Chinese ethics constitutes an especially heinous crime. The rascal throws his sworn brother into the Yellow River and supposes him safely drowned. He promptly marries the widow. Living in a city well removed from his wife's parental home, after a prolonged pregnancy from her first husband she has a child, who at maturity passes an official examination, becomes a judge, and ultimately sits at trial of his father's supposed murderer. Actually, the father has escaped and lives to be united with his family. But this is for the last act.

Midway in Act One a second unfortunate man seeks refuge from the storm. This provides the play with its hero and chief foil to the antagonist. After killing a man under just provocation, he is exiled, a halter about his neck. In this pitiable condition he is taken into the custody of the old people's household. A less specious character than the first recipient of their charity, he continues under a cloud of suspicion. In due time, however, he becomes the head of a Buddhist monastery. Meanwhile a fire destroys the house of the wealthy old people, leaving them in extreme poverty. They in their turn are driven out as beggars into the winter storms. Their grandson, when on a visit to the capital, offers a disposal of alms, primarily food, to the oppressed. In a scene of some conventional complications, his grand-parents appear as mendicants. The recognition is effected. The final act presents a remarkable instance of dramatic virtuosity. A general reassembling occurs, with recognition all round. All have been in one state of misery or another and all are in the end exalted, with the exception of the hypocrite and murderer, who is duly condemned to a death not represented upon the stage. This, by a theatrical convention, is postponed "to the following day." This scene proves considerably more complex than the familiar finale first of all because three generations instead of the usual two are present. Much is made of the extreme age and venerability of the grandparents. The scene is not in the conventional sense romantic. It presents no marriage, only the reunion of the three generations. The morality here is completely typical of Chinese thought. The virtuous one of the two suppliants for the aid of the old people is brought into the final scenes as the Buddhist leader. Three persons of official rank are assembled to pass judgment upon the criminal and for further pomp and good measure a special legate from the Emperor is brought in to pass the final sentence and pronounce the last word. The closing scenes are in a romantic setting, amidst high mountains, infested by bandits. Much is done to dilate the scene and its imagery. Whereas many great Chinese plays, as *The Orphan of the Family of Tchao*, in their basic simplicity suggest small groups for chamber music, *The Divided Tunic* suggests a full orchestra. Elemental themes are developed with sophisticated technique. Ethical values are powerfully expressed with refined art. They are, accordingly, without banality and completely removed from specious dialectic.

The play's title, *The Divided Tunic*, refers to a stage property that with pleasant surprise relates this work to many successful dramas of the West, especially within the tradition of classical comedy. It provides good stage business, an intimate touch, and a moving image or symbol. Such properties have played their part in recognition scenes from the time of Sophocles to virtually the present day. The fragment of clothing introduced as a property into Synge's *Riders to the Sea* merely transposes the comic to the tragic scene, separation instead of union being the experience symbolized. The ways of dramatic art, it seems, are astonishingly alike the world over. What is commonplace in one culture is likely to be commonplace in another and what is imaginative in one remains imaginative through the vast ranges of space and time.

Artistically considered, the austere *Orphan of the Family of Tchao* and such an expansive work as *The Divided Tunic* stand almost as far apart from each other as possible where two works remain essentially sound. *An Heir in His Old Age* occupies a more assured and comfortable mean between the two. Few Chinese plays, if any, express so well the most typical and prominent values in Chinese society. The play is intensely moral but never moralistic. Scarcely a line lacks its strong burden of commentary upon human values. The central figure, an old man by name of Lew, represents, among much else, the wisdom that at last succeeds in turning its possessor away from money-getting to a genial and just conception of the true value of property and wealth. In general, the play exalts the supreme value of family piety and cohesion. A shallow young man marries into a family thinking that since its head is old and without a son he will through his daughter inherit the estate. He is deceived. The old man has a second, or subordinate, wife who finally presents him with an heir. His daughter, who is loyal, knows of this woman's pregnancy and of the hatred in which the expectant mother is held both by the first wife and the dishonorable son-in-law. Out of loyalty to her father she sends the woman to a secret place of refuge, where she and her son can live in peace. At the end of three years the secret is revealed.

Meanwhile the father has repented his avaricious ways. He has also discovered that a nephew, who by rights belongs to his own family, is more pious and loyal than his calculating son-in-law. This nephew combines the character-types of aspiring scholar and prodigal son. Although harshly repudiated by his uncle, in the chief scene of the play he performs pious offices at the ancestral graves, while daughter and son-in-law are neglectful and arrive late. The prodigal's soliloquy at the tombs gives a clear picture of the play's ethical and dramatic qualities. This man is speaking :

Since the day when my uncle gave me the two pieces of silver, I have been living about the potteries. Now is the season of the Tsing-ming, and all ranks, both great and small, perform the sacred rites at the tombs of their respective families. My uncle said to me, Yin-sun, if you diligently honor the graves of your ancestors, in one or two years you will become rich. Surely, he must have deposited some treasure there. When I reflect that my own ancestors, beside my father and mother, are interred in these tombs, it would be strange if I should wait till my uncle told me to go ! —Though I am poor, I am still a scholar, and therefore could not possibly be deficient in this essential point of duty. I have been to the paper shop and obtained some gilt paper by singing ; I have been to the wine shop, and procured this half-jar of wine ; I have been to the eating shop, and obtained this piece of bread. Thus, then, I have not neglected my uncle's advice. From a neighbor I have borrowed this iron hoe, and now proceed to the rites : to burn the paper, and to trim the earth round the graves, to perform the other ceremonies of oblations, and thus fulfill the duties of a son. In the midst of my meditations, I have arrived, it seems, at the place of tombs. Ah ! Lew-tsung-sheu, in spite of your great wealth, where have you a son who shall visit your tombs ?—(*performs his adorations*) Ye parents of my father, your lives being ended, after death be immortal ! I make this oblation to your shades.— Here lie my father and mother ! —I, your child, the victim of poverty, reflect that during your lifetime you turned the partial affection of my grandfather and grandmother for you, to the disadvantage of my uncle and his wife. Now, that you are dead, all the ill consequences fall upon me !—My parents ! why do I repeat the maxim : "Possessing property, do not exhaust it entirely, but refrain from one portion in ten for the sake of your children". I repeat this because you made use of all your property and now I severely suffer for it. But "in one or two years I shall become rich."—Yin-sun has no other way of performing the duties of filial piety than by throwing a little fresh earth on the graves ! I may be compared to the iron hoe which I hold in my hand ; but the disposition of my aunt is so unrelenting that even if I were composed of iron or stone I could not forbear to complain. They have directed my cousin, Chang-lang, to take care of the family, while I am sent to dig the ground, and to labor. Now that I have thrown up the earth, I may proceed to the rites of oblation. If I offer this cake only to the shades of my grand-father and grand-mother, those of my parents will have none. —What is to be done, to prevent their contending for it ?—This I can easily manage : I will divide the cake, and offer half to one and half to the other.—Having poured out the wine, burnt the paper, and finished the oblations, I am to eat what remains of the provisions. —One hundred and five days after the winter solstice, observe the rich, with what splendor they have performed the rites of the tombs. I alone am poor and destitute. —The graves of my ancestors are not heaped with dried hams and other meat offerings, nor with fragrant wines. With this iron hoe I have performed the duties of the season. —(*Taking up the wine*)—This wine is cold, and not fit to drink. I will go to one of the neighboring cottages and warm it. Having done this, I will return for the iron hoe. —Now to warm the wine. (*Exit*).

The old man and his wife are much impressed on seeing this act of piety and completely reverse their views of the two young men. In the end she is even more hostile to the son-in-law than is her husband and even more favorable than he to the reformed nephew. The play becomes somewhat out of the ordinary in stressing this note of reformation. It proves to be an educational drama. Everyone, even the villain, learns to think more justly of life. This antagonist is not actually punished, indeed he has in reality committed no heinous crime, though he has comprehensively mistaken the true values of life.

This is strictly a domestic drama. Yet at no time, its insistence on morality notwithstanding, does the morality obtrude on the art, as is the case in almost all so-called "domestic dramas" in the West. This, to repeat, is because of certain ingrained qualities in Chinese thought and art. The moral earnestness is all the more effectual for being seasoned with much salt of wit. There is no hero in the sense that there is an infallible character. The young scholar, who comes nearest to winning our complete sympathy, is, after all, much of a ne'er-do-well. The audience identifies its own ideas with those of the playwright but at no time identifies itself with any of the characters. Hence there is no room for romantic sentimentality. The old man is irate, abrupt, short winded; his mannerisms and delusions are distinctly ridiculous. Yet he is essentially a congenial figure. The wife's role has at least a broad resemblance to that of Katharine in *The Taming of the*

Shrew, but she is, to paraphrase another Elizabethan title, a woman redeemed by kindness. The play's morality somewhat resembles that of Thomas Dekker in his celebrated play, *The Honest Whore*. But, again, the Chinese work is firmer, more sharply pointed, more realistic and less pathetic. To a truly remarkable degree, it expresses the consciousness of the Chinese people as they have for so long remained faithful to their deeply ingrained traditions. A more essentially ethical drama or a more effective one within this category would be hard to find.

This is a statement with more than one implication. Undeniably the ethical phase of life is but one of life's phases. It is an aspect largely overlooked by the great Sanskrit dramatists, who are at heart spiritual, metaphysical, religious, and concerned with refinements and expansions of the emotional and the imaginative life. *The Palace of Eternal Youth* and *The White Snake* may be mentioned as two masterpieces expressing Chinese thought far removed from ethical considerations. They chiefly reflect the Taoist way of thinking, the essentially spiritual element in the Chinese consciousness. Beside such works, or, to refer to a third, beside the emotional sophistication of *The Western Chamber*, both *The Divided Tunic* and *An Heir in His Old Age* appear timidly confined to a middle-class, bourgeois point of view. They deal with the palpable, the measurable and the strictly ascertainable. They may, at least according to some delimiting conceptions of the word, be said to lack "poetry." Be this as it may, they are built with an extraordinarily firm craftsmanship and are built to last. Their substantial frames are successful containers for values by which countless persons of some sensitivity and certainly great depth of conviction have lived and long will so continue to live. They stand among our most perfect monuments to our work-a-day world. To construe them as merely moralistic would be to neglect the deep pleasure which they are capable of transmitting both to their readers and audiences. They will long remain as examples to encourage later writers to whom ethical content seems important, above the niceties of an abstract or, shall we say, a merely vacuous form ?

7 / Dramatic Characters

It is virtually inevitable that in the course of any survey or analysis of dramatic literature the nature of the characterization shall enter the discussion. In recent years this has more than ever proved the case. We know that individual actors perform as individuals—unless there is the currently unfamiliar condition that they present ideas allegorically. The public is only too well accustomed to consider its favourite actors as distinct personalities. There is no more commonly accepted view of the theatre than that it presents an arena where personalities are created and displayed. Yet all this to the contrary, thinking on the subject remains peculiarly inconclusive and little general understanding exists as to what may be signified by the word "characterization" or what in general the categories of characterization may be. Much of the confusion stems from romantic, nineteenth-century conceptions. According to familiar views in this tradition, individualization becomes one of the major goals not only for the playwright and his actors but for all persons in real life. Moderns are well acquainted with the cult of individuality. In Ibsen's phrase, he is the strongest who stands the most alone. A peculiar virtue attaches to uniqueness. The individual is instructed, in Socratic terms, to know himself; even more, he is encouraged to be himself. Uniqueness becomes intrinsically desirable. A novel or play is to a great extent valued according to its success in bringing before us the illusion of having encountered in the mind real and distinctive people. Of late critical theory has called some of this familiar thinking into account but its force still without doubt remains strong.

Before examining the special aspects of this subject as presented by Chinese classical drama it will be profitable to consider the matter further in general terms and especially in its historical perspective. Insofar as these ideas enjoyed currency in the times of Shakespeare, for example, the term "character" first of all suggested the stock "characters" of the *commedia dell' arte* and the psychological "characters" described in such well-known authors as Theophrastus. In short, this very idea of character precluded the uniqueness of personality. A character was a concept based, to be sure, on a faithful observation of life. But life was presumed to be systematically understood. Emphasis fell on the typical; the unique was entirely out of the question, regarded as presumably unrealistic and at most essentially unimportant. The same character had lived in a thousand books and plays, was part of the commonly accepted folklore and simply borrowed by each writer pragmatically to serve his momentary ends. The romantic attitude toward personality was yet to be born. According to this view, one of the outstanding facts of life is the uniqueness of each human soul. One knows an individual not by some physical birthmark, superficial characteristic or mannerism but by the complex of personality. A major function of literary art, say the romantics, is to create such unique beings, whose natures clearly are known not rationally but intuitively. Each character is a spirit or soul carrying a full conviction of reality though this is in the end too comprehensive to admit definition. Theophrastus and the *commedia dell' arte* are left far behind. In fact, romantic characterization stands in complete opposition to what may be termed classical characterization. Romantic characters are persons to love or hate, not necessarily to understand. They are not types or masks but unique entities. Noh drama admits some two hundred masks; the *commedia dell' arte* admitted a very fair number of types or species. Romantic drama, on the contrary, glories in the notion of personal character as multiplied to infinity. Its basic assumption is both naturalistic and irrational. It presumes that we meet and know persons in art as we meet and know people in daily experience. More than this : if the writer is inspired, we know his characters not merely as casual acquaintances but as our intimates, either as friends or foes.

In general, the Oriental mind and especially the Oriental drama share little in this romantic theory. They are, instead, in the camp of the classical. The individuals projected on the stages are as a rule conceived as types, not personalities. To such a marked degree is this true that whereas the *commedia dell' arte* represents only an episode and a more or less minor episode or digression in the development of Western drama, its basic suppositions are astonishingly pervasive in the drama of the East. The Chinese theatre in particular cherished the notion of types. The names were, to be sure, generally individualized ; in this respect the *commedia dell' arte* appears the more radical and logical. But in such theatrically important matters as make-up, gesture, and speech-delivery each type followed rigid prescriptions. Little or no incentive was offered the playwright or actor to invent new types. The problem of the theatr econsisted first of all in refining and perfecting the old.

It might well be of value to explore the causes of this outlook of the Orient, with the "closed societies" as their base, but the subject, if broadly considered, would usurp an enormous amount of effort and time. Only a few suggestive considerations call for further attention here. The typical mythologies of the East and West prove especialy pertinent where the imagination in art is concerned. Western religions as a rule show the imagination particularly active in creating divinities with palpably human characteristics and with sharply distinguishing marks of characterization. In short, theology itself becomes strongly humanized. This is, indeed, true of most folklore, but the Oriental religions go far beyond folklore. Of the typical attitude in the West the Greek mythology, so potent a factor in Western culture, proves the most conspicuous. The warriors in the *Iliad* are by no means as sharply distinguished from one another as are the gods. The goal of all the fighters is much the same : to destroy the enemy. Some, like Ulysses, prefer to accomplish this by guile ; others, like Achilles, by brute force. But they all bear a strong family likeness, as well indicated by the vase-painting of the age. With the gods the case is reversed. The family of Olympus is one of the most heterogeneous assemblies of mortal-seeming gods ever projected by the human mind. Not only does each deity serve a unique function. Each clearly has a unique nature;

and the abstraction introduced into European thinking by Christian mysticism at least carried with it the conception that God was also man and that Jesus was an historical person. The saints, too, were individuals, though Christian thinking, in many respects less imaginative than the Greek, failed to establish between the saints the vivid conviction of individuality which the ancients won for the all-too-human inhabitants of their Olympus.

These conditions are strongly reversed in the Orient. How can one conceive as an individual a god such as Kwannon, who flourishes in at least thirty-three manifestations and may be either masculine or feminine? The prevalence of animal manifestations among the gods further divorces them from personal realism. Mythology becomes not a series of tales resembling man's daily life but a riotous world where universal forces play upon one another without respect for personal identity or idiosyncrasy. Life's object, according to Eastern religion, is not to imitate Christ, who is man as well as God, but to submerge the individual into the infinite, thereby escaping from personal consciousness. In brief, for Chinese drama the individual clearly means less; society and the universe signify more.

The use of the word "historical" in the course of the foregoing remarks must lead to a more intimate view of the subject with reference to some of its most significant features, Shakespeare in his fluctuating but vigorous commerce with history affords a practical source of reference, for the English dramatist weaves his way in and out of historical material with much virtuosity and in ways highly noteworthy. In a word, as he approaches an historical view, he approaches an acceptance of the advanced view of personality in drama; as he clings to a more purely aesthetic view, he remains conservative and divorced from such an outlook. Both outlooks he could nourish from the Renaissance infatuation with the classics. Theophrastus first defined the conventional notion of stage figures; Plutarch defined the historical attitude toward characterization that was in time to develop into the full romantic conception of the personality imaginatively and intuitively conceived and in due time to burgeon into a new doctrine of heroes and hero worship. Modern Shakespeare criticism has come almost yearly to fuller realization of the degree to which the figures in his comedies owe their being to comic tradition, especially as crystallized in the Christian images of classical comic conceptions, the Italian *commedia dell' arte*. The purest examples of Shakespeare's comedy, as *Twelfth Night, As You Like It*, and *The Taming of the Shrew*, are virtually conventional comedy given the new richness of an English dress with the new splendor of the Elizabethan poetic tongue. The figures in the great tragedies, once viewed by nineteenth-century thought primarily as individuals, are now usually conceived according to an outlook stressing ideas of pure poetic productivity as the embodiment of primal emotional forces virtually of universal or cosmic significance. Lear, Hamlet, Othello, Romeo appear to us less as unique persons and more as crystallizations of those vital powers that, in our quaintly naturalistic phrase, "make the world go round." Recent criticism discovers these magnificent figures close to mythological beings and much farther than had previously been supposed from the psychologically refined creations of modern naturalistic fiction, Hamlet may be more real in the sense of being more emotionally convincing and relevant than Hedda Gabler or Miss Julie but the Scandinavian women are no doubt more faithful to human nature as reported by the contemporary psychologist. Shakespeare's tragedies and comedies are in a very real sense more "poetic" than his "histories." They depend much the less upon characterization as this is today commonly understood. Falstaff and his followers, the English kings and princes as delineated in this great series of plays, rivalled in their field only by Strindberg's plays on Swedish history, have, on the contrary, a personal reality not strictly matched in the English poet-playwright's more typical and in the end still more remarkable work. In his histories he was the more ahead of his times ; in his great tragedies he even more conspicuously outdid himself.

This theoretical relation between "history" and "characterization" has distinct relevance for the analysis of Chinese drama. The commonly received view that history is a more or less faithful narrative of public events that have already transpired is the most useful view of it in a consideration of literary and dramatic methods. Such writing falls midway between the plain chronicle that merely follows a calendar without the organization implied in the word "narrative" and the philosophical inquiry into the basic cause of human events. History considered in these popular terms is commonly a story of persons who have caused or effected events. It is, in fact, much more likely to be personal than sociological, for social science is a field well beyond history as usually understood. To Shakespeare, for example, history meant first of all the story of the English kings as related in volumes easily accessible to him and Plutarch's *Lives,* his favorite source for knowledge of the ancients. More than this, to him and to most persons until comparatively recent times the distinction between fictional narrative and factual statement was as a rule cavalierly drawn. Thus the *Aeneid* related the history of the early world of the Romans in much the same terms as Livy or Tacitus treated their own subject matter. The Middle Ages used the word "history" quite indiscriminately in reference to the fictional and the comparatively authentic. The important issue to readers everywhere was not the documentation of events but the force and conviction with which these were narrated. Where people of the past were made to appear to live before men's eyes, were made to appear vital, breathing and speaking persons, the requirements of history were fulfilled. To revive the voice of the past had long been one of the leading aims of the classical historians themselves. The writers made history speak, as messages by radio across the years, giving the supposed words of important persons on important occasions and for the most part on moments of crisis and contention. This practice in itself made long strides toward the dramatic. One of Shakespeare's happiest discoveries was that he needed to do little more than to utilize the harangues in Plutarch to create brilliant passages for the English stage.

The conception of history as closely related to drama has been current in the West from the earliest historical times. Aeschylus's *Persians* is the resplendent beginning of a line of "historical" plays whose ending is certainly not yet in view. Persons eminent in history have in turn become vividly realized characters upon the stage. Few stage characters have lived more convincing lives than they. Especially up to the Romantic Period these characters ranked with the most fully developed in respect to personality. They were the puppets of neither farce, comedy nor allegory. They escaped from the routine conceptions of the *commedia dell' arte*. They were of necessity naturalistic, as the fictional characters were not. Moreover, they inhibited on the whole the more serious parts of the stage. Men as a rule refused to accept the view that history was a farce or that its narrative was mere fantasy. By long tradition serious plays were most favored when hardened by the inference of history and thus almost all tragedy, or drama in the grand style, prior to the nineteenth century was in some sense also historical. Its scenes were laid within an historical framework. Shakespeare's tragedies, for example were presented as at least plausible "histories" and his most mature tragedies, as *Hamlet, King Lear, Macbeth, Antony and Cleopatra,* and *Coriolanus,* are quite obviously historical. The figures are conceived as "real." Not so those of comedy. Classical doctrine itself made this distinction, as shown, if not in Aristophanes and the "old comedy," at least in the works of Menander, Plautus and Terence and the "new comedy." Still, tragedy remained more devoted to a psychological exploration of the passions and to the purgation of the audience by pity or fear than to its secondary assumption of personal verisimilitude. This assumption strongly distinguishes the "historical" plays as written, for instance, by Shakespeare and Lope de Vega, from the works generally classified as pure tragedy. The historical plays took on a form of their own, less committed to such conventional plot or story-telling as found, say, in the Romeo and Juliet plays by both Shakespeare and Lope and more in keeping with the serial events unfolded by history's own natural course. What this signifies for dramatic form need not at the present detain us, chiefly because Chinese playwrights, who rejoiced in narrative as well as poetic license, failed to take historical narrative seriously enough to experience the sobering influence felt by the Europeans. But the almost inevitable focus upon character or personality in all such historical narratives does concern the present argument. Here, at least to some extent, East and West share common ground.

Being traditionalists, an eminently literary people, and living with full benefit of printing, the Chinese from early times had many incentives for the love and cultivation of history and, indeed, few peoples have for so long a period given themselves so devotedly to it. Their more sober and scholarly minds respected historical truth. Their playwrights belonged here in a somewhat different category, writing not in the scholarly language but in the vernacular dialects and aiming first of all to entertain. But the sense for history necessarily became a part of their mental nature. By their plays they aimed to gratify the curiosity of their audience concerning Chinese history, to make this history come vividly before their eyes, and to exploit its obviously dramatic possibilities. The great majority of the plays, to be sure, are in no sense historical but a considerable number are so. It is in these plays that the first notable departures from purely conventional type characterization are to be found. The distinction may not go far, but it is clearly observable. By this road persons came upon the stage who not only bore historical names but performed actions which the audiences at least credited as historical. They brought to the theatre a special conviction of personality. Like the conventional comic type figures, they moved from play to play but unlike them they escaped the more rigid conventions of thoroughly artificial comedy. The audiences evidently felt warmly toward them. One credited their reality, much as one believed in the reality of the gods. But they were more tangible and human than the Oriental gods, who of all divinities are the most clearly fabrications of the creative and unregimented imagination. They become more three-dimensional than the more explicitly fictional characters. In them one begins to see in more developed form the complex of emotions that constitutes what we have come to regard as the human psyche. Without intellectual embarrassment, one only too easily talks about them as if they were human beings.

An objection might be raised here that many of the Chinese plays offering themselves to the audience as "historical" are themselves subject to a dense mass of purely theatrical conventions. Most of these plays fall into the class known as "military plays." War they present as a highly stylized dance. They are also costume plays, with a glamour and splendor almost beyond credibility of Western audiences. One thinks of a glitter of head-dresses with dancing balls and pheasant plumes.

Visually considered, these dramatic spectacles may appear to deal no more with characterization than does a ritual, a dance, or a circus. This is all indubitably in the Chinese manner and signifies negatively insofar as characterization is concerned. But this is far from telling the whole story. Beneath the extravagantly decorated surface and dazzling ornament the Oriental audience in many and important instances throughout their dramas discerned the heart and character of both man and men. They grasped the words as well as the spectacle. And even the spectacle became in many instances symbolical of aspects in the individual constitution of a stage-character. Thus in the historical plays and, I assume, in these only, there are individual characters who wear unique make-ups and carry special symbols of their identity. Ts'ao Ts'ao is such a character. He has as much personal identity as a Greek god or a fully developed character in a modern psychological novel. He is not only a dancer and a singer but a man, peculiar and unique. He achieves that personal identity in the folkmind which Pirandello so loved to discuss and which makes a fictional character even more "real" than an historical one. Yet this imaginative reality of Ts'ao is itself clearly owing in no slight degree to his initial historical reality. There is another important consideration here. He not only possesses this quality in himself ; he appears to confer it upon those who surround him. An entire play moves in a special atmosphere of credibility where the persons are concerned. Even where the plot seems in our eyes fantastic from a political point of view, the character remains human. This condition provides much of the play's attraction, for historical plays, both East and West, often lack the aesthetic form or symbolical power evident in more poetic, dream-like and idealized works.

Ts'ao appears in many plays, only two or three of which need be examined here. He is always the villain and warlord but, like other villains, he is made, largely by a sense of humor, to some degree ingratiating. He himself has humor, ability, gusto, and a vast love of life. He epitomizes the positive, aggressive, unscrupulous forces in human nature, a diabolical monster evincing the monstrous and the diabolical that in some measure lurks in all human breasts. To himself he deals in no lies or inhibitions, though in dealings with others he can be the complete hypocrite and pretender. He exercises a supreme magnetism over most of those with whom he comes into contact. Only the gravest and most profound strategists can defeat him and thus save the imperial throne from falling into unholy hands.

One especially memorable play depicting him has been entitled, *The Capture and Escape of Ts'ao Ts'ao*. It shows his success in outwitting his captors and his extreme cruelty, treachery, and self-seeking. Owing to his conspiracy against the reigning Minister and hence against the throne, he has been sought, captured, and bound. But Ch'en Kung, the administrator of the province in which he is taken captive, proves no match for his wiles. Ts'ao persuades Ch'en Kung that he is simply attempting to overthrow a corrupt minister and is in no way hostile to the Emperor. Ch'en accepts the promise of a substantial reward in the regime presently to be established and rides off with Ts'ao. Shortly they arrive at a village where the chief figure is Lu Po-she, a sworn brother of Ts'ao's father. This genial host offers the two travellers a warm hospitality. But despite the hereditary family friendship, Ts'ao is wrongly suspicious. As he himself acknowledges : "All my life I have been suspicious of everybody and everything." The good host has gone to the market to buy wine for the feast. Meanwhile Ts'ao hears the servants at the back of the house sharpening their knives to cut up a pig for dinner. A complete egoist, he fears that they sharpen their knives to cut him up. In mad fear and suspicion he proceeds to murder the entire household in cold blood. Later he treacherously kills his host. Nothing troubles his conscience. Gay at heart, he is off within a few hours to further adventures.

As already indicated, in all such plays not only the chief warlord but persons around him take on the three-dimensionality found in comparatively naturalistic characterization. The figures in this particular play have as much verisimilitude as characters in the most realistic parts of *Don Quixote*. The host is a singularly warm-hearted, genial and convincing character. But even more "real" in the literary sense is poor Ch'en, whom Ts'ao has so completely duped. The study, completely ironical, is of a man of weak judgment but good intentions, fascinated and deluded by a sinister person of great power. He lacks even the decision of a Hamlet. Ts'ao sleeps soundly after his mass murders. Ch'en, at last convinced that he has committed a most grievous error, vacillates between the decision to kill or not to kill the evil man. His position closely resembles Hamlet's while standing beside the king at his prayers. Moreover, Ch'en's soliloquy has almost as convincing psychological insight as the best of Strindberg. It must be quoted entire :

He has fallen asleep. Ugh, how I abhor him ! The bright round moon is shining through the window and my heart is as tangled as hemp. But it is too late now to repent. I am a wanderer, wavering and unsettled. Too late to repent ! We went to Lu's home as guests and our host truly deserved to be called a man of lofty principles. He killed a fatted pig, bought wine, and made ready to entertain us handsomely. Who could have foreseen that Ts'ao would prove so mistrustful and put his whole family to death in the twinkling of an eye ! The blood of that poor old man was mixed with the yellow soil. It was a sad end ! After suffering such a wrong his spirit will have to be propitiated. But why should I suffer ? I was not the culprit. There are spirits roaming about in the void who can testify to my innocence. The drum in the watch-tower strikes the second watch. The more I ponder, the more acute is my sense of the injury. Too late to repent ! I have abandoned my official post and even my robes. I have absconded from my magistracy, discarded my official robes and headgear. I fancied that Ts'ao Ts'ao was a person of broad intellect and consummate ability, that he was the very man to reform the Dynasty and confound the traitors. (*The third watch is struck*). Ts'ao Ts'ao sleeps like a log, like a frog in a well. He is like a waterdragon, his body covered with scales. He is like a fierce tiger, shorn of his claws and fangs. If I don't strike him now that he's asleep, it will be like letting the tiger loose to return to his lair and destroy more victims. (*He draws his sword and is about to strike when Ts'ao turns over*). I was just about to cut off his head. (*Ts'ao turns again and continues to sleep. Ch'en sheaths his sword*). Ah ! That was a risk, another foolish blunder ! Wo, stay your hand ! If I kill him, when

daylight comes, will not the people of the inn be implicated ?
What's to be done ? Ha, I know my course. Here are pen
and ink on the table. I'll write a few lines in verse. But
what theme shall I select as a warning to him ? Ah, I have
it ! I'll take the Fourth Watch as my theme ! (*Writes*).
  The Fourth Watch strikes ; thick night's still overcast.
  My office and its robes are of the past.
  To kill Lu's innocent family one and all
  Is Ts'ao Ts'ao's crime, and he is bound to fall.
(*Calls*) Your Honor, your slumber's very sound. I know
you now for what you are, an execrable traitor ! (*He reads
his lines*). Well, I had better look for my horse and make
my escape. (*He takes the lamp and does so*). I, Ch'en Kung,
repent my folly. Why should I accompany this rebel to
the ends of the earth ? The flower may float with the current, not I. (*Exit. The fifth watch is struck*).

Another play gives a revealing picture of Ts'ao and a still
more revealing portrait of one of his attendants. It has been
entitled, *Beating the Drum and Cursing Ts'ao*. This brief
piece is more an episode than a play and was presumably
a segment in a series of plays or acts, as determined by their
manner of presentation. In any case, it belongs to the Ts'ao
saga. The lesser figure politically who plays the major role
dramatically is the scholar, Mi Heng. Most scholars in Chinese
drama resemble the effeminate Chao Ch'ung in the already described play, *Madame Cassia*. Mi Heng is of a radically different
nature, so that he stands out in the world of the Chinese
theatre with strong individuality. He is arrogant in the extreme. Although Ts'ao has in no conspicuous way provoked
him, he decides against all precedent to insult his superior.
On being introduced into Ts'ao's august presence, he reviles
both him and all his aides and fellow-generals. Ts'ao does not,
as might be expected, at once order Mi's head severed from
his shoulders. There is even an intimation that wicked as
Ts'ao is, he feels a smart from the justice of Mi's audacious
rebuff. But the general is no one to yield or confess a fault.
As return for the insult all that he requires is to have Mi
appear at the New Year's feast arranged for the following day
in the servile role of drummer. The scholar accepts the order

but with a plan of his own. Such a role should, of course, be performed with due ceremony and in a becoming costume. To do otherwise would be to insult Ts'ao still more deeply than by merely verbal rebuke. So Mi enters the environs of the court chamber clad in a shabby dressing gown. At the dramatic moment he throws even this aside and, stark naked, beats a terrifying assault upon his instrument. This brings the play to its climax. It is now clear that the decision must come. Mi's patron advises him to follow a conciliatory course. Ts'ao decides to act slyly by offering him the position of envoy to a distant province. This Mi accepts, though the audience knows far better than he that Ts'ao intends in due time to eliminate so objectionable a servant. Ts'ao's action resembles Claudio's treacherous order removing Hamlet from the court. This play shows the underside of Ts'ao's character. He is no hero. Its focus falls on Mi, admirably delineated as victim of an extreme pride of learning. He is a plausible though extravagant man, a superior scholar gone mad with the vanity and arrogance of his profession. In all parts of this short play psychological discernment is by any standard whatsoever truly excellent.

Another drama showing the superior work found in characterization in the pseudo-historical plays, *Lord Kuan Goes to the Feast*, has considerable charm. The focus is sharply maintained. As often, two hostile camps face each other across a river. On one side is the army of the Kingdom of Wu, led by the Minister Lu Su, on the other, the army of the Kingdom of Shu, led by Lord Kuan, Governor of Chengchow. Sharp debate takes place over the terms of a truce. Neither side will yield as to either the principles or the details to be negotiated. Lu Su and his followers finally conceive the obvious though treacherous plan of inviting Lord Kuan to a feast, with the intention of murdering him. The Lord is too proud and confident to decline an invitation, though he suspects full well the intended ambush. He trusts in his own strength of arm and, more than that, in his commanding and overpowering personality. His foes are strong but he is stronger. By his personal magnetism and supreme majesty of mien he frustrates the wiles of his enemies. After a visit in which all the due ceremonies are observed, he returns triumphantly to his own men across the stream. Thus the play, unlike most successful works for the stage, really shows no decisive action in the usual sense of the word. Negative in action, it stands at the antithesis to melodrama. A storm threatens only to pass over completely. Lord Kuan's action is really less active than passive. His personality and his presence, not his deed, confounds his foe. Several fine Chinese plays deal with similar audacious military visits, usually exemplifying the Chinese unwillingness at any time to relinquish the prospect of a feast. *Huang Ho Lou*, or *The Yellow Crane Tower*, is an excellent example. In all such plays vivid sketches of well known personalities appear yet none, perhaps, places so strong a focus on the mind of any one character as *Lord Kuan Goes to the Feast*.

One of the chief persons in the aforementioned *The Yellow Crane Tower* is the hero who has well been described as the special favorite of the Chinese people, Chu-ko K'ung-Ming. This redoubtable minister and tactician is Ts'ao Ts'ao's most successful opponent. The latter being the very essence of the hated warlord, is the evil genius within the Chinese theatre ; Chu-ko K'ung-Ming, the magician and strategist, who conquers by force of mind and not of arms, is its good genius. But in Chinese eyes Chu-ko K'ung-Ming is by no means a mere symbol or personification. He is a more convincing realistic character than either Ulysses or Merlin, both of whom in important aspects he resembles. His witty thoughts and words spring from him alone and are the unmistakable manifestations of his personality, ever serene in the midst of direst peril. He talks and sings as no one else on the Chinese stage. Since he appears in almost countless plays, it would be impossible in a brief compass to do full justice to such a statement. A single, very typical instance of his extraordinary appeal must suffice. An episodic drama, *Grass Boats Borrowing Arrows*, tells of his triumph over Ts'ao when all odds seem in Ts'ao's favor. Ts'ao has a vast and well equipped army ; Chu-ko K'ung-Ming finds at his disposal a weak army especially ill equipped with missiles. The issue appears to lie in the armory itself. The commander-in-chief over Chu-ko K'ung-Ming is in despair. But the wizard offers his plan with sublime confidence. He requests a fleet of flat-boats loaded with mounds of grass. These he proposes letting loose to float down the river. Having received these appointments, he takes no further heed to the matter, though he has wagered his own head upon the outcome. No one knows what is in his profound mind. Day succeeds day and he remains in what seems preposterous serenity. At the close of the last day which he has stipulated for the fulfilment of his plan, evening descends with dense fog. The boats are cut adrift as the loyal army raises an immense clamor. Ts'ao's men fire virtually all their arrows into the darkness. These affix themselves in the bales of grass. The wind changes and the boats return, Ts'ao's men now being without their arms and the loyal forces being well supplied. Chu-Ko K'ung-Ming calmly accepts his triumph. When his fellow-generals ask how he has known that fog would descend and the wind blow in their favor, he makes only the bland remark : "A general who is ignorant of astronomy and geography will never rise above mediocrity." A more delectable line would be hard to find. It provides also the very epitome of the character of its speaker. Chu-Ko K'ung-Ming is no less demonstratably an individual than his deadly foe and final victim, Ts'ao Ts'ao. Such figures as Li Ka-yung, the henpecked husband in the historical play, *Chu Lien Chai*, or *Pearly Screen Castle*, or Mo Ch'eng, the faithful servant, in *I P'eng Hsueh*, or *A Double Handful of Snow*, are other instances of exceptionally vivid portraiture.

In conclusion, it must be admitted that had the exploration of history been closed to the Chinese playwrights there is still good reason to suppose that they would have achieved some insights into psychological discrimination. Their historical outlook considerably aided but did not altogether determine their position. In all literatures "characters" in the literary or the dramatic connotations of the word are commonly conceived through excursions into certain areas, the most widely favored being, perhaps, the erotic. A more delicate and penetrating study in this field where drama is the literary form can hardly be found than a dramatic monologue from the Ming Period made famous by Mei Lan-feng, *A Nun Craves Worldly Vanities*. The title sufficiently suggests its contents. In both theme and technique it strikingly parallels the most inspired work by August Strindberg. Characterization, in short, though by no means its foremost accomplishment, is far from negligible on the Chinese classical stage.

8 / *Extravaganza*

THE SOPHISTICATION of the ripe Chinese culture as found from the earliest periods of our historical knowledge has nourished a drama endowed with all nuances, as romantic sentiment, refined humor, and even psychological characterization. China's tenacious hold upon an advanced civilization owes as much to sturdy foundations grounded in the very elements of human nature as to its assiduously maintained elegance and grace. A type of drama or at least a mood in drama developed for which no precise parallel occurs in the West. It has elements of farce and of burlesque but the word "extravaganza" possibly describes it best. It has more emotional vigor than a theatre of nonsense ; the popular designation, "theatre of the absurd," hardly proves descriptive, indeed that term is misleading in many of its applications to Western plays themselves, for such works as Genet's *The Blacks* have in fact only too grave implications. For such the word "poetic," as distinguished from "rationalistic," would be more appropriate. Under whatever term this phase of Chinese drama is designated, it indubitably expresses the ebullience of the Chinese spirit. To an elemental energy is added the gift for strong exercise of imagination and fantasy, with a talent for the grotesque and the bizarre. In their more elementary aspect the plays are largely intended for the eye, with much dazzling color, clowning, and pantomime. In their more developed form they make truly remarkable contributions to comic literature and to the humorous theatre of the world.

One deals here with shades of meaning quite as often determined by the producer as by the playwright. It is well known that in many instances of plays throughout the world the same text may be presented in a serious or a comic vein, given soberly or in burlesque. In this regard a play may have a long and surprisingly varied history and while it would be inaccurate to say that the best works of the imagination can be the most gravely misunderstood it is doubtless correct to say that they can be the most variously interpreted. An instance is afforded by a Chinese play that has apparently been given in several dialects, throughout several centuries, and in a variety of styles and which in the course of its history has even been known by several titles. The most recent of these is translated in the phrase, *"The Fisherman's Revenge,"* a title that suggests the violence of Chinese social and political life during the last half-century. In some versions it is comparatively serious, in others, broadly farcical. A commentator writing in the volume supplying the most recent translation, that by Yang Hsien-yi and Gladys Yang, sees the play as sober political propaganda. He writes : "This drama shows that the fire of revolution can never be extinguished. In the second scene, Hsiao's friends pose a number of questions to the landlord's steward. 'This fishing tax, was it granted you by the emperor ? . . . by an order from the ministry ? . . . Then what is your legal right ?' This expresses the rebellious spirit of the peasants under the oppressive exploitation of the time, and the writer's indignation over decadent, feudal rule." No doubt the comment states one of the playwright's thoughts correctly. But from it no one would infer the truth that even in the version offered by Yang Hsien-yi and Gladys Yang the play is above all a roaring farce. As produced by the company of Mei Lan-feng it actually had less of the spirit of extravaganza, for the great actor himself played the secondary role of the romantic daughter.

The story is of a fisherman who, either because he cannot or will not, simply does not pay his fishing tax. When he presents his complaint to the district court, the local lord has him whipped. In return, he crosses the river to the lord's mansion and puts this petty tyrant to the sword. These are the bare facts of the case. But the play is much more than bare fact. All characters are presented with extreme gusto and the majority seen for the most part in attitudes of lusty farce. Since this must to some extent be read between the lines, a brief description may be desired.

The least farcical figure is the daughter, the part not only performed but enlarged by Mei Lan-feng. Yet the conception is deliberately trite. She represents filial piety extended to the uttermost degree. From one point of view she is a parody of the female warriors who enliven so many of the military plays, from another she is merely a timid girl. The inconsistency here leads to her chief scene, one of the play's most delicious episodes. She has bravely insisted on accompanying her father on his journey of vengeance to the lord's mansion. Yet with much incongruity she voices a sentiment wholly antithetical to her father's view of the situation ; with feminine delicacy she expresses her horror of bloodshed. She is, in fact, frankly opposed to the expedition. With the feminine privilege of changing her mind in mid-stream, she voices her wish to row back. She is the perfect, gentle heroine, shortly to be married. On one hand she represents the modest maiden dutifully awaiting her husband ; on the other she is a valorous Britomart. The humor of the incongruity makes the part what it is. She comes nearer to pure comedy and digresses further from rude farce than the other figures. Her superiority is nicely symbolized by the ornament which she wears, the lucky pearl, which in some older versions gives the play its title. It is on the pretense of showing the tyrannical lord this magic jewel that he is ultimately killed and his household with its evil ways wholly extinguished. Such is the play's kernel.

Her father, assuredly the chief figure as imagined by the playwright, exists in the condition of extravaganza rather than pure farce or burlesque. Not he but his enemies are satirized. He is a true hero yet one whose every move fills the theatre with laughter. First of all, he passionately loves conviviality and hard drinking. We see him carousing with his boon companions, the much idealized bandits, and on the morning after his feast arising late in a complacent, half-drunken condition. He always appears as drunken-happy. This association of broad comedy with deep drinking is a much used convention in the Chinese dramatic extravaganzas. Its appearance will be found much more conspicuous in the next play to be examined, *Li K'uei Carries Thorns*.

In addition to being a toper, Hsiao En is that conventional character in comedy throughout the world, the man who is the opposite of what he appears to be : a peaceable old man pretending to be weak, though in reality lusty and powerful almost beyond credulity. His soft-spoken ways lure on those fools who are his natural opposites, the empty-headed braggarts. The audience knows it is being fooled and delights in being fooled. Hsiao play-acts and pretends to tremble with terror ; the boxers rage with arrogance. In the twinkling of an eye it is he who will be aloft and they prostrate. A single old man defeats a throng of lusty young men. The jest is that the tables of probability are completely overturned. The wisest calculations of mice and men go oft aglee. The audience loves it, since mankind is at heart inveterately romantic and irrational.

So well is the entire action of the play integrated that when the main role is understood all other roles fall naturally into place. The lesser characters are defined by their relation to him as he is to them. The boxers are all obviously fools and, as entirely befits the conception, the leading boxer, being the most boastful, is the greatest fool of all. The jovial crew of bandits are clearly the apotheosis of an extreme romanticism. Enemies of the state and the only true friends of mankind, they express in humorous terms man's inveterate anarchism, nourished by long acquaintance with mankind's inability to establish any political institutions remotely equivalent to his own ideal of justice. In ancient China, containing one of the most rigidly established and authoritarian governments the world has ever known, this zest for anarchy makes itself the most stridently expressed in the imaginative life. "The Way of Heaven," it seems, is equally in the hands of the bandits and of the state, of the romantic followers of a creed essentially Taoist and the classical followers of a faith explicitly Confucian. In the classical dramas the bandits are almost without exception figures of theological and philosophical significance. Their aim in life is not theft, murder, and cruelty but the disinterested confirmation of Heaven's Way. They are not land pirates but unselfish philanthropists. In perverse and occult fashion, like Robin Hood of England, they rectify the world's injustices and inequalities. All this is perforce depicted in a spirit of extravaganza and self-conscious optimism, for everyone knows in the back of his mind that the dramatic convention violently conflicts with the world's actuality. This art is indeed Aristotelian. It presents life not as it is but as it ought to be. Bandits in reality are no more philanthropists than old men are strong as Hercules.

These and like considerations assist in defining the character and spirit of the humor of such plays. They are not burlesque because they are fundamentally creative. They are not primarily satirical because they are in fact extravagantly idealistic. They are completely without the astringent irony of such fantastic plays as *The Beggar's Opera* or *Tom Thumb the Great.* Although they emphatically contain political propaganda, that in itself is by no means of primary importance for as works of art they immeasurably outdistance any editorial function. They possess an immense gaiety. Nothing can be further from them than the harsh, realistic, literal-minded, hate-inspired satire of the Latin tradition. It would be wholly inaccurate to describe their social and political propaganda as oblique, for it is almost naively direct. But the essence of the work clearly lies in its hilarious extravaganza and it is this which should first meet the attention of anyone considering them as works of theatrical art. Rarely if ever in the West is such a paradoxical brew concocted. The West is almost as deeply intoxicated with logic as the Orient with illogicality. Robert Burns's dramatic cantata, *The Jolly Beggars,* for example, has some properties in common but still clings comparatively close to the Western satirical tradition. *The Fisherman's Revenge,* or, as this writer would himself prefer to call it, *The Luck Pearl,* is above all essentially Chinese. The former title, incidentally, seems to have been given it only since its enhanced popularity under the Communist regime, when emphasis has naturally fallen on its political "message." Belief in "luck" comes closer to the traditional Chinese outlook, which accords with the whirlwind of irresponsible vitality blowing through these hilarious scenes.

Some of this vitality and euphoria is witnessed in one of its explicitly poetical features. Nature imagery is conspicuous and pervasive. It accords with the elaborate pantomime that in particular concerns the imaginary rowing of a boat across a stream. In the play are a few lovely songs and metaphorical flights of fancy concerning the life and scenery along the river. We hear that the fishing has become bad because the stream is low. The whole country suffers from draught. In a rice-growing land this, of course, threatens starvation and death. The fish die, the crops wither. Nature's face under these circumstances becomes grim. The old man is urged to give up his hard and unrewarding work. Yet it is clear that he views the river and its scenery with passionate affection. The rippling water, the willows bending over the banks, the sky brilliant by day and star-thronged at night, the mist, with its mysterious and exquisite movements, concealing and rediscovering nature's face, fascinate this nature-lover to the innermost depths of his heart. To read or to imagine this play is equivalent to unrolling a Sung scroll-painting of a river's long, sinuous course. In addition to being a riotously funny picture of humankind, this is a delicately sophisticated tribute to nature and the physical universe. Nature's harshness is not denied but its beauty is conceived as predominant. The same attitude is apparent in *Li K'uei Carries Thorns*. These plays are both excellent works of art fundamentally because of their power of expression and their admirable view of life. The distinction between them, or at least between their most accessible versions, is that one play as a work of literature is relatively crude, the other, its lusty mood notwithstanding, is remarkably refined. *The Fisherman's Revenge* is commonly known in its version as a Peking opera of relatively recent date. It has of late been considerably rewritten and older and more refined versions—though probably no more vigorous—left behind. Moreover, no one will describe any of its translations as poetically inspired. As English poetry there is little to choose between the equally competent and uninspired versions by Arlington and Acton and Yang Hsien-yi and Gladys Yang. Both are more or less prosaic. J. I. Crump's spirited rendering of *Li K'uei Carries Thorns*, on the contrary, faithfully represents an ancient play in a translation that as literary art far surpasses that enjoyed by any other English rendering of any Chinese play whatsoever. It affords a peculiarly favorable subject for analysis for readers who are not dedicated specialists in the peculiarly difficult language of the Yüan theatre.

This play has much less of political value than *The Fisher-man's Revenge*. Again we encounter a company of noble bandits but the playwright shows no disposition to dwell upon the general theme of social and economic injustice. His bandits are merely dedicated to furthering "Heaven's Way," though in precisely what fashion does not appear. The only evil persons are a pair of undistinguished rascals masquerading as bandit chiefs, who emerge out of nowhere and at the play's end are justly condemned to lose their lives after experiencing the most sanguinary torture. Their crimes have been to impersonate others and persons far better than themselves and to impose upon an aged and devoted father, whose daughter they spirit away for three days of sexual enjoyment. The father is distressed but little or no evidence is given that the daughter, who is, of course, the most immediately concerned, shares his feelings. Instead, she weeps at her final separation from her ravishers and seems little comforted by her father's promise that he will in good time find her a respectable and more desirable husband.

In its dominant mood the play is even more hilarious than *The Fisherman's Revenge*, though the level of poetry is incomparably higher. Possibly it gains as art from being less complicated by politics. Be this as it may, it has less the quality of a moral tale and more that of innocent folklore. The kernel of the plot lies in a wager of heads, Li swearing to offer his own if the scoundrels who have violated Man-t'ang are not proved to be the bandit chief, Sung Chiang, and the ex-Buddhist monk, Chih-shen, while Sung wagers his head to the contrary effect. The father, Wang Lin, rightly declares that Li is mistaken. Li has been far too impetuous to do good, primarily because he has, as usual, been drunk. As he is about to lose his life, the father abruptly appears with the news that the impostors have returned bringing his daughter in safety. The heroes readily capture the rascals, whom Wang Lin has reduced to a drunken stupor, and all ends happily and justly, the rascals giving the remnants of their bodies to the dogs and crows and the bandits and the innkeeper joining in an hilarious feast. It is possible that the play was written for production as part of the festivities for the holiday on which its action is represented as occurring.

Drinking, more or less incidental in *The Fisherman's Revenge*, becomes a dominant feature of the Dionysian play on the desperate adventures of Li K'uei. This work is a satyr play to no small degree dedicated to the wine-god. Drinking bouts are celebrated in the mountain heaven of the bandits. The only scenes set in what appears to be our normal world are laid in Wang Lin's tavern, where drinking proves much more conspicuous than eating. The play's hero, Li, is shown as intoxicated at all times. The distinction is only in the degree of his intoxication. This pervasive atmosphere of the wine-cellar helps enormously in sustaining the extravaganza of the play as a whole. Its plot is wholly incredible in rationalistic terms. It meticulously follows well-trodden paths of folklore, brazenly deserting the ways and conventions of life as reported in the sober pages of history. It follows the moon-struck, wine-drenched poetry of Li Po, not the sober, Confucian realism of Po Chü-i. Both ways are, of course, equally indigenous in Chinese culture. One leads to such masterpieces as *An Heir in His Old Age*, the other, to such delectable extravaganzas as *Li K'uei Carries Thorns*.

The genial travesty of old age implicit in the delineation of Hsiao En is carried to much greater extremes in the portrait of Wang Lin. The story invites the introduction of this romantic father's blindness, though foolish as he is he proves not as mentally blind as Li K'uei. Of course he is not totally blind but is in a condition that makes the imposture passed upon him comparatively plausible. In their make-up the knaves should by no means closely resemble the noble leaders whom they impersonate. This the text makes abundantly clear. The rascal playing the role of the Buddhist monk does not even take the trouble to shave his hair. In all scenes the old man's pitiable condition enables the actor to perform elaborate pantomime, groping about the stage in humorous discomfiture. When finally put to the test, however, even he can distinguish between true and false heroes. He is described as timorous, as are almost all comic old men ; yet even he cannot be intimidated by Li K'uei's insistence that he is not telling the truth, however much he was earlier deceived by the bold liars. The wheel of comedy comes full circle.

Goodness and optimism are, of course, the essence of the

play's spirit. It is further delightful and paradoxical that an habitual drunkard such as Li should undertake so chivalrous an adventure as to defend the honor of a tavern-keeper's dubiously virtuous daughter and even sacrifice his own life for the happiness of such a pitiable old man as Wang Lin. Human goodness has seldom been celebrated so exuberantly as in this remarkable play. The bandits are heroes, the drunkard is the greatest hero of all, the father, "honest though poor," is utterly devoted to his daughter, the daughter is at least spared for a respectable marriage, and the only criminals live outside society and without too great difficulty are within three days brought to condign punishment, leaving the atmosphere as pure as Eden before the fall. This is a rapturous extravaganza. No wonder its scenes abound in gay music and delectable song and the scenery of its vales and hills is blest with verdure of early spring. In short, the play is a pure lark. This, however, is in no way "the theatre of nonsense." Although it is difficult to imagine an action more extraneous to the sober history of humankind than the play's story, nothing can well be closer to the human heart. In other words, the action, when literally considered, is wholly absurd, whereas the motives are the very soul of normality. To love one's child almost to the folly of excess, to be devoted in friendship, to respect pledges at all costs, to be generous even to strangers, to enjoy the pleasures of life to the very uttermost, and to detest brutality are basic properties in human nature at its best. It would almost appear that the degree of imaginative conviction in the story depends on the artificiality of the setting that encases it. The jewel becomes more authentic as the setting becomes more fanciful.

The play's excellence lies, of course, in the execution. The extreme artificiality of the technique harmonizes admirably with the similar artificiality of the story. Continual interplay occurs between verse and prose, song and speech, together with the addition of a species of verse recitative.

These abrupt transitions contribute immensely to the excitement and vivacity of the performance. None is casual; all are calculated. Moreover, especially delightful to encounter in the course of the play, like green fields in a mountainous terrain, are the songs, usually in warm appreciation of some of the beauties of nature. Li K'uei shows himself especially appreciative in this regard. The contrast between his rude exterior and actions and the delicacy of his sensibility constitutes a great part of the charm of the scenes. His exclamation on the scenery of Liang-shan and defiance of all who fail to agree with him is a sufficient instance.

All roles are delectable comedy but one of the most attractive is the minor role of the Buddhist monk turned humanitarian bandit. The irony of the conception intrigues the mind. The man of contemplation throws his asceticism and meditation completely aside to revel in the active life. Quite clearly, brother Lu Chih-shen is the Friar Tuck of Chinese folklore. The sturdy divine is, in fact, a universal theme in comedy and even in tragedy. We find him in the novels of Henry Fielding, in *The Song of Roland*, and in such medieval farces as the admirable, *Johan, Johan, Tyb and Friar Johan*. This universal character appears in the Chinese extravaganza at his best.

The play's mood calls for the chief attention. Admirably worked out as its innumerable and studiously calculated details may be, the spirit of the piece gives it its primary distinction, setting it off from the great majority of even remotely analogous plays in Western drama. It also affords a valuable commentary on the genius of the Chinese comic spirit, arising from a people rich in human understanding and entirely unimpeded in their art by the prosaic pressure of mere logic. On the one hand Chinese playwrights compose works of such delicate and reserved humor as *The Western Chamber*, and *Madame Cassia*, on the other, works of robust extravaganza, such as *The Fisherman's Revenge*, and *Li K'uei Carries Thorns*. The distance between them affords a measure of the vast scope of humor within the Chinese mind.

Like all other types of legitimate art, this is composed of many component parts often paradoxically related. The effect of this species in the theatre is obviously humorous. The audience laughs and is happy. The mood is not only gay but seemingly irresponsible. An overhasty critic might pronounce the entire show nonsense and absurdity. But the residuum left from such an entertainment is much more than entertainment. Amusing the actual experience certainly is yet the after-effects may safely be regarded as substantially

more than frivolous. Admittedly the extreme artifice of composition and presentation on first direct acquaintance leads only
to hilarity. Beneath the gaiety, however, lies the substratum
of the solid appraisal of basic values in life. The warmth,
geniality, generosity and even the spontaneity act as effectively
liberating forces from the cold, formal, cynical, and calculated
temper that life, especially in a mechanized or mercantile
society, is only too likely to assume. In the manner in which
all the literary arts are oblique, the more serious ends of society
itself are served. The most amoral of plays may thus in the
end have a morally salutary effect. Nonsense cures by a purgation of a great nonsense, as pity by a purgation of a still deeper
pity. The ideal goal of a robust poetic comedy is won.

9 / *Mythology*

IN THE twentieth century the student of the world theatre is easily prone to forget the degree to which the world's drama has hitherto been dedicated to religious thought. The farther backward the eye glances, the more likely is this to be true. The classical and medieval dramas of Europe, the stages of ancient India, and of Japan at least up to the seventeenth century were preponderately religious. China presents one of the extremely few dramatic literatures with a classical age that fails to give priority to religious experience. At least to Western eyes it at once impresses us by its secularity. The central theme is man, not the gods. Yet there is much eminently supernatural in the subject-matter of the Chinese stage, where magic, folklore, superstition and a genial mythology appear from the Western outlook to supplant the more strongly spiritual inspiration of other classical stages. A more refined problem, however, is presented here that intimately concerns a broad view of Chinese drama. Its themes from daily life are happily lightened and relieved by these many excursions into supernaturalism that enliven the entire picture and accordingly contribute much to the over-all tone and spirit of the Chinese theatre. It may possibly be held that the testimony of drama reveals the Chinese people not as deficient in religious inspiration but as taking much of their religious life with a lightness of heart foreign to more psychologically perturbed cultures. The Chinese possess a poise hardly found among the more tense Japanese. Though as a people the Chinese indubitably have undergone their full share of hardships and distress, hardships have left fewer apparent marks on their natural character than, say, upon the religiously obsessed peoples of India. Their poise resembles that of an aristocracy to the manner born. As for the comparison with Europe, no image comparable to the crucifixion haunts their racial consciousness. Much of their religion takes the form of a worship of luck, a placation of supernatural powers in the frankly avowed interests of worldly blessings and gains. In India the religious mind is centered upon the universe, in China, upon the family. The family itself may be the universe in epitome but viewed from the imaginative standpoint of Chinese civilization the universe exists for the family, not the family for the universe. Indians and Chinese look through much the same telescope but in India it is the fashion to look through one end of it, in China, through the other. The Chinese magnify what is near, the Indians, what is far. To Westerners the longer vision appears the more religious, the shorter vision, the more secular. Indeed, it is difficult to escape the conclusion that such is a reasonable interpretation. But from an aesthetic point of view, the residuum of the religious element in popular Chinese thought holds great importance. Confucianism itself obviously has a strongly religious foundation and Taoist and Buddhist thought are clearly of much importance for all phases of Chinese artistic life. If the base of the Chinse food is derived from the substance of this world, it is nevertheless of much significance that this secularity is leavened by an infusion from the supernatural and the irrational.

No play of consequence wholly escapes these trans-mundane features. On the one hand, none clings more strongly to a vision of this world and the ethical aspects of Confucianism than *An Heir in His Old Age* Yet, on the other hand, its action centers in the ritual of prayers for the dead. Some religious element proves all but inescapable. Accordingly the subject is both vast and in its totality unwieldy. To explore it extensively would be far beyond the scope of any work in a single volume. For present purposes it must suffice to examine a few of the more suggestive features and in particular one of the plays that springs the most clearly from myth and folklore. In this way the temper and tone of Chinese supernaturalism should become to some extent illuminated and some light shed on the imaginative areas of Chinese drama as a whole. To the element of the supernatural this drama owes much of that lightness of touch which so greatly distinguishes Chinese drama from that of other lands. Such religious element as actually present is also less insistently theological and more clearly personal and human than is the case in dramatic literatures reflecting cultures where theological abstractions flourish abundantly.

It should first be recalled that a fair amount of the supernaturalism on the Chinese stage is found in plays and scenes that have attracted even less attention than usual as literature. To begin with, no traditionally trained Chinese actor or acrobat has ever entered the stage without offering a prayer to the protective deity of the theatre, an emperor who was its traditional founder. All performances traditionally commence with a quasi-religious ceremony that should definitely be regarded as more than perfunctory. Opening scenes often possess a mythological complexion, as the truly exquisite opening episode in *Madame Cassia*, previously discussed. As a national institution, the theatre has long religiously observed many festivals of the Chinese year, these being celebrated with appropriate dramatic interludes. Most impressive of these events was—and still is—the autumn festival in honor of the annual meeting of the Spinning Maid and the Cowherd, which occasions the play, *T'ien Ho P'ei*, or, *The Mating at Heaven's Bridge*. This captivating work tells the tale of two lovers, manifested astronomically by two stars who once a year meet after one of them crosses the heavenly stream known as the Milky Way. The passage is effected by a bridge made of the wings of birds. It is popularly believed that birds will by men be rarely seen or not seen at all on this day because they have gone to heaven to offer their pious wings to the two loyal lovers. Behind this starry tale lies a delightful legend of a singularly earthly complexion. It concerns a friendly ox, giver of excellent advice to his pastoral friends, a herdsman, the spinning damsel, a wicked stepmother, a group of maidens bathing in a stream, and a large family living amid considerable hardship and poverty. Seldom has a more eminently human group of figures been lifted into the sky, or, to put the case more literally, rarely have the stars been brought down into a more intimate converse with men, women and children. The entire story is rich in pathos, warmth, and the intimate human touch. It possesses equal value for young and old. It proves to be religious only insofar as it is supernatural but homely as the homeliest barnyard tale. Its mood is far more playful and tender than exalted or sublime. As literature it stands nearer to *Alice in Wonderland* than to *Paradise Lost*. One is here much closer to the magician than to the preacher. It is true that in all gravity and earnestness Chinese lovers invoke the Cowherd and the Spinning Damsel as protective deities. Such a petition, for example, occurs in an eminently serious passage in *The Western Chamber*. Yet in the original legend are humor and fantasy as well as piety and compassion. These petitions are wholly typical of the element of religious consciousness in Chinese dramatic imagination. Although some Western thinkers may deny the relevance of the word "religion" here, their objection itself seems equally humorless and unreasonable. It is religion seasoned with levity or, to put the case metaphorically, the same familiar egg whipped into a highly rococo fluffy omelette. Much of the charm of the Chinese theatre is defined by such thinking as this. So far as a formula exists, this is a wedding of heaven and earth, of fantasy and human society. The Cowherd is also a star. Even the legends themselves have this duality, so foreign to Western thinking. In the theatre it is generally what is seen that is out of this world, as the fabulous costumes, artificial gesturing, and mincing steps. The shrill singing more nearly suggests the notes of birds than the voices of men. The words constitute the chief force keeping the play attached to the world. The Chinese theatre is thus a fantastic kite held, with aid of a magic string, in a warm human hand. The rainbow-colored kite, soaring among clouds and stars, is the Chinese mythology; the kite veers capriciously with the wind; it is, nevertheless, controlled by the man on the ground, the family man, who lives his ordered life under Confucian laws. So far as a separation is to be acknowledged, this chapter concerns the kite, the supernatural. But the game itself is all one and its proper subject, man.

Many Chinese plays deal with a pure magic that, it is true, seems repugnant to the commonly received conceptions of religion. Dragons flaunt themselves upon the stage. Such incidents are neither so slight as the usual Western fairytales nor so grave as Western sacred books. Fantastic episodes occur under water, as in the comparatively modern dramatic fantasy, *The Brass Net Plan*. There are revolving towers, rainbow clouds, disappearing mountains, such imaginings as a rule, however, expressed by some brilliant stage pageantry and, in modern terms, even by stage spectacle, as if the spirit of the Kabuki were avenging itself on the more reserved Chinese stage. This is parlor magic taken into the open, public view. Inasmuch as these exceptions to the general rule usually make small demands on language, they lie outside the province of this investigation, concerned, as it is, primarily with dramatic literature. In our field of reference the language need not be in itself peculiarly refined or in any sense rhetorical but language must at least be conspicuous. These pages do not present a study in theatrical pageantry or decor.

Those earthly custodians of religious truth, the priests and devotees, play roles that should in this context be briefly examined. By and large, they fail to account for any considerable proportion of figures on the classical Chinese stage. Even where scenes, as fairly often happens, are laid in monasteries, as in *The Western Chamber*, the play's chief subject-matter as a rule is not religious. The monastery becomes less a temple than a hostelry. A fair number of the comedies, as of the farces in medieval Europe, show monks in highly secular guize. Their profession to the contrary, they are depicted as seducers, as in the entertaining comedy, *The Jade Screen Mountain*. Such pretenders to religion are soundly ridiculed. Here the Chinese drama stands at the antipodes from the Noh Plays. There the monk is invariably a sympathetic character and the life within the temple is invariably presented in a completely serious and favorable light. Sages are frequently seen in the highly idealistic Sanskrit plays and almost always revered. In Chinese drama, on the contrary, religion more often wears the secular garment of folklore and needs no priestly class for its support, inasmuch as all society accepts it as a statement of reality. The monasteries stand apart, as retreats from society. Priests are relatively inconspicuous. Devotion, which is highly important and sincere, becomes a function of the family, commonly centered at the family shrine or the family tombs. The Chinese have the sociable habit of taking the divine for granted. Their affable deities become as familiar as persons daily encountered in the street.

No play better reveals the value of Chinese mythology for drama than the popular, *White Snake,* an old work frequently revived by Mei Lan-fang and one of the standard pieces in the repertory of the remarkable child-actors performing in the mid-twentieth century on Formosa. The version discussed here will be that currently used and translated by Yang Hsien-yi and his wife. Here the theme, like that of such plays as *The Butterfly Dream,* and *At the Bend of the Fen River,* belongs not merely to China but virtually to all the world of folklore. The story is of the snake-woman, a legend which John Keats in writing his *Lamia* derived from Philostratus by way of Richard Burton. A sense of magic pervades the Chinese play, though many of its scenes, as the initial episode of the lovers meeting under an umbrella during a summer rainstorm, have all the qualities of social naturalism. To judge the nature of the myth it is necessary to keep at least its broad outlines in mind. The inner meaning can only be examined after the images themselves are clearly perceived.

A paradox for which rational explanation is conspicuously lacking occurs in the figure of the snake-woman. She is pictured as in her own mind wholly benign yet endowed with a strange, venomous potency that on certain rare occasions, magically induced, causes the prostration or even the death of any man who has the misfortune to be her lover. Through her ancestry, again a matter unexplained in the play, she is part snake. It is especially to be remembered that in most Oriental creeds the snake is not venomous spiritually but, contrary to his physical properties, is essentially a good spirit, indeed the foremost deity of healing. So in one capacity the White Snake proves benign, in another, sinister. Her will is wholly sound, her loving heart wholly pure. But if her lover is indiscrete, he will be crushed by great misery. The Snake as Woman may not inform her lover of her true nature or warn him in advance. This is at least rendered partially plausible in that should she confess her true nature, her lover would presumably shun her. For him she feels only the deepest devotion. Hoping the best, she perforce lets fate run its course.

This Snake Woman we shall henceforth call "White," the name given her by the playwright and symbolically associated with the supernatural, with ghosts and with grief or mourning. Her faithful companion, a less ideal being, whose thoughts are closer to human fallibility and to our earth-bound life, is called "Green." They are "sworn sisters." For a thousand years White has been one of the attendant spirits of the moon, where, like the heroine in *The Palace of Eternal Youth*, she serves as deity of music and dance. As destiny revolves, she finds herself incarnate in the guise of a beautiful woman and feels happy to be so since she appears born to love, cherish, produce and guard her offspring. Some further developments of the thought occur. A complex of vegetable myths runs parallel to those of the stars. White's husband is a modest dealer in medicinable herbs and she herself especially skilled in this profession. They set up business where she attends to the patients and the husband, Hsu Hsien, apparently for the most part in good Chinese fashion, tends the accounts.

A melodramatic plot thickens. A Buddhist abbot by name of Fa Hai conspires against the lovers, or, as he more humanely expresses himself, attempts to save Hsu from his own tragic destiny. Paying Hsu a visit, he tells him that his wife is a deadly snake-deity and that he must utterly desert her. His sole prescription is that he flee to the monastery and become a devotee with the prospect, no doubt, in due time of becoming a monk. Hsu scorns the suggestion. But the abbot has his reply. If on a certain festival of the year Hsu gives his wife a glass of wine containing realgar, the spirit will reveal her true snake form and the blow will mortally wound him. Hsu, of course, wishes to believe nothing of this report and attempts to dismiss it from his mind. Nevertheless, the seed of his unrest has been planted. He has at least bitten into the fruit of knowledge. Full marital bliss is not for him.

The day of the festival arrives. The two spirit-women know their danger. White induces Green to fly into the inaccessible hills but is herself, ironically, too much in love with her husband to be separated from him even for a day. Besides, she is well advanced in pregnancy. The indisposition which she is suffering because of the curse that besets her

Hsu at first ascribes to her pregnant state. His apprentices have presented him with some wine as a gift to his wife. The more he tries to induce her to drink, the more she becomes alarmed. He is himself somewhat intoxicated from the festivities of the day. In a moment of weakness she yields and drinks not only one but several glasses. She retires to her chamber, as her husband believes, merely overcome by the wine that adds to her natural pain from her pregnancy. The abbot re-enters and dares him to draw aside the curtains over his wife's bed. On doing so, he faints. No stage direction specifies precisely what, if anything unusual, he sees, but from a later development it appears likely that he beholds a white dragon that has magically evolved out of the belt that White has been wearing. In any event, the venom has had its way and the sight prostrates him completely. The abbot has apparently won his case. Hsu lies as if dead upon the floor. White sees but one course open to her. This is to journey back to a magic mountain rising in the regions proper to the sky and return with a magic herb of healing. She attempts the perilous trip, is at first repulsed by two deities, one in the form of a stag, the other, of a stork, but her intrusion and theft is finally pardoned by the all-powerful Star Canopus. She is mercifully sent back to earth with the herb to cure her husband. The cure, as far as it goes, proves effective and the couple resumes conjugal relations.

Still, Hsu has learned a lesson and can no longer love completely. When the abbot once more visits him, he becomes increasingly doubtful of his condition and agrees to a trial visit to the monastery. On this visit he seems at first willing to settle down into the monastic regime, though shortly he grows restless in longing for his wife. Meanwhile White leads a raid on the monastery. Outside the walls White and Green encounter the abbot and his followers. Their verbal debate is followed by a pitched battle in which the women are worsted, partly because of White's pregnancy. In vain the women summon the Water Spirits to their aid. Green is all the while loyal to her mistress but antagonistic to Hsu and presumably to masculine company in general. Hsu escapes from the monastery. Beside the bridge where the lovers first met on a spring morning they compound their differences and for a short while once more look forward to a happy married life. By the next scene, their child being a month old, a ceremony is being held for the wife's emergence from the chamber of the childbirth. All goes well until the abbot abruptly appears with a magic almsbowl. The rays from this golden bowl have an overpowering effect on all. Green Snake attempts to resist the abbot but is worsted by the Guardian Deity. Deprived of Green's protection, White, as usual, becomes powerless. She is temporarily imprisoned in the golden bowl. Hsu is brought to his death and the abbot is for the time being triumphant. He sees to it that White is buried beneath Leifeng Pagoda with the understanding : "Only when the lake dries up and the pagoda falls shall she come out again." Hsu is last heard uttering in despair the word "Wife !" his sister addresses White with the exclamation, "Sister," and White herself exclaims : "Ah, husband ! sister ! son !" Son and sister survive and possibly flourish but we see and hear no more of them. The popular modern version of the play provides a happy ending. A hundred years later Green has mustered sufficient forces among the mountains to assault the pagoda. Aided with these loyal spirits, she attacks this monument, which stands at the mouth of the Chientang River. The Pagoda Spirit comes out to fight but is vanquished. From the remains of the smouldering pagoda, burnt to the ground by the fairies, issues White Snake, young, immortal, beautiful as ever. The last scene is presented largely as a dance and spectacle. It connotes a victory for the Spirit Woman in terms of immortality, though scarcely a victory in terms of mortal life. Hsu's end is tragic. Son and sister have survived at least for their mortal span. So ends this episode in Chinese popular mythology.

The play is strangely moving. Much of its theatricality springs from its stage business. Of this, the role of the heroine provides the core, for the part must be performed with gestures on the one hand serpentine, on the other, completely feminine. A typical instance of the stage business is provided by the magic belt. To reassure her husband after her first transformation she conceives the plan of hanging this belt from a beam of the house and describing it as the dragon of good luck. She tells Hsu that he has altogether mistaken her true nature ; that she is no snake ; that, on the contrary, she brings for their mutual protection this divine guardian over their household. The stage business with the umbrella and the storm in the first act and with the magic almsbowl in the last contributes typical incidents to the play's great and lasting vitality. In the first act, too, is a typical boating scene. The lovers hire a boatman to transport them through the waters in the park and on to the landings in the city. This is also a dazzling costume-play, where all costumes are symbolical, as the color-symbolism the most clearly attests, especially in the use of green, white and gold.

In what spirit is this strangely beautiful play to be conceived and interpreted ? Is it naive fantasy or philosophical symbolism, bright nonsense or tragic doctrine ? Has it or has it not psychological significance ? Is it designed for the most popular or the most esoteric audience ? Or is it conceivably all things to all men ?

Although an affirmative answer to the last question would possibly be nearest to the whole truth, the subject should repay much further and much more analytical consideration. The question of the component media through which the play operates is distinctly pertinent. First for the words, the version now most commonly performed quite lacks the literary or poetic distinction even of such an extravaganza as *Li K'uei Carries Thorns*. Mime, dance, spectacle and music carry much of the weight. Yet comparatively frail as the verbal texture may be, it is not weak. When read with any degree of imagination and sympathy, the play is poetry as well as spectacle. For the imagery is deeply meaningful. It has the essential properties of poetry that renders religious sculpture also poetic, making the facade of Chartres a religious epic as well as a monument in stone. Poetry does not require rhetoric or even the finer niceties of verbal nuance to be itself. Elegance would manifestly be out of place in the present case. The legend springs directly from folklore and thus from the folk mind. It is appropriate that the language in which it is couched should share the qualities of the mink from which it first sprang.

How far its author or one or another of its original audiences was conscious of specific philosophical meanings is for the most part beyond the possibility of our knowledge or at least beyond the ability or ambition of the present writer to decide. From its first appearance cultists may well have been in a position to give learned meanings to its images. Their explanations would certainly not have agreed in literal terms with any which the speculative reader in the twentieth century is likely to advance, although in general it will be agreed that whatever meaning is legitimate today will not deviate at least in substance from that of earlier times, when symbol would presumably have been laid over symbol rather than any rational exposition provided. William Blake would certainly have believed in the validity of the myth, as in his own explanation of it. Current exposition will be in all likelihood indebted to Jung and Freud. Some truth presumably pertains to all these approaches.

The story, so clearly beautiful in the sequence and balance of its parts, presents a philosophy of life certainly much indebted to a philosophy of both love and sex. An exposition might run as follows. Men and women are fated for each other yet destined to conflicts beyond complete resolution. Only in contemplation, which is the wisdom of eternity, can the contentions be fully resolved. The woman is by nature both the most faithful and the most fickle or contradictory. In her resides the supreme power of survival, for she is the mother-symbol and her potency, though according to one criteria terminating first, according to another survives the longer, inasmuch as her sexual drive outlasts her sexual fertility and in essence is stronger than that of her partner. He is thus outdistanced in the competition, equally confused by feminine caprice and fatigued by feminine endurance. He is also outdone by feminine devotion. The chief factor in the success by which their love survives their passion lies in their offspring. Nature triumphs while the individual falls by the wayside. Friendship also survives. The companionship of friends, indicated in the intimate relationship between White Snake and Green Snake, outlasts the relation of husband and wife or in any case symbolizes the most enduring aspects of this relation. In this play society is sustained as the sister of the husband takes the heir into her custody.

The myth may in another of its aspects be described as the

history of two rival powers, Eros and Anteros. Of one, the husband is symbol, of the other, the Buddhist abbot. For the average man the monastic life fails to give satisfaction but for the exceptional man, capable of overcoming the desires of either worldly or fleshly life, the life of contemplation is the strongest and best. This way of life has the most assurance of survival, for at least its institution, the religious creed or establishment, survives. Nature herself provides survival only through generation, that operates through birth and death. In the eyes of the world the monastic ideal appears grim but not so in the eyes of the spirit, or the third eye on the forehead. From causes sufficiently obvious, asceticism allures the man, not the woman. The ultimate strength of the religious ideal considered in terms of society lies in its realization of mercy and compassion, symbolized by the Buddhistic almsbowl, before which even the full strength of the feminine principle sinks into temporary submission. Although White Snake and Green Snake triumph in many an open contest of arms, Buddha's almsbowl is the invincible weapon wielded by spirituality against all powers of the mortal world.

It is footless to attempt a final appraisal of the value of this symbolical interpretation for the aesthetic potency of the actual myth or, in other terms, for the play itself. It is doubtful if the analytical interpretation on the whole either aids or impedes the aesthetic experience. When confronted with such art as *The White Snake*, being pure mythology, the intellect is actually inoperative. This marks the best possible distinction between the intellectual art-form, allegory, and the intuitive form, myth. For the one, as witnessed, say, by *The Divine Comedy*, the rational meanings materially enhance enjoyment, indeed, the pleasure is definitely mulcted where these meanings are not grasped. The contrary holds true for myth. The success which the excellent troupe of child-actors recently established on Formosa has had in performing *The White Snake* gives striking evidence of this contrast. Surely, these children have not been conscious of any such analysis as the foregoing. Yet the play as art they grasp, enjoy, and admirably perform.

Analysis may not add to our pleasure in the art but does presumably add to our understanding of its excellence and judgment of its aesthetic worth. It is by no means rash to presume *The White Snake* a finer work of art than Keats' *Lamia*, roughly speaking, devoted to the same theme. Keats' poem, too, has a content, in this instance rendered only too explicit. It is the story of a philosopher whose presence frustrates the pure joys of the poet's intuition. Keats proposes that analysis freezes delight. Lamia's double nature signifies on the one hand pure beauty, on the other, beauty itself contaminated by intellectual consciousness. To think is to destroy. The poet openly says as much in the lines of the poem and creates a symbol for his abstraction in the poem's own story. This is all simple enough, so that the tale as told by Philostratus becomes a simple parable, or exemplum. *The White Snake*, on the contrary, presents a vastly more intricate complex of symbols. By virtue of its elaborate design it wins superior position in the artistic hierarchy. Moreover, at the same time that it invites a philosophical interpretation it welcomes a naive experience. Keats points a moral and actually introduces an abstraction in the midst of his enthusiasm to condemn abstraction. After the manner of the moralistic and intellectual poetry of the school of Dryden, whose style he emulates, he tells what his age termed a moral tale. The meaning is only too clear. No child would really relish so brazen a regimen of instruction. On the contrary, it may be presumed that even the child when enjoying *The White Snake* is unconsciously acquiring an intuitive feeling for the main issues of life which it so eloquently expounds.

By no means all Chinese plays dealing with materials of folklore, myth and legend have the depth or brilliance of this acknowledged masterpiece. Yet it is far from standing alone. Many of its leading features are shared with plays already examined at some length in these pages, in particular *The Palace of Eternal Youth*. It is appropriate and refreshing to conclude these surveys of Chinese poetic drama with analysis of a work so conspicuously poetic and so clearly universal in its attraction to the poetic mind of all lands and ages within the span of civilized consciousness. Certainly a more mature and profound drama than that celebrated English dramatic fairytale, *A Midsummer-Night's Dream*, it possesses a singularly catholic charm.

PART TWO

The Japanese Classical Drama

I / *The World of Astonishment*

It can hardly be an overstatement to describe the Noh drama of Japan as the nearest of all schools of the theatre to being unique, like no other school yet significant for all presentational artists throughout the world. It closely resembles nothing in Asia and naturally stands still further removed from the stages of the Western World. Concerning its origins in dance, ritual and recitation there is more speculation than assurance and the Kabuki is only indirectly its heir. Imitations in the West have been comparatively remote from the Japanese drama itself and the relatively few Japanese plays designated as "modern noh" are only in minor respects faithful to their more famous predecessors. Insular Japan evolved a type of play much more idiosyncratic, for example, than England created in the times of Shakespeare partly because during the period of the Noh's evolution Japanese contacts with the continent at its side were considerably weaker than English contacts in the sixteenth century, or, to take a slightly different view, than English indebtedness to the Renaissance. True, most of the thought-content of the Noh plays remains remarkably close to the Chinese and its strong religious elements are only superficially Japanese in origin. The art, however, especially in its more theatrical aspects, remains peculiar to Japan. Although innumerable individual features are with small difficulty traced back to earlier semi-dramatic forms or forward to the Kabuki, the general complex of the Noh stands forth in pronounced independence.

Nothing so baffles criticism as the quality of being unique. The most impressive reactions to this drama have been emotional : warm admiration in the West and deep veneration in Japan. That it has an atmosphere or, to use a stronger word, a spell of its own has nowhere been doubted. It perplexes the twentieth century in being highly paradoxical, at one and the same time surprisingly succinct in its speech and leisurely and slow-paced in its performance. The text is brief and action on the stage economical of movement though not of time. It is obviously decorous and dignified, a drama of stately ritual and devout feeling, yet fired with the most intense passion. Westerners in particular in the presence of this religious mystery have discovered a vague pleasure and a critical incertitude. Seldom have works of art induced such an ample measure of praise or so slender a literature of rigorous analysis. This book undertakes the task of enlarging the area of analysis and especially of describing whatever significance the Noh plays may have for the development of modern drama and art. Although complete novelty will scarcely be expected, the broad generalities and somewhat monotonous repetitions common in existing criticism should at least be avoided. Though all art is a mystery, awe and critical hyperbole need not obstruct useful comment. There is much of importance in the content of the plays that may well be taken for granted or left to speak for itself without further critical intrusion. The circumstances call for specific statements rather than over-all appraisal or critique of work by general consent deserving of admiration. On the one hand, discussion of particular features should not fracture them into trivial detail, with the result that one deals with shards and not with works of art ; on the other hand, when dealing with such highly accomplished works, cross-sections themselves may prove rewarding. The aim is not an ultimate appraisal but some answers to the practical questions : what particular attractions and values have the Noh plays for the mind of the twentieth century ?

One of the first problems is to determine the relative value of the plays as documents, as imaginative literature, and as theatre. As documents they are reservoirs from which may be drawn ideas of various kinds, aesthetic, social, historical, philosophical or religious. From such a viewpoint the plays are seen intellectually and studied rather than enjoyed. As

imaginative literature they are poems, works to be read and
contemplated in the study. As theatre they are, of course,
works in actual performance. To a notable degree the tendency in recent years has been to regard them as subjects for
study and above all for a theoretical aesthetics. For many
minds they have existed primarily in speculation and even for
speculation. Viewed in this light they have exercised considerable influence on poetic drama outside Japan, beyond
whose islands they have rarely been seen and more often
than not read in translations of debatable merit. Many discerning Western writers have commented upon them without
ever having witnessed an adequate performance or a performance of any kind. They have become a favorite field
for reference and allusion. Moreover, it becomes of special
note that they have generally been viewed as stage productions even when they have not been actually experienced as
such. They have as a rule been seen in the mind's eye as
hypothetical plays, not read as dramatic poems. Thus they
have been regarded as a unique and fascinating kind of theatre,
not as closet drama.

Much encouragement for such an outlook is clearly present
in the plays themselves. As the West experiences drama, the
Noh plays are uncommonly brief, even parsimonious in their
verbal texts. In a production considerable periods occur when
the stage is almost static and only the musicians are active.
Or the spectacle shifts from these frozen tableaux to become a
scene for dances of various kinds, as a rule stately and slow-
moving, though on occasion violent and even frenzied. These
practices discourage reading from the strictly literary point of
view, tending to give the plays the look of a libretto. The
reader places himself more in the position of a hypothetical
producer—say Gordon Craig—than of a man of letters ;
he speculates on the ideal character of the poses, the costumes,
or the dancing. Though the texts themselves offer little
resembling stage directions, it is precisely the mental application of such directions that gives such readers a peculiar
pleasure. In their presence the mind easily becomes fascinated
with problems of theatre technique. The page supplies a
scaffolding across which the student, with spider-like diligence
and ingenuity, constructs the web of his own thoughts. The

process is certainly intriguing and doubtless in some instances rewarding.

It should be added, however, that these speculations are more stimulating than conclusive, more likely to affect the productions of a new stylized drama than to result in thoroughly successful revivals of the old. Even in Japan scholars may understand this and that about the plays and still be insecure in producing them. The sum of these perceptions may not lead to a completely satisfactory projection upon the stage. There are few plays that thoughtful persons are more pleased to discuss and few that they seem so reluctant to patronize in performance. In Japan all but a cult of devoted enthusiasts regard them as somewhat esoteric. The performances, generally on Sundays, resemble the exercises of a religious sect primarily aesthetic in its observances. It is the Kabuki that for some three centuries has been overwhelmingly popular, not the Noh. For this the powerful religious sentiment of the Noh, as a rule Buddhistic, must in part account. Most audiences find this sentiment uncomfortably austere. Another obvious and quite different discouragement to readers and listeners alike lies in the archaic language, presenting at times serious difficulties even to advanced scholars. The texts, with their patina of years, discourage modernization and confront translators with peculiar obstacles. Even Chaucer is, it seems, more readily transposed into twentieth-century English than these contemporaries of Chaucer into current Japanese. The reader may derive what he takes to be an idea while missing the original inflection. In short, the text is more often consulted than read. Nevertheless, so far as the West is concerned a radical change in the picture has recently occurred. Quite possibly a sympathetic reader of the equally brilliant and faithful English translations by the Japanese Committee for the Translation of Classical Texts may come as close to the intentions of the playwrights as the average student of the original work.

There seems no escaping the difficulties in performance. If sincere effort is made to achieve fidelity to the tradition, the music demands considerable research, even on the part of the performers. Still harder problems confront the dancers. From causes such as these a wide popularity for the Noh as theatre seems doubtful in Japan and still more difficult to imagine elsewhere. Abroad a few amateur and academic productions are possibly the most that can be expected in the near future. But excellent prospect exists for an ever increased attention to the Noh on the part of thinkers, lovers of the stage, and progressive minds actively employed in the rapidly changing theatres of the world.

It is quite another matter to consider the plays as poetry, as literature, as works to be read not only for instruction but for pleasure. The aforementioned translations of thirty of the chief plays into English executed by the ablest and most conscientious of Japan's scholars and enforced with extensive and reliable commentary, places this question in a new and much more favorable light. The new translations are much more attractive to the modern spirit than the work of Arthur Waley, which now seems under considerable romantic influence. The plays offer probably the finest body of short lyric dramas in the literature of the entire world. They are poetry of the first water. An analogy that may at least be suggestive is offered by William Butler Yeats, who favored the inclusion of certain of his pseudo-Noh plays into the volume of his Collected Poems. Contrary to what may be the general record of recent history, or more specifically, the problem as posed by the first half of the present century, it now appears that the plays may confidently be read in the Western languages as poetry. To this several factors so far unmentioned contribute. Although the times may be out of joint for widespread performance on the stage, the contrary seems the case for their prospects in the library.

The plays are written, so to speak, in short-hand, with a severe compression in style distinctly agreeable to the prevalent manner in modern verse. Similarly, just as modern verse dispenses with rhetoric that savors of Victorian or Renaissance patterns, the terse, symbolical statements of the Noh are at least as language plain and straightforward. This further assists the translator. Whatever real and substantial difficulties the Noh plays present to him, they seldom embarrass him with elaborate metaphorical expression, such as Shakespeare, for example, often employs. Like modern poetry, the Noh prefers symbol to metaphor, the structural image to the decorative embellishment. The Noh indeed favored elaborate decoration in costume but not comparable ornament in speech. The subjective character of thinking in the Noh, the strong inclination to the metaphysical, further flatters modern taste. The subject-matter is much more personal than political. It offers exercises in spiritual therapy, a helpful gesture for a period as conscious of personal maladjustments as our own. There are, then, many features both in the form and content of the Noh attractive to the modern mind.

Without speculating on details, a reader reasonably aware of the conduct of stage-production in general can gain much pleasure from the Noh. Probably he will require little more actual awareness of the imagined stage than induced by a reading of Shakespeare. A distinctly lyric type of drama has been by no means unpopular in the twentieth century. The late plays of Strindberg, much of Schnitzler's work, and plays by Pirandello, Brecht, Lorca, Synge and Yeats, all afford admirable specimens of the short, poetic drama. In times favoring short poems, a natural tendency on the stage has been for short plays to be closer to poetry, long plays, to fiction. The public is learning more and more to read between the lines. Playwrights restlessly experiment in dramatic forms unknown to their Western classical tradition. This experimentation proves especially fruitful and prevalent where pantomime, dance and music are added to the straight-forward, conventional conduct of the spoken play. There is increased fondness for "the open stage." These new types of theatre assist us today not only in seeing but in reading and imagining such drama as the Noh. Good reason exists to presume that all classical Asian drama will in the next few years be increasingly read in translation in the West and that no form will be more warmly received than the Noh. The most striking shift in the reception of the Noh will almost certainly lie in this area. The plays will as books presumably be continually searched for new ideas and the plays as theatre continue to be relatively neglected by producers ; in these respects one can foresee, even at the most, comparatively slight changes ; the chief development to be expected is their increasing attraction in the study, or as dramatic poems.

It is true that in some circles there lingers a prejudice against

such poetry inherited from Victorian times, when an emasculated type of closet drama was favored by an emasculated
minority of the reading public. Such playwriting signified as a
rule a lame blank verse and a pale imitation of both the neo-
classical and the pseudo-Elizabethan tradition. But small
cause exists to transfer these infelicities to a reading of Noh
plays as poems or to consider that such reading betrays either
stage or poetry. The general history of dramatic literature
completely invalidates such prejudices. As the prevailing
criticism overcomes a passing bias, the Noh plays must emerge
more clearly to their rightful and rather unusual position.

From a perspective of dramatic theory it is further important
to observe that rigid distinction between a theatrical and a
literary view of a play is in plain violation of fact. Dismissing
from consideration writing merely in dialogue form, no intelligent reader is likely to examine a play while entirely neglectful
of its theatrical aspects. No one, for example, will read even
the most talkative play by Bernard Shaw in the spirit in which
he reads an imaginary conversation by Walter Savage Landor.
Where stage directions are absent, the reader's mind in substance supplies them. The nature of the dramatic text compels
him to see the gestures and to hear the speech and other
imagined sounds. It is further to be recalled that the Noh
plays have from their very beginning been received as works
of literature no less than of the stage. No schism exists. The
most that can be said is that the reader enjoys the better
opportunity to contemplate the play and to meditate upon
it, the spectator, to receive the stronger impact of its sensuous
reality. The kernel of the experience remains much the same
in whichever medium it is encountered.

The Orient itself has wisely favored an analysis of drama
based on the two-fold appeal to eye and ear, sight and sound.
This unique property of the stage may well supply the basis
for its critique. Noh playwrights are lavish in gratifying the
visual imagination. Here a distinction must be made between
images entirely poetic, that is, presented in description of
scenes wholly imaginary, and the images actually visible
as objects on the stage, as the actors, their costumes and
gestures, and the stage properties, the last being in the Noh
few in number but often highly important. Almost all Noh

plays contain vivid descriptive passages, as a rule evoking impressions of nature. How these images are incorporated in the play's inner meaning must be examined later as one of the Noh's most distinctive features arising from the Oriental philosophy and manner of experiencing nature. The point to be insisted upon here is the unsurpassed vividness of the images themselves, frequently attended with tactile and even olfactory values together with the ocular. Even the mere reader of the Noh play is invited to conjure up images vivid in color and sharp in profile.

Dancing clearly supplies the most prominent and exciting feature on the imagistic side. Not all Noh plays include dancing but by far the greater number do so. Moreover, the dance is likely to be the emotional climax of the work. It is noteworthy that it does not ornament the conclusion of the play, as often in classical and neo-classical comedy or in an American musical show; it expresses the emotion at its height, when the dance climbs to the summit of emotion more readily than words. Miming, though no more important, is even more prevalent than dancing. This is usually introduced while the chorus or some character not engaged in the miming recites lines illustrated by the mimist. The burden of the poetry falls to one actor, that of the movement to another. The chorus itself is never permitted to duplicate in gesture what is expressed in its words or song. On the contrary, it usually parallels the action of the main figure. Miming is primarily in solo. There is virtually no pantomime or dumb show, as seen on the Renaissance stage or in *commedia dell' arte*. Attention is strictly focused on the individual performer. Here is a good instance of the principle everywhere observed in the Noh plays, an economy of statement together with a synthesis of the arts. Music, poetry, and dance, or miming, are completely integrated. They are, however, held somewhat apart and not chemically fused, as they are fused in the Sanskrit theatre. Neither the musical line nor the line of speech is seriously interrupted and impressive action is almost continually provided, either as pure action, as miming, or as dance.

The appeal to the ear exists on several levels arranged in the most careful gradations with a sophistication hard to match in the entire history of the stage. Although some prose is used in minor or more naturalistic passages, the greater part of the plays is in verse. Though at least three levels are observable in the voiced parts, namely a less stylized manner for the prose, a highly stylized manner, approaching recitative, for the poetry, and a singing voice used primarily in the choral passages, differences are less marked than in roughly analogous patterns in the West. In short, all the dramatic speech appears more or less musical and all the dramatic song somewhat declamatory. Just as there were few, if any, ensembles in pantomime, so, with the exception of the chorus, there is relatively little polyphonic or part speaking or singing. But the Noh playwrights are not without their brilliant innovations. The leading character, for example, may have from one to a dozen followers who engage in choral speaking or chanting. These attendants constitute a chorus on the stage. The chorus proper sits to one side.

The instrumental music for the Noh guides the rhythm of the actors' motions and accompanies their words. It is much less demanding in its own right to be heard than lyrics of Chinese opera or the musical lines of any Western production designated as opera. Extraction from the play of this "music for use" and its emergence as a pure music proves almost unthinkable. Although volume and tone are somewhat more substantial than in the delicate music of the classical Indian plays, the Noh music is in general less strenuous than that of the Kabuki and vastly less obstreperous than that of the traditional stages of northern China. Thus the poetry is accented but never obscured and from the generally received point of view a remarkably well balanced harmony is obtained. No part is pressed forward to the disadvantage of the whole. A balanced weight is maintained, for example, as some of the finest verse is rendered by the chorus at the same time that the dancer gives the play its most powerful visual and emotional appeal. Of course there are clearly artful modulations on both sides. Certainly at the entrances and probably the exits, both protracted in time, the music and miming take ascendancy over the words.

No device of the Noh to insure its monumental unity of affect is more striking or more likely to astonish the Westerner than the splitting up of single phrases or sentences between two or more speakers and even the apparent transference of one man's statement to the role of another. This achieves for the play a high stability as a poem at the same time that it deliberately renounces a naturalistic style or any illusion of naturalistic character delineation. To judge from much Shakespearean criticism, the character, not the play, is the thing. The Western play frequently seems a vehicle to portray characters or individuals. Incidentally, or perhaps quite deliberately, the star actor is favored. The Noh play, an aristocratic form, in this respect as in all others, favors the total value of the work. Even its major actor is subordinated to the affect of the whole. Its words are never strictly dialogue in the Western sense, for they more nearly resemble a musical pattern where the disposition of the notes follows its own law. With their eye on universality, the playwrights show little or no interest in distinguishing individuals. To their own end of a centralized focus they use in their speeches many highly conscious devices. To mention a few : one formula often employed divides a passage into three successive parts, commenced by two actors and concluded by the chorus ; one person appears to understand another so fully that he speaks for him ; two characters thinking alike speak not together but pronounce two parts of the same sentence ; frequently the chorus or one of the characters utters the thoughts of another person who for the time being turns dancer ; or the chorus voices the thoughts which the actor entertains but for some reason does not himself express. The last-mentioned practice uses the chorus to the ends achieved in Western drama by the aside. Eugene O'Neill met these problems rather less successfully with his use of masks in *The Great God Brown*, and with asides in *Strange Interlude*. In these areas of stage artifice no school of playwriting approaches the Japanese masters.

The leading characters themselves are not simple but projected on lines of double or multiple exposure. This, of course, is a common practice, not an invariable rule, and applies chiefly to the hero or central figure. Yet the technique sufficiently expresses the whole purport of the Noh plays, unified in concept but elusive in execution. The central character is simply not what he seems. First, he may be a mortal and later a god, or first a mortal and later a ghost. Much of the aesthetic pleasure springs from the observance of variations on a given theme, of the skill whereby the playwright presents on the first appearance of the hero in disguise intimations of what he will become on his second appearance, or revelation, and on his second appearance reminiscences of what he has earlier said and done. There is thus an interweaving in time as well as in speech. Furthermore, the chief incident in the play is frequently viewed itself as duplication of some earlier incident in myth, in history, or in classical poetry. The play provides a series or mirrors in shrewdly placed locations reflecting a unified idea through a conjugated series of images. This is essentially a symbolic poetry, not a narrative according to the manner, say, of Shakespeare's *Romeo and Juliet*.

Mental realization of space is no less artful. The main scene or action does not as a rule shift. Thus in an important phase of its execution the playwriting is classical and conservative, not romantic and liberated. There is far less moving about of the principal action than on the Chinese stage or even on the Sanskrit stage and incomparably less than on the Kabuki. The question is much deeper than one of mere length. A large number of Noh plays begin with an imagined journey, which the actor mimes while walking about the stage. This preliminary scene of motion, so unlike the rest of the play, resembles a bird's flight to a distant point at which it alights. The audience is exhilarated by a display of free motion but still greater stimulus is felt in that the stylized motion has led to the precise spot where action may proceed on a mental basis to the point of greatest intensity. The dramatist commands a mobility in excess of his bare necessity. He husbands his powers to good purpose. Later scenes taking place in other localities than that of the main action are commonly described in speeches that are in themselves pure narrative or reminiscence. The play has potentially free and abundant motion all directed to a conclusion that is without motion, the still point of whirling, concentric wheels. This strategy seems strikingly modern. It is the manner of a metaphysical theatre where the most violent action is to a far greater degree mental than physical.

The specific place or scene of the action is usually of great importance, indeed the typical play becomes in one of its most vital aspects a celebration of place. Often one of its most significant figures is "The Man of the Place". Generically, the Noh plays owe much to the celebration of a certain feast in a certain temple, the shrine memorializing its own fame by a play and dramatizing the principal legends associated with it. European drama presents perhaps only one masterpiece of vaguely similar orientation, Sophocles' *Oedipus at Colonus*, where the title itself indicates the importance of place. In the Western sense of the words, the Noh play has no stage scenery yet the scene itself in the poetic sense proves of immense value, far beyond its usual weight in the West, and serves also to aid the phenomenal use of nature imagery in the Noh, an imagery humanized to a much greater degree than is the nature imagery in the romantic or sentimental poetry of Wordsworth and his school, so strongly colored by an ego-centric outlook on life and the "pathetic fallacy" in its view of nature and landscape. Place in the Noh indeed signifies a geographical place but one whose meaning has been deeply felt in the most eminently human terms. It is almost invariably a secondary figure, not the major figure, who in mental action moves so rapidly from place to place; the main figure, in contrary manner, obsessed with a sense of place, haunts the scene where he or she has performed memorable acts or met a tragic death. The rapid passage from one location to another celebrates not the importance of the scenes so impatiently passed by but the prime importance of the location held sacred and never for a moment overlooked, where the traveller at last comes to rest and the leading character attains enlightenment.

The treatment of time is no less artful and likewise presented with double exposures. Clearly, no such simple and direct technique as the throw-back common in Western drama and film can be found. In an essentially uncommitted stage, where no one place or time is pedantically insisted upon, quite obviously the entire scene cannot at any time be revolved from past to present or present to past. It is of the essence of the spiritual realism and fidelity to experience depicted in the Noh that no moment or place is ever wholly sufficient to itself. The soul is conceived as a deathless organism threading its way as a moveable cell through the universal body of time and space, which has therefore in itself no mastery over the soul, spirit being in the end superior to all tangible aspects of the material world. Thus an old woman imagines she is young or that she is actually a man, her lover of years' past. A warrior's ghost fights again the battles of his youth. A hero as ghost re-enacts his heroic death in a scene that may legitimately be conceived as a dream of death. An entire play may be considered as the dream of one of its more passive characters. One autumn epitomizes all autumns, one spring a symbol for all springs. A flowering tree, whose blossoms are one by one dissipated by an April breeze, becomes symbolical of all life's pride and death's tyranny. Seemingly all gradations of time are represented in subtle conjugations, from plain reminiscence to reincarnations so vivid as to surpass by far the impact of literal, present prosaic reality. Changes of mask, costume, music, and movement, flowing from speech to miming and from miming to various forms of dance, define the movements within this eminently live and plastic world.

Motion within the world of the Noh may at times give a Western eye an impression of painful slowness ; movement, like that of an hour-hand, may even appear to cease altogether and the stage be frozen into complete passivity. Examined more attentively, however, the movement will be found within its own terms to be phenomenally free and rapid. Prosaic fences are wind-blown to earth ; the imagination moves with the force of a capricious wind, now high, now low, the horses of its chariot at all times held in leash within the hands of art. If occasion calls, the spectator may find himself swept into the sky, as in the incomparable last episode of *Hagoromo*, or transported as if by magic from one side of the Japanese islands to the other, as in the change between the first and second parts of the celebrated drama, *Takasago*. In Noh's awareness of space there is no cumbersome shift of scenes or rumbling of stage machinery. To the sensibility of its play-wrights all such movement would seem pedestrian. The image, "time flies," becomes here more than merely meta-phorical ; through areas of time and space the imagination of the Noh proceeds not on foot but on the wing.

Most conspicuous among the means whereby this liberation is achieved is the use of ghosts. Here the spectator is almost induced to believe this resort to superstition a conscious artistic device rather than a surrender to popular belief. By this usage a heightened actuality is given to the past, which becomes not merely more alive than the historical past but than the present. Is not the ghost in *Hamlet*, though briefly seen, the most vivid and vital figure in Shakespeare's play ? What appears almost a happy accident on the Elizabethan stage becomes a favorite practice on the Japanese. The world of the Noh is the world of astonishment, itself the property of the most moving art. In all these affects the Noh plays achieve ends to which the avant-garde theatre of the West at present aspires.

The attainment of an ideal toward which the West moves with an uncertain footing, a metaphysical drama, is happily exhibited in the highly prevalent nature imagery of the Noh. The plays not only celebrate place ; they almost always celebrate a physical scene, a landscape, a season of the year, even a condition of the sky or heavens. The grasp of nature in these plays is more literal and less spiritual than that in the great Sanskrit dramas, for the Japanese imagination is more given to concreteness than the Indian and less strongly fired with the compelling force of seasonal myths. In Japan the blossoming tree itself becomes virtually a deity, while Sita, as Earth Goddess, is wholly forgotten. Thus in distinction from Indian drama, the Noh stage is by no means a great mythological drama. At its best it deals with symbols of nature and with men and women quite obviously human, not with gods, demi-gods, and religiously conceived heroes such as those who populate the Sanskrit theatre. Behind the Indian stage move as spectral forms the prime forces of nature itself. Man is merged in nature. Supporting the Noh, on the contrary, is the belief that nature is itself an infinitely spacious assembly of souls. Thus in one play, *Basho*, the central figure is in fact a tree. This tree appears first disguised as a woman and as a dancer. As the play draws to its climax her true identity unfolds. Only in appearance is she a woman, in this manner accommodating her to the necessity of the stage. Her human aspect is a mask or disguise. In reality she is both a spirit and a tree. The natural is supernatural. All things are in reality spirit. This conception of the world can better be described as animistic than as theological. It seems to us closer to the primitive than the typical cosmologies of the Chinese and the Indians.

It would be impossible for the Noh poets to comprehend the pathetic fallacy, or view that nature sympathizes with man or in any sense duplicates man's own nature. The universe of the Noh is at heart not man-centered but with all its infinitely varied parts is centered upon itself alone. Its favorite religious text is the *Lotus Sutra*, which teaches that all things possess soul and that the soul passes successively through all things. Human nature is thus only a way-station, though an advanced one, to the All, to Buddhahood, or the divine. The more fully man becomes aware of the infinite forms and manifestations of the divine around him, the closer he approaches the divine "Way". Natural forms are not, as in Christian thought, merely symbols of an over-world of the spirit, as they are made to appear, for instance, in *The Divine Comedy*. There is no allegory in matter. The forms are themselves instinct with spirit, just as man himself is, and live in a boundless universe of concentric circles about the central Buddha, with a focus as austere as the pearl on Buddha's forehead. If a non-human being appears on the stage or in vision, this is its courtesy in speaking the language of humanity. It has as much right to be the spirit that it is as man in his turn has to his own soul.

Thus nature and nature's forms readily become leading elements in the plays. Matsukaze in her ecstacy takes a pine-tree to be in actuality her dead lover. The twin pines of Takasago and Suminoye are virtually two lovers, not two trees in our common understanding. These trees are depicted as reincarnations of the two principal human figures in the play. Or shall it be said that the figures are the trees ? Behind all four images lies the seminal belief in the transmigration of souls and in the power of the spirit to manifest itself even simultaneously in innumerable forms. The souls assume their different forms as the actors assume their different masks.

The sadness of autumn and the misty, salt-laden atmosphere of Suma Beach are of the essence of Matsukaze's own grief. She is the place and the place is herself, for places no less than things have souls. In the play bearing her name they do not resemble her. She is the spirit of the shore and she and the shore become one. *Toboku* similarly is a play dedicated to a garden. Again, in *Miidera* the magic beauty of the harvest moon shining on a vast, outspread valley is itself the peace and salvation of the heroine's soul. Here is no background scenery. The scene itself moves forward, takes the central and most active position upon the stage, to become the force impelling the decisive motion in the heroine's soul. The peace that passes understanding exists first in nature and, aided by the magic of a temple bell, enters and possesses the heroine's breast. The thinking is completely animistic. Nothing could be further from the thoughts of such a good Christian as Dante or as Wordsworth, though Saint Francis may have had intimations of the mind of the East. At least Dante himself virtually suggests this as, in his famous eulogy on the saint, he associates him with the sun at dawn and the radiance of the Eastern sky. The patron saint of the birds cannot well be described as a Christian humanist.

In this regard the identification of winter with old age in *The Dwarf Trees* proves typical and noteworthy. In the celebrated drama, *Sotoba Komachi*, the main argument in the dialogue establishes a virtual identity between a stupa and the aged heroine, the stupa having the form of a fallen tree. Obviously, this is more than metaphor, imagery, or even symbolism. It is animism with the Buddhistic interpretation of nature at its roots. Of course not all Noh plays are equally eloquent in this field of thought but most of them share in it and on the whole the most famous and most poetic are those participating in it the most fully. Western thinking customarily associates nature as subject-matter with non-dramatic poetry while the theatre is dedicated explicitly to the human or even the social scene. But not even the rich non-dramatic poetry of Japan surpasses the Noh drama in awareness of nature. The Noh plays reach a high point in such thinking, for they are considerably more inspired by nature than the Kabuki, more obviously occupied with it than the Sanskrit plays (though Kalidasa is at all times unsurpassed as a nature poet) and far more concerned with it than the socially inspired theatre of the Chinese. Man has always to some degree been occupied with his imaginative relations to nature. Even in an age of atomic science this remains true, possibly even with promise of becoming increasingly important. The Noh plays must always constitute an outstanding monument to man's penetration of nature and the inevitability of his collaboration with it, whether as herding sheep or flying rockets to the moon. In Western terms, the plays exhibit "nature poetry" in one of its rarest and most superlative manifestations.

Still another important aspect of the Noh relating it to contemporary thought and to the contemporary needs is its emphasis on the therapeutic values of art. Especially since the imaginative thinkers of the West have to so marked a degree despaired of the effort to save the ship of state and become preoccupied with the effort to save the individual, their works have resembled life-preservers cast on stormy waters for the use of whomsoever they may reach. Their art is still propaganda but propaganda for the soul, not for organized society. Its uses are deemed personal. Art offers a form of therapy. At times this includes an egocentric confessional ; at other times it becomes a discipline whereby the soul is purged of its diseases, whatever they may be, whether, for instance, self-pity, fear or terror.

The Noh makes an impressive contribution to this persistent faith in art as therapy. It offers a special discipline for the soul in its quest for salvation. The main distinction here is, of course, that psychiatry, a secular discipline, proposes a personal cure for a private affliction, whereas the Noh, a religious discipline, proposes a universal cure for the universal ills of collective mankind. Yet insofar as the process of art is concerned, the paths are by no means dissimilar. In the typical Noh play the hero gives comfort and inspiration to the spectator by passing from tempestuous and destructive emotions to peace discovered on his road to Buddhahood. Man's tragic condition is dissolved by initiation into religious enlightenment. Passions are given full rein, are exhausted and allayed. In the end, religious truth takes possession of the soul, all passion and all attachment spent. Whether or not these particular terms of salvation prove acceptable to the modern man, at least the play's general direction is distinctly acceptable.

Again, this description of the Noh fails to apply equally to all the plays and to some of them it scarcely applies at all. There are "Congratulatory" pieces and pieces of an eminently public reference. Yet it faithfully describes many of the strongest and if there is considerable difference in the violence of the passions displayed, there is never the least doubt felt as to the idealistic attitude and a spiritual resolution is of the play's essence. The so-called "Mad Women's Plays" are the darkest, beginning the farthest back in tragedy, and proceed most sensationally along the path of therapy. These are also among the most striking of all Noh plays, *Aoi No Ue* offering a ready example. Congratulatory plays, on the contrary, such as *Tamanoi*, which as a rule assume felicity from the very beginning, seem to Western observers less true dramas than pageants, spectacles, masques, and to be much less moving, less poetic, and less distinguished. As court rituals, belonging to a literature of praise for the Japanese state, they hold a relatively modest place in the estimate of the drama of the world.

So frequently has the art of the Noh been commented upon as regards its extreme economy and compression in the use of its media, its employment of intimation where the West prefers direct statement, its art of conveying emotion by images of repression, that little need be added here. Nevertheless the playwrights' nuances are almost infinite. The style is oblique without being obscure. It has not been generally noted that the prevalence of disguise or some artful presentation of reincarnation, occurring in nearly half the total number of pages in the literature of the Noh, greatly aids these effects. In all such scenes meaning is more intimated than expounded. The Japanese propensity for emotional secretiveness accounts for much of the powerful and almost painful conveyance of emotion to the audience. Suppression of direct statement is carried to degrees unimaginable outside Japan. The more than Spartan attitude is well illustrated in the last moments of the play, *Miidera*. A mother who has recovered her lost son postpones admitting her good fortune even to the child while the two are among a large group of people. The chorus notes this and encourages her to speak as she really feels, observing that spontaneous expression may rightly be indulged on rare occasions. The exception provides the most eloquent evidence for the force of the rule. Broadly speaking, the view of art in the Noh holds that emotion is best expressed obliquely and with considerable suppression, the romantic view, that it is best expressed spontaneously. Fortunately there is agreement as to the ends though not as to the means.

The ultimate test of any work of presentational art is the power of the emotional tones which it evokes with affects akin to the emotions experienced in active life but not precisely duplicating them. The aesthetic life of the presentational arts is itself an emotional life. This is most clearly perceived in the case of music, where successful compositions induce tones of feeling gratifying to the hearers, modulated along the entire gamut of emotion from delight to pain. The distinction of the art becomes commensurate with the validity of the feeling. Where there is no feeling, there is no truly successful art. Where the feeling is in any degree spurious or concocted, as in the case of sentimentality, the art-product becomes to this extent vitiated. The Noh carries the conviction of major achievement in the dramatic form primarily because it projects the strongest emotional tones, clear of all sentimentality or spuriousness in any form. The plays ring with absolute purity of tone. The heart responds to them fully. We discover in them a major aristocratic art, wholly free from a vulgar overindulgence of feeling. The commonly received opinion that the Japanese puppet drama as written by Chikamatsu is the high mark of the Japanese stage cannot be rightly sustained. Zeami, as master of the Noh, is the purer and greater poet, for his works, unlike those of Chikamatsu, are emotionally sound and wholly without vulgar sentimentality. This absolute conviction of soundness in the Noh is its chief assurance of its lasting worth and fame.

A final aspect of the Noh deserving at least passing mention is its profound preoccupation in subject-matter with the theme of the aesthetic life itself. In this respect it closely resembles much recent poetry and imaginative prose throughout the world. A woman, as Eguchi or Lady Izumi, though sensual in the extreme, attains salvation through her poetry. *Takasago* is on one of its levels a celebration of two famous anthologies of verse. The hero, Tsunemasa, is dominated by his lust for poetic fame. Hagoromo and Yamamba are presented primarily as dancers. In *Tsunemasa* and *Atsumori* music is celebrated. *Haku Rakuten* announces the Independence of Japanese from Chinese poetry. The Noh plays like so much modern art and speculation upon art present the creative process as a road to salvation, an escape from the mundane and material world, a way towards Buddhahood.

Despite the deep significance of the Noh drama for the mind of the present century and indeed for any century, it must be in the end acknowledged that a general revival of it on the stage is not shortly to be expected. Doubtless it will be increasingly studied for certain of its remarkable qualities but can hardly be recovered as a widely successful vehicle for professional performance. This is owing above all to two of its features, which even detract from it as poetry : its ritualistic form and its religious content. A ritual is a social usage, an aspect of the manners and institutions of a people and can only in external respects be recovered after the period of its historical burgeoning. The abstract element of dance may to some extent be extracted and preserved yet the inner content will have been dissipated. Much in the Noh plays, especially the formula for the Introduction, is ritualistic, depending upon well-established, deeply ingrained tradition. Thus passages of secondary importance are virtually identical from play to play. In such work a grasp of the playwright's intention to any degree of fulness depends on long familiarity with his artistic form, which is also a social formula. The scholar specializing in the Noh may possibly recover a partial understanding but the general public, whether in Europe, America, or even in Japan, cannot be expected to grasp even as much as this. These ritualistic plays also demand of the actors a peculiar discipline in style today difficult to realize. In Japan the romantic Kabuki lifts its imposing form between the present and the past. Elsewhere the passage backward is, obviously, even more arduous. Most stylistic conventions so deeply affected by the passage of time derive from religious usage. The religious attitude, giving the plays much of their substance and intensity, also discourages a popular reception.

These plays are in their view of life one of the most austere and ascetic of all species of drama. To be sure, in their original uses they were as a rule given in conjunction with two or three comic interludes, or Kyogen. But such a practice is unlikely to be recovered today partly because of the strong local coloring in most of the farces, not to mention their occasionally violent explosions of eroticism. The Noh is antiaphrodisiac and as a rule expresses a profound religious disaffection with the human experience as commonly understood. The emotional life, though profoundly expressed, is at least in the playwright's avowed intention not celebrated but decried. This may be seen in the depiction of such militant heroes as Atsumori and Sanemori. In some plays, it must be acknowledged, the pride of life assumes the upper hand at least in the passages of reminiscence, as in *Kagekiyo* and *Settai*, in *Eguchi* and in several slashing plays dealing with the redoubtable Benkei. These very contradictions in the Noh are the ultimate cause of their intensity, their tension and their disillusionment. On the whole the austere and dark tone strongly prevails, especially in the older and more poetic works. The inner struggle is that of Japan itself, unwilling wholly to accept the mystical doctrines of the Asian continent. That singularly tender and beautiful play, *Izutsu* (*The Well-curb*), is a fair instance. This comes as close to a love story in the romantic sense as any of the Noh dramas. Yet the two lovers never meet before our eyes. The heroine is not a woman but the ghost of a woman, who recalls her affection, extending backward in time even to the innocence of childhood, when the two children played about a well-curb and observed their youthful faces reflected in the water. Near the play's end the woman, as ghost, re-enacts this incident in their childish play. Afflicted by her madness, she puts on the head-dress of her lover and on looking over the well-curb imagines that she sees his face instead of hers. The tragic irony, almost unspeakably intense, is bitter in the extreme. One suspects that in the Noh passion is so high-pitched that annihilation affords the only solution to its dilemmas. The mysticism of the Noh plays is not the fully accomplished mysticism of the Sanskrit scriptures on which its thought is ultimately based. The dark night of the soul dominates the thinking of most of the great Noh. In comparison the Sanskrit drama appears vastly optimistic and even *King Lear* is, as

Yeats described it, gay. The world at large is reluctant to embrace a drama so desperately austere, its consummate art and profound insights notwithstanding. It is possible that the English are happier with their Chaucer than the Japanese with Chaucer's illustrious contemporary who was a still greater artist, Zeami Motokiyo.

2 / *The Dramatic Principle in Noh Plays*

ON ANALYZING the form of the Noh plays we are almost immediately confronted with a distinction between the lyrical and dramatic. The Noh is by and large probably the most lyrical of all types of drama. This does not mean that it is musical—though such is certainly the case—but that it comports with the basic conception of lyrical form, which signifies the greatest concentration of expression possible in a presentational art that is also evocative of emotion. An art both warm and concentrated is likely to share some of the properties of music and hence of accentuated rhythm, which in turn lends it further affinity to the dance. Although it may possibly expand beyond the expression of a single feeling, it will still be sharply contracted upon itself. It renounces digression, narrative, argumentation, and all excursiveness. Lyrics are the pinnacles of the edifice of poetry, the spires that rise with their chimes into the sky. Lyric form already stands at its place of destination. As with the travelogue of the typical monk in a Noh play, the journey is presented as completed ; the momentous point has been reached. Whatever development ensues is conspicuously within the framework of the piece. The lyric has its analogue in sculpture or in the still picture, whereas drama has its analogue in the motion picture or the dance that unfolds a story. Time in the lyric is not so much absent as arrested. A lyric may be retrospective or prophetical, may look backward or forward, but may not actually traverse these territories stretching about it on all sides. Lyric poetry is obviously analogous to song, drama to the more extended forms of music, as the sonata, the symphony, the oratorio, and, most obviously of all, the opera. All lyric poetry is, as it were, in process of becoming song, all poetic drama, in the process of becoming theatrical music.

Drama presents further distinctions. Its development in general implies both suspense and, the virtually inevitable accompaniment of suspense, surprise and climax. The lyric, to be sure, has beginning, middle and end but not a climax, as drama does. Also, drama in general implies conflict, a meeting of opposites, at least a duality of focus, a protagonist and an antagonist. The lyrical form tends to be private, personal, introverted, the dramatic, to be plural, public, extroverted.

Although it would be folly to overlook their important distinctions, it would be almost as grave a mistake to extend them to doctrinaire positions. All form in art observes certain general principles ; a lyric, say a poem by John Donne, may often be described as a drama in miniature, or a particular type of drama, say a masque by John Milton, as a lyric in magnification. All these distinctions serve less to delimit than to describe and none is of absolute applicability. The generalization itself approaches an abstraction. It is here that the Noh stands forth conspicuously, for in no instance is it absolutely lyrical nor dramatic and even to a surprising degree it moves freely between the two poles of reference. Some Noh are remarkably dramatic, others, remarkably lyrical. By and large, taking world-drama as field for comparison, the Noh, however, appears astonishingly lyrical. As already urged, it is probably the most lyrical species of drama known, not in the sense that it is sung or attended by music throughout but in the more analytical sense thus far defined. All Noh plays are spectacular and theatrical and all to some measure unequivocally lyrical, yet many deviate in surprising degree from the condition here described as dramatic.

Some distinctions must be allowed between the actual affect in the theatre and the verbal text. It is conceivable that a Noh play essentially undramatic in its text should be dramatic in performance by virtue of the dancing or miming. Occasionally where a Noh play is divided into two Parts, the verbal text for Part Two shrinks nearly into insignificance while dance and spectacle rise to an impressive climax. It is of the play as drama, or dramatic literature, that the present study here, as always, deals.

Much of the spirit of the Noh springs, then, from its musical and choreographic origins. Its roots were not in another type of drama but in other forms altogether, as the festival song, dance and ritual. Moreover, the tap-root is not only religious but Buddhistic and Buddhistic ritual in Japan is considerably less dramatic than, say, the Catholic mass. We deal here with a religion of quietism, contemplation, mysticism, whose goal is Nirvana, a religion aspiring to abstraction. The rituals from which the Noh gathered so much of its inspiration were as a rule stately and slow-paced, impressive as spectacle, not as being dramatic. The dances seem for the most part not to have been narrative or dramatic dances but, as far as they possessed subject-matter or content, were lyrical dances expressing a well established mood. To Western ears the music for the Noh also does not seem especially dramatic, does not, in other words, suggest program music. The music does not characterize the persons as the music in operas by Mozart or Wagner does. To most ears in itself somewhat monotonous, it serves the valuable function of pacing the production, perfectly accompanying the gestures of the actors and movements of the dancers. It also, of course, paces the very considerable passages of miming. This miming is presumably both theatrical and dramatic but the music attending it is fundamentally neither. As a medium of expression in itself it fails to produce any dramatic affect whatsoever. At most it serves a dramatic end; it does not itself achieve such an end or provide a positive contribution to the affect.

In Western understanding of the terms, at least according to classical doctrine, a play has a plot and presents an action. Especially in the domain of comedy, it has an intrigue. Little or nothing of this nature is to be found in the Noh. There is no narrative line. At most there are two panels: in Part One a person is presented in his humble manifestation, a peasant, a ghost, a spirit essentially in disguise. In Part Two the same person is presented in a higher manifestation, as a hero, a god, or an historic figure of high significance. The mask is shifted. But the process of shifting the mask is itself a transformation, not a development. The eye passes from the panel on the left to that on the right. In this shift there is no sharp climax. The second entrance of the Shite is from one point of view dramatic yet it would probably be better said that it is highly spectacular. What motion there is here does not violate the statuesque affect, the essentially static presentation.

And yet, as already indicated, striking differences exist in these terms within the Noh plays themselves. Some are far more lyrical than others, some far more dramatic. Despite all the remarkable integrity of the Noh form, very great distinctions occur in this regard. In general, for example, plays in two Parts are more dramatic than those in one. Some plays are almost entirely lyrical. We shall presently review a dozen works ranging from the most essentially lyrical to those which seem more lyrical than dramatic and yet present the lyrical elements in reduced strength. Following this we shall review a similar series of works proceeding from those most emphatically dramatic to those still more dramatic than lyrical yet in which the former element is well short of its highest potential force and the latter correspondingly more conspicuous.

That all the plays possess something of the severe focus of an ideal lyrical art is clear. For this austerity of form the almost unique dedication of the Japanese spirit to aesthetic manifestations of life must chiefly account. As far as the dramatic element represents a spirit of conflict, the Noh plays have at their philosophical base an even alarming instance of spiritual contention, one that always remains such and is never, perhaps, fully resolved in the plays into a solution bringing contention to rest and therefore in substance to its termination. The strong infusion of the dramatic element in the Noh ultimately derives from a condition for which a philosophy of society must account.

It is important in an understanding of the peculiar flowering of the dramatic spirit within the Noh to consider some of the peculiar qualities of Japanese thought. If one can speak of a schizophrenic culture, Japan would be a fit candidate for such a discussion. Indian philosophy, like the system of Kierkegaard, is established on a conception of opposites but of opposites successfully reconciled and held serenely in poise. The flesh and spirit are defined and distinguished but are not ultimately at war. The continental Asian mind as a whole achieves in its psychology a remarkable equilibrium. Not so the insular Japanese, a people that conspicuously would eat its cake and have it too. The chief theme running through the Noh plays is the opposition between the worldly and the otherworldly existence ; on the one hand are the feudal virtues and the sophisticated sensuality of a courtly life, on the other, a devout belief in Buddhistic mysticism. A nervous incertitude underlies the scene. This conflict does not describe all dramatic conflicts within the Noh plays but is the chief underlying factor in their manifestation of the dramatic. The tempestuous stories of the plays reflect these unresolved conflicts within the soul. Japanese manners were clearly more indigenous than Japanese thought. The former were largely insular and provincial, the latter, largely borrowed and acquired from the continent. Life did not sit easily on the shoulders of a people whose ideals themselves reflected a divided loyalty. One result was the development of intense repressions. Emotions were held in check. But it is within the law of nature that emotions cannot be repressed indefinitely. The conflicts behind these repressions were sure to break forth in moments of violent climax. These climaxes provided the ultimate source for the dramatic scenes in which the Japanese stage so conspicuously excels. The Sanskrit theatre is the theatre of poise, built upon a religious foundation. The Chinese theatre is the theatre of entertainment and serene delight. The Noh stage is the theatre of spiritual conflict, of psychical unrest. Although it may not be the most gratifying theatre of the East, it is in the present sense of the word the most luridly dramatic. In it the dramatic principle is frequently pursued to such a degree that it may, in the minds of some persons, be carried to excess. Emotional values are at times painfully forced on the Japanese stage, as they are never forced on the stages of China and India. (One can almost imagine that Ophelia wrote half the plays). Nevertheless, the great art of the Japanese goes far to tame the violence of their content. Zeami's own precept that the actor even in his most violent scenes shall move with poise, as though he carried flowers in his hair, is, surely, one of the most elegant maxims ever educed for the perfection of an art style.

On the one hand, then, certain factors in Japanese thought encouraged a full realization of the dramatic idea within the theatre, and on the other hand, other factors resisted its rise. The form enjoyed much of its initial impulse from temple ceremonies that were presumably for the most part decorous and serene. There is a monastic flavor within the Noh ; quite literally, the monastic element provides a framework. In a large proportion of the plays travelling monks play a part. Sometimes the monk or monks take the stage at the play's opening and have throughout a secondary, choral value. They introduce the work and assist it on its way. Sometimes, too, they take a more important part. A monk becomes the Waki, a figure of secondary importance only to the leading character, the Shite. The monk strongly supports the action. Frequently his prayers result in the salvation of the hero's soul, which is the spiritual goal of the entire performance. The chorus, always appearing in Noh plays, has a priestly aspect ; its chant tends to have a religious tone. Ritual may, of course, be itself highly dramatic and certainly is almost by definition spectacular but it is not the ideal container for the more restless dramatic principle as described in this study. Especially a religion of quietism, as Buddhism, favors rituals of a less than explicitly dramatic character.

Ritualism and lyricism are far from the only factors in the Noh retarding the development of a purely dramatic style. By virtue of its religious origins, the Noh in addition to being ritualistic and musical is also theological, allegorical and, to some degree, didactic. As long as the ideals in a play remain primarily in the realm of pure ideas, divorced from the personal, the play's spirit will be more philosophical or theological than dramatic. A contention of pure ideas is not the contention of pure drama. Ideas, of course, often impel and inspire drama but cannot in themselves constitute it. As will presently be shown, the Noh plays offer extremely clear instances of this distinction. Certain of them are as close to sermons as others are to lyrics or to true dramatic actions. These theological works may be extremely beautiful as treatises on the value of life, as poems or even as theatrical recitations or spectacles ; nevertheless, they lack the tang of drama as we generally understand it. However successful they may be, they fail to realize that unique and peculiar flowering of the stage which we consider the dramatic.

Allied in some degree to this lofty category of theological stage-treatise is the highly Asiatic form of the fable. Especially the religious element of the Noh favored the rise of a group of plays that may be described as fables or parables. They simply project into the theatre a type of non-dramatic writing of a narrative sort already highly perfected elsewhere. The result may be a quite successful vehicle for the stage but a work, like a court masque, more theatrical than dramatic. Such plays are likely to be low-pitched emotionally. *Kantan* is by far the most celebrated instance of such work in the Noh.

A perceptible tendency towards allegory in the more overtly religious plays withholds such works from the fullest realization of the dramatic. An allegory is, broadly speaking, a work inhabiting a mid-region between abstraction and concretion, the speculative and the aesthetic. Its figures are outwardly human but the full breath of life has not been breathed into them. They are not intended to convince us of their reality. Their purpose is to confer warmth and beauty upon ideas. Although the figures may contend in many a fierce battle, or psychomachia, fighting with sword and bow, their contentions lack the true vigor of conflict in the more fully achieved drama, not to mention mythological and epic poetry. Allegory has invaded the stage but never happily dominated it or become completely at home there. In the history of Sanskrit drama, for example, it represents the last and decadent period. As warmth receded from an over-conscious stage, the figures were chilled into abstractions of philosophical allegory. There are, as we shall see, at least traces of this condition in certain Noh works. Although the playwrights at times win superb success in giving a full-blooded life to ideas, at times doctrine shoves drama aside. The artifice may still be great but the spark of dramatic conflict is missing.

Finally, the brevity of the Noh plays and the limited scope allowed their authors inside their rigid frame encouraged works that seem to modern eyes rather scenes from plays than plays themselves, chapters, as it were, out of popular narratives. They were themselves originally presented in sequences but are not so read today. So much satisfaction, also, was to be had on so many sides from highly skilled acting, from music, dance, spectacle and indoctrination, that the additional stimulus of dramatic tension or climax was unnecessary. Many plays mount on a superb crescendo. Others proceed relatively quietly and impress us as episodic. Even the Japanese are not always infatuated with montage or climax. Possibly a strong head of steam cannot conveniently be secured within so brief a period. But enough art and content is achieved without this ultimate contribution of dramatic art. Were it not that almost everything related to the Noh seems strange and astonishing, we might be surprised that playwrights capable of such intense dramatic affects could well afford on occasion to dispense with them. To the contrasts that are the essence of all intense drama they add the contrast that in their own work they can also be non-dramatic and still successful artists for the stage.

A grave difficulty confronts the presentation of conflict in the Noh in that as a rule the protagonist has no visible anta-gonist. By at least common practice, in the Noh, Macbeth cannot physically confront Macduff; Othello, Iago; Hamlet, his uncle; Brutus, Caesar. Structurally, the plays are as close to a dramatic monologue by Browning as to a play by Shakespeare. Yet in the case of some of the most dramatic Noh the ingenuity of the dramatist was capable of creating exceptions to the rule. Thus at the very end of *Atsumori*, the hero, or Shite, discovers in his interlocutor, the Waki, his former antagonist. It is distinctly to the point that in this instance the antagonist is no longer such. On the con-trary, the play ceases when the impulse to struggle ceases and, ironically, when the antagonist is first recognized. To describe this conflict as between two individuals would only be misleading. It is between two ideals, feudalism and Bud-dhism, but in this instance the ideas have been fully realized in personal terms, so that true drama and not allegory results. The play brilliantly exemplifies drama as conflict. It is at once a philosophical work and a dramatic poem.

Sometimes the Noh play, as already urged, resembles not so much a lyric as a didactic poem, as becomes notably the case with the so-called "Congratulatory Pieces." This is true of the celebrated fable in Noh form, *Takasago*. Dramatic in one sense of the word is, of course, the transformation of old laborers into poetic sages and trees into men or gods. This splendid pageant-drama progresses and unfolds its fabric with an art of which Aristotle might have approved though he would hardly have regarded it as dramatic. There is emphatically progress ; there is motion ; there is climax ; but not conflict. As result, the play becomes a masque or pageant, a moving ritual, a court ceremony. Dramatic in the strictest sense it is not. It illustrates, however, the semi-dramatic principle of contrast so commonly found in many Noh plays divided into two Parts, where humble characters in the First Part turn out to have been exalted characters in disguise. But in the purest drama contrast is raised into conflict. The opposites must meet in an opposition that is positive. Contrast is negative opposition, producing art in space ; conflict is positive opposition, producing art in time. The latter belongs more particularly to the stage.

Of plays predominantly lyrical *Hagoromo* is the happiest example. The brief tension between the fisherman and the Spirit of the Air hardly constitutes the chief feature of the play. The work is a dance, a song, a spectacle and a poem— all before it is a drama in the strictest sense. Its spirit is the peace and brightness of the spring landscape and the lightness and grace of the spring breeze. Its background is a cloudless sky. The rude fisherman is barely a foil to the central figure. Nor can it well be argued that there is a contention between earth and heaven. It is true that Hagoromo is temporarily bound to earth and therefore unhappy and that her mood changes abruptly on the recovery of her winged robe. The weight of water and earth symbolized by the fisherman scarcely signifies beside the lightness of air and sunlight radiated by Hagoromo. Especially is this clear in the play's later section, where drama, if it has ever existed, dissolves into pure poetry. This is lyric theatre in the strictest sense.

Hagoromo is really a play about a bird-spirit in the form of a girl, a phoenix disguised as a maiden. *Basho* is a hardly less moving play about a tree disguised as a woman. The point of the latter work is made abundantly clear : it is simply the doctrine of the *Lotus Sutra* that all things possess a soul ; that the universe is animistic ; that man is in this regard in no way unique. Even the thought itself seems lyrical : it is the thought of the great canticle, *Benedicite omnia opera*. The only conflict here is between the night of ignorance that denies this vision and the rays which dispel the darkness. The play exists largely to disclose a dancer whose limbs and garments suggest the limbs and foliage of a tree. The work is supremely theatrical, exquisitely choreographic, but in only the most secondary sense dramatic.

Yoroboshi offers a good example of a lyrical drama in one Part and virtually in a single mood. Its germ, as customary in such pieces, is an idea given a material manifestation. A blind child sees with the eye of the mind, religiously inspired, more than the average man sees with normal vision unaided by spiritual enlightenment. At the play's end the child, who is temporarily lost, stumbles into the arms of his father. The play explores the depth of its idealistic theme to the full. The boy reveals his piety in eloquent poetry depicting the landscape beside the islanded Japanese sea. The reunion with his father is little more than an appropriate happy framework to an idealized stage-portrait, a graceful means of dismissing the hero from the stage. The pathetic mood is exquisitely set in the imagery of the first few speeches, comparing the father's alms with the blossoms falling from Kwannon's sacred trees. As the play moves forward, we merely advance further into the sensations and feelings of the tragically blinded child. The whole is a lyric in dramatic guize. A powerful imagination and high sensitivity place the tone closer to the true lyric than to the "dramatic monologue" as realized, for example, by Browning, whose mind tended more to an intellectual and analytical approach to experience than to lyrical intensity.

Tamura provides another singularly clear instance of lyrical drama as well as of the religious roots nourishing the genre of the Noh. There is no plot. A young boy piously sweeping fallen blossoms from a temple floor is finally revealed as the deity of the temple. The play is a hymn in praise of the temple, the cult, and the myth on which the cult is founded. That in its last moments an address by the chorus accompanying a dance by the god introduces a louder and more emphatic tone than any heard previously in the play merely brings the whole to an impressive conclusion. Although this lyric drama enjoys a moving finale, there is no dramatic climax in the customary meaning of the term. It would be difficult to discover a play simpler in its basic form or more completely of a piece.

The two plays, *Sanemori* and *Tomoe*, having much in common, carry on in a quite different emotional temper the type of lyrical integrity represented by *Tamura*. Each is at the same time lyrical in spirit and emotional evocation and strictly focused on delineation of a single heroic figure. The hero of *Sanemori* is an aged warrior unwilling to surrender to the indignity of years, eagerly maintaining the full animation of his youth. On entering a battle which he rightly presumes his last, he dyes his hair black and wears a gorgeous costume virtually amounting to a disguise. He wages war against his own infirmities. The theme has universal significance ; its expression is narrowed and sharpened to the point of a needle.

Tomoe similarly depicts an episode in human nature where the spirit's valor rises above material and physical infirmity. The courageous soul of a dead warrior passes into the breast of his wife who survives him in battle and successfully disperses their foes. In the end she puts aside her own armour but at the same time assumes her husband's robes and makes no formal renunciation of the role of warrior. This role is for the time being no longer demanded of her in action since her husband's death has been immediately followed by the utter rout of their enemies. Tomoe is a Japanese Britomart. The entire play is in substance a secular hymn, a paeon, an heroic song in her praise. From Western standards this is not properly a play—not even a typical one-act play. Rather, it is an episode given the splendor of an essentially lyric poem.

Toboku and *Tadanori* are lyrical plays in praise of lyrical artists, one likewise having for its central figure a woman, the other, a man. Their form may better be said to unfold than to develop. The lyrical simplicity of such a work may be symbolized by the stem of a flower. The blossom unfolds its petals. It moves from within but not from without. In other words, though the motion reveals not only life but powerful vitality, the stationary nature of the phenomenon shows that we are confronted with a form that is lyrical, not narratory or in the more technical sense of the word dramatic. In each instance a paradox, a dichotomy, even a certain conflict is present, yet the conflict never remotely resembles the conventional dramatic plot. In each case irony lies in the ambiguous position of poetry and art in the Japanese, or Buddhistic, philosophy of life. Poetry is conceived as at once a vanity of the material world of illusion and a gateway to the immaterial world of the spiritual and the divine. The last infirmity of the noble mind is not, as Milton presumed, fame, but art. Like sex, poetry may lead the way to spiritual understanding and in some degree woo the heart away from material things. Art is both within the material world and a force in the transcendence of this world. In *Toboku* a woman who was both courtesan and poet becomes, years after her death, virtually a saint, revered and worshipped by her enlightened followers. Deeply as in her lifetime she loved things of this world, such as the cherry-tree that constitutes the focus of the play's symbolism, she passed from the mundane to the ultra-mundane, from darkness to enlightenment, from the vulgarity of this world to the Buddhahood of the Western Paradise.

Though less ideal and metaphysical in its thinking than *Toboku*, *Tadanori* presumes the same idealism. Its hero is a man who feels distress because fame for his poetic gift has been denied him. His chief poem is indeed famous, since it graces the pages of the most profoundly esteemed of anthologies, a collection bearing imperial endorsement, but there the poem is given as anonymous. The glamor of personal fame may at first sight seem the focus of the play but beyond this lesser fame shines the glory of poetry itself. Personal fame is acknowledged to be a vanity, deeply human and emotionally compelling as it may be. Implied is the contrast between the personal and the impersonal, or, more accurately, between the egotistical claim of the individual or the personal in art and a transcendent impersonality or the condition of the humanly universal. A touching episode is unfolded : a monk promises to exert his utmost to secure the correction in the anthology ; more important, his prayers finally enable the poet to purge his soul of vanity and to attain, again through strength of his art, the condition of salvation. It becomes almost accidental that, as in *Tamura*, towards the play's conclusion a warrior's dance heightens the scene's animation. This is the shrewd and invariably observed convention of Noh dramatic technique, in keeping with an almost universal practice demanding an added force and increased tempo for the conclusion. From first to last the play focuses on its dominant thought. Tadanori's brief poem runs through it as a refrain. The play is itself a song in praise of a song. To Western thinking it appears less a contraction of a play than an expansion of a lyric.

The lovely play, *Tsunemasa*, differs but little from the preceding except that emphasis falls more upon music than upon poetry. This unusually brief work depicts the dedication to Buddha of a lute named "Green Hill," the pride of a warrior who has recently died. His ghost returns to expatiate on the irresistible affection which as a man he felt for his music and to confess at once the vanity of this love and its healing grace, in some occult way acceptable to Buddha, the proponent of Nirvana. A more compact work for the stage breathing the soul of music more forcefully would be unthinkable. *Tsunemasa* is a lyrical tribute to the essence of the lyric.

Eguchi is a lyric drama combining the idealized aestheticism of the foregoing plays with a mystical and romantic conception of passion. It praises courtesans who are themselves mistresses of music, poetry, and dance, indeed of all the arts, as well as of erotic love. The play is essentially a vision, an apparition, a revelation of a religion as mystical as that of Saint Paul though wholly different in orientation. It is the quintessence of lyricism.

Matsukaze represents another equally valid aspect of the lyric drama, a perfection in the expression of a single mood. The theme is love's coldness, marvellously evoked in a poetry dedicated to the landscape of early spring, with frost and lingering snow upon the ground. This is beyond question a masterpiece.

Finally, *Ikuta* exhibits the lyric drama through the most complete simplicity of its action. A son, grieving for his lost father, is granted an interview with his father's ghost. This is all. It proves enough for a moving play, but a play using only a small fraction of the multifarious elements entering into such a work as *Hamlet*. It represents the Noh in its simplest and doubtless in its earliest form.

With the notable exception of that exquisite lyrical play, *Hagoromo*, the explicitly dramatic pieces in the Noh are on the whole more famous than the lyrical. It is among these that the largest number has been adapted by the *kabuki* and other more recently developed forms in the Japanese theatre. To Western eyes the more dramatic pieces far more closely resemble plays as known to the West. As already stated, these Noh plays never wholly desert the lyrical tendency and never wholly conform with Western conceptions of the dramatic. Yet they undoubtedly show an advance in theatrical evolution.

The works that are the most explicitly plays of action share this advance most strongly, even though these commonly have a more specious and less philosophical character than the more lyrical or conservative pieces. The arch-hero of this most conspicuously dramatic type is Benkei, the ideal warrior, supreme strategist, and valiant servant of his lord. He, it will be recalled, is hero of *Ataka*, the dramatization of the famous episode of the twelve warriors disguised as travelling monks, forcing their way through a barrier. The play presents a most dramatic contention, that between the followers of the Hogan, led by Benkei, and those of their opponents guarding the barrier. The scene is singularly rich in theatrical action and affects, as the beating of the Hogan disguised as a baggage-carrier, the dance simulating intoxication, the threatened clash of arms, the disguises, and the reading of the imaginary proclamation. Religion, which in the plays thus far considered is treated with great sincerity, is here the occasion of ironic jesting. Abruptly we discover ourselves almost wholly removed from the world of Buddhism and plunged precipitantly into that of feudalism. The basic theme is military strategy. We have emerged from the world of spiritual contemplation into the material world of physical action. The latter proves less poetic than the former but even more theatrical. We have virtually a new type of dramatic art.

It is instructive, parenthetically, to contrast the supremely dramatic *Ataka* with another piece still secular but much less developed along the lines of dramatic action. *Settai*, a companion piece, presents a similiar group of characters under very different circumstances and with a completely different affect. It is also a supreme instance of the art and spirit of the Japanese theatre. Its power lies in presentation of the most intense emotions stoically or even abnormally repressed. The same disguises are used. But here the accompanying group of characters is friendly instead of hostile. In place of the threat of death the travellers face only the (doubtful) danger of recognition. No blood-thirsty commander but an aged woman and her orphaned child stand before them. They are recognized, or rather, confess their identity but there is no fundamental opposition. A touching episode at the end gives only a fillip to the action. The heroic child who wishes to join the troup in which his father served and died has to be put off with tender evasions. This action is clearly episodic to the play, though it finishes it off very artfully. *Settai* is, in fact, itself an episode highly theatrical but not in the strict sense of the word dramatic, since the element of conflict is muted. A quiet, singularly beautiful scene and to a perceptive mind perhaps no less rewarding than the sensational and melodramatic *Ataka*, it is according to our definition incomparably less dramatic—as it is also less famous. In further contrast with *Settai* and in much closer agreement with *Ataka* is *Funa-Benkei*, a melodramatic work in which the enemies of the Hogan who have long been dead arise in the waves of a severe storm at sea to threaten a vessel containing the Hogan, Benkei, and the faithful retainers.

Already in process of defining the concept of dramatic conflict the play, *Atsumori*, has been analyzed. It is a fine instance of a Noh play attaining an ample share of the dramatic temper. Similarly, as a play of action, narrative and conflict, *Hashi-No-Ki* deserves study. Here the familiar division into two Parts is carried out in a more drastic manner than usual. In Part One an old couple, once prosperous and now reduced to poverty, grants hospitality to a man beset by a harsh snowstorm who appears in the guise of a travelling monk. In Part Two the traveller is revealed as the Prince. He summons the old man to court to confer high honors upon him. Time, action, and sentiment are treated with a freedom comparatively rare in the Noh though distinctly in keeping with practices of the Western stage.

Western critics and readers of the Noh have taken special pleasure in *Aoi-No-Ue*, the lurid drama of the supernatural dealing with one woman's jealousy of another and with the tragic incidents resulting. There is a protagonist, whom the audience never sees, though presented by a symbolical garment, and an antagonist, a ghost whose malignant curse has by some strategy to be allayed. The play abounds in action, in oppositions, in violent shifts of mood. It immediately strikes us as dramatic, no matter how lyrical are certain episodes, especially those of magic incantation.

The noble little play, *Kagekiyo*, affords a good instance of strikingly orthodox dramatic procedure according to the terms of our definition. Representing, as it does, a reconciliation between a blind and exiled warrior-father and his devoted daughter, it immediately reminds a Western reader of Sophocles' *Oedipus at Colonus*. The embittered old blind warrior also suggests the hero of Milton's *Samson Agonistes*, itself in large part modelled on Sophocles' work. In the Japanese play are two strong sources of dramatic conflict, the hero's struggle with his daughter and his contention with his decrepit age, the struggle in each instance springing from his heroic pride. At first the father rejects his daughter, who fails at the time to recognize him. Later he accepts both his debt of affection to her and, in some extent, his debt to nature and to destiny. The play has a most dramatic movement. It is clearly more dramatic than lyrical and one of the most powerful works in the literature of the Noh.

Equally powerful and still more famous, *Shunkan* shows the dramatic element so far as the Noh is concerned at its height. This brief, vivid work presents more than mere contrast: it develops both inner and outer conflicts. Within is the disparity in Shunkan's own heart. With admirable contrivance, a passage early in the play discloses him as the most self-controlled, philosophically-minded and idealistic of the three exiles on their lonely island. As the action mounts to its climax, however, he completely breaks down, falling into the most abject despair. His companions are released while he is forced to remain. The theme is expressed much later in a play by that gloomy Elizabethan, John Marston, where a stoical hero who has preached control breaks down and confesses in tears : "Man must break out despite philosophy." The conflict outwardly expressed appears in Shunkan's despairing efforts to push through the waves and board the departing boat by force. *Shunkan* is the very epitome of the dramatic, condensed to highest pressure. It is almost a miracle that within such narrow confines so great force can be engendered.

A fair number of Noh plays similarly develop in terms of dramatic action. *Yuya* provides a case in point, even though a brief poem, that may be described as its lyric capsule, forms its core. A courtesan wishes to visit her mother, ill and dying in a far-away province. Her prince, on the contrary, wishes her company on a spring festival, where she is to entertain him with dance and love. After viewing the spring blossoms, she shows him a poem that by implication associates the dying parent with the falling flowers. At last the prince's heart is touched, so that he gives the girl leave to go. This play, then, presents an action. Moreover, there is an appropriate shift of scene. While in his palace, the prince is obdurate. When at the mountain shrine surrounded by the sacred trees, he yields to his kindlier nature.

Other plays dealing with women have markedly a dramatic spirit. *Yamamba* contrasts a devotee with the divinity that she worships, who appears at first in disguise. The woman on her pilgrimage performs a sacred dance with some passable competence but when she sees the deity herself execute the dance she confesses how little she has herself grasped of the inner meaning of her own creed. Here the progression to enlightenment is by degrees sharply defined and essentially dramatic.

The conception of montage is in itself dramatic. This may be seen in the remarkable play, *Miidera*. A mother searches for her lost son. At length she discovers him in a temple. The reunion is effected only after a revelation. Her grief has driven her mad. Yet a moment of extreme excitement and ecstacy effects her cure. This occurs as, in her mad joy at the autumn moon and its dominance over the landscape, she rings the temple bell. The act cures her of her insanity and shortly occasions the reunion with her child. One immediately recognizes here the presence of heightened drama.

Surely one of the finest of all instances of montage in poetic drama occurs in *Sumidagawa*, another play on a mad woman in quest of her son. This work is in its imagery both subjective and objective. Had it remained wholly subjective, it would only questionably have been dramatic. But the child is not merely dreamed of by his mother. In succession she hears his voice, sees his form, and, briefly, at last converses with his ghost. The mounting succession of events exceeds the lyrical and becomes indisputably dramatic.

The celebrated play, *Sotoba-Komachi*, affords a final instance of a subjective or metaphysical drama transcending its lyrical quality and becoming dramatic. Had Komachi merely dreamed of her lover, we would have a lyrical soliloquy. But she puts on his clothes, wears his mask, and imagines that she is he. Her performance in this regard is considerably more drastic than that of Matsukaze in the play bearing her name or than that of the maiden in *Izutsu*. With such sensational action played out before our eyes, there remains no question as to the play's basic quality. The gold of essential drama is found here in a high degree of purity. From an aesthetic point of view we are far indeed from the lyrical perfection of *Hagoromo*.

The conditions of the Noh drama which have just been described have their moral. This drama was created at a time when dramatic art was in formation. In our own times this art is in a state of reforming itself. Our own condition brings us close to the Noh and makes the Noh a singularly stimulating field for thoughtful consideration. Once again drama is in a state of becoming. It can only be hoped that drama today will find a solution to its problems as felicitous as Zeami found for his own age and culture.

3 / *The Lyric Capsule*

ONE OF the chief organizing features of the typical Noh play may be called the lyric capsule. This is a quoted poem or section of a poem, always brief, but always of much dynamic force for the play in which it is found. This technical procedure becomes one of the outstanding mannerisms of the playwrights. To be sure, there are various degrees in its use, since no aesthetic device can ever be employed mechanically or with complete uniformity. In many instances the passage clearly amounts to the core or kernel of the play, the seed from which it develops or the goal to which it moves. In other cases the capsule's value is less phenomenal. Although still of much importance, it colors only a part of the play, not the whole. Sometimes the capsule states the play's theme with an almost logical precision. Its primary value is inescapable. On other occasions it shares in the indirection and intimation constituting so distinguishing a feature of all the more intense forms of Japanese poetry and of the more lyrical phases of its style. The chemistry of the capsule itself may, in short, be relatively simple or highly complex. Whatever phase manifests itself, this is always one of the most brilliant and distinguishing features of the best Noh playwriting. No other dramatic fruit has quite this kernel. It becomes one of the outstanding insignia of a Noh.

Were the Noh sermons, which, in fact, they occasionally are, the capsule may be regarded as the text. This analogy is even closer than may at first appear, for something of the deep regard for authority inducing Christian preachers to base their utterances on a verse or two from the Bible induces

193

the Noh dramatist to base his poem not on some statement of his own but on a statement borrowed from older and more venerable writings, carrying in themselves an enlarged authority, some of which happily descends upon his own work. Although the capsules are from the classics and occasionally carry a rational force, rationality proves one of their least common features. Unlike the text of the orthodox preacher the quotation is as a rule favored not because of its philosophical, theological or moral value but because of its poetic value. Such a text belongs more explicitly to the gospel of beauty than to that of truth.

The entire procedure lends additional strength to the Noh's solemn and liturgical quality, epitomizing the depths to which the Noh is grounded and established on tradition. The poet refrains from composing a theme of his own ; he prefers to borrow a poem from an old master and develop it afresh, discovering wider, newer meanings in a theme long valued and long familiar. Of course the technique further encourages the pleasure of recognition, the distinction of a cultish poetry, favorable to a learned few. Yet it is easy to fall into a misunderstanding of this convention. The learned in the Noh audience may take special delight in recognizing a quotation. They may even at times enjoy the still more delectable pleasure of filling in phrases omitted in the actual text of the play. This device, incidentally, is employed by Dante, who at times quotes the first lines of a canticle, assuming that the enlighted reader will supply what he leaves unsaid. Nevertheless, it is more to the point that in almost all cases the little capsules are in themselves strong and clear. Their meaning remains usually unmistakable. It is of secondary importance that they are learned quotations but of primary importance that in themselves they are powerful and memorable poetic utterances. Like so much else in the Noh, they have a pronounced lyrical value with an inescapable analogy to music. In short, they provide the dramatist's leading themes. If his play were a piece in Western music, it might be variations on a theme by Handel, Bach, Vivaldi, or Monteverdi. To change the metaphor completely, each is the central jewel in the crown worn by each play. This is one of the ultimate devices for making much of little, for turning frugality into opulence, with a succinctness of pointed statement that is no less a characteristic feature of Japanese craftsmanship than the overtone, half-tone and intimation.

Although the prevalence of the device must be sufficiently obvious to anyone in the least acquainted with the Noh, some demonstration of its inspired use is not only rewarding but in itself pleasurable. An anthology of these quotations should be revealing as an introduction to an analysis. Like the typical quotation itself, the process should be in its own way a legitimate short cut to truth. The passages are admirable in themselves and much more significant when considered in terms of their context. Taking, in accordance with our custom in these essays, as basis for discussion the thirty plays in the versions by the Japanese Society for Translation from the Classics, it will be found that twenty-six of them afford excellent examples of the convention. The round number itself has a natural though illogical attraction. In this survey four quotations are accordingly added from four plays found in versions by Arthur Waley. Let us examine these precious particles one by one, particles that may almost lead us to believe the medieval superstitions regarding the magic potency of gems. Lest the enumeration become clumsy and defeat its own purpose, some further division of the topic is useful. We shall examine first a dozen or so clear cases of capsules central to their plays and afterwards examples less perspicuous or powerful for the general meaning but still highly significant and in various ways unusual.

In *Takasago* we read this quotation from the *Ise Monogatari*:

Long years have sped
Since first I saw
The Pine of Semiyoshi by the sea.
How many years has *it* seen?

The essence of the play is here. The reference is to the Pine which is the play's central image, that is, a manifestation, first, of the old man in Part One, second, of the deity in Part Two, and which symbolizes, among much else, the Manyoshu anthology. The Pine is ancient but to all appearances indestructible; its foliage is always green ; no one knows its exact age but only that it remains ever venerable, yet sturdy and young. The familiar legend that the poem was composed by an emperor on a visit to the Semiyoshi shrine contributes also to the play's important political meaning, for it is a congratulatory paeon to the imperial power. As the pine-cone connotes the pine-tree, so this short poem both epitomizes and begets the play.

The Japanese playwright is economical though not parsimonious. In *Tamura* two quotations possess almost equal value, the first stressing the importance of the idea of beauty for that of divinity, the second, the saving, supernatural power of the compassionate divinity himself. The flowers and the gift of mercy rain equally from heaven, Kwannon being both patron of beauty and lord of all charity. The play unites these two conceptions so frequently combined in Japanese thought in general and in the Noh plays in particular. Witness Part One, especially with its thanksgiving for the spring : a pious youth sweeps up the fallen blossoms from the precincts of the temple. In Part Two we discover that the youth himself has been a manifestation of the Holy One. Beauty predominates as theme in the first half, theology in the second. The first quotation is from Su Tung-po :

The scent of flowers,
A hazy moon,
A single spring evening
Are worth a thousand pieces of gold.

The second poem proves to be less a statement than an exhortation. It is quoted from the *Shin Kokinshu.*

Have faith in me,
Ye, who are like moxa-weeds on Shinizi Moor,
While yet in this world I dwell.

The last line refers, of course, to Kwannon's deferment of entrance into Nirvana so that his lingering proximity to mortals may aid his service in the salvation of souls. More pertinent to the present analysis is the repetition in a new key of the motif of fallen blossoms. Men are, to be sure, weeds, not flowers; yet like flowers they fade. It must be clear to anyone studying the play that it resembles a twin foetus: with these two allied poems the play's total meaning becomes clarified.

The same duality—the exception and not the rule—appears also in *Kiyotsune*. This passionate domestic tragedy deals with a woman whose mad infatuation for her lord, who has committed suicide and left her a lock of hair as keepsake, subdues her heart to earthly vanity. The idea that such a keepsake proves to be less a gratification than a source of misery is repeated in many Noh plays and, together with the appropriate gestures on the stage, has strong tragic value. The first distillation of the thought is as follows:

Each time I look upon this lock
Grief tears at my heart;
I bid it hence return
Unto my sorrow's fountain-head.

The second is also from an anonymous poem, in this instance from the *Kokinshu*:

The keepsake brings new agony,
Recalls afresh to the bereaved
The loss she had else forgot.

These poignant expressions transfix the heart and establish the play's poetic force. A poem extremely similar to the last quoted stands at the heart of another important Noh drama, *Matsukaze*.

The exquisite play, *Izutsu*, is a tissue of quotations, its heroine being herself a poet who composed many famous verses to her beloved. The hero in this pair of lovers does not actually appear; even the heroine appears only as a ghost. But indirection merely enhances the final affect. The play's title, meaning "The Well-Curb," indicates the chief focus of the imagery while at the same time pointing unmistakably to the quoted poem holding the central position. From childhood the two have been familiar with a well-curb. In the last episode, the ghost on looking into the well imagines that she sees the image not of herself but of her lover, so firmly is her thought fixed upon him. At the time of their courtship the two exchanged poems dealing with their favorite meeting-place, the well. The boy's poem shyly indicates his climbing towards maturity. It is quoted from the *Ise Monogatari*.

> Standing against the well-curb,
> As children we compared our heights,
> But I have grown much taller
> Since last I saw you.

The poem sets the key to the singularly delicate artistry employed throughout, as well as to its chief symbol and chief stage property.

In a still more striking sense the key-poem in *Eguchi* constitutes the focus of the whole. A monk much taken by the charms of a courtesan felt injured and wronged by her rejection. Whereupon he composed these bitter lines, actually attributed to the monk, Saigyo :

> Hard may it be for you, a woman,
> To cast the world far from you,
> Yet even for one night
> You grudge me your temporary lodging.

The courtesan's reply, according to the Japanese custom of courtly verse, uses much the same imagery and explains that her refusal has been owing not to any want of love but to her veneration for the monk's sacred profession, which should dissuade him from fleshly indulgences. The action develops along the altercation between these two viewpoints, its conclusion resting in the assumed superiority of the woman's position, for the play bears her name and celebrates her ultimate grasp of Buddhistic teaching. The impetus setting it in motion comes from the monk's verses ; the clue to its resolution, from the woman's reply. Since her words are merely a variation played upon his, the man's poem must be regarded as the kernel of the work. Eguchi's highly contrived entrance occurs as she protests, at first with a voice heard from off-stage, that her true motive has been misinterpreted. She was not niggardly in exercising her profession as courtesan ; she was herself entering upon her road to Buddhahood as she turned her own verses against him. It is this truth which her ghost aspires to teach to posterity.

Sumidagawa, one of the most deeply pathetic of the Noh, depicts a mother in search of her lost son. In the end she finds only his grave and his ghost. The family lived in Miyako. The poet, Narihira, unseen hero of *Izutsu*, in his verses addressed birds as messengers to his beloved, calling them "Miyako birds." The mother imagines that she sees in the same birds possible messengers between herself and her son. In the play's final lines, that incomparable instance of montage in drama, the spectators of the scene imagine that they hear the cries of "Miyako birds" joining in the Buddhistic prayers. The last petition of the dying boy is that he be buried near the highway leading to Miyako, so that shadows of travellers to and fro from the city may pass over his grave. The quotation from Narihira follows :

O, birds of Miyako,
If you are worthy of your name,
Tell me, does my love still live.

A more poignant reference from past to present would be unthinkable. These outwardly simple lines provide one of several high-points in the course of the play.

A still better example of a short poem guiding the course of a longer and more complex one is supplied by *Tadanori*. Here the hero is a warrior-poet, who even beyond the grave laments that his most famous piece should through political causes have been included in an imperial anthology as anonymous. The poem and the poet's attitude toward it become the play's main subject. In itself the poem charms partly through its simplicity :

Belated
I lodge beneath a cherry-tree in bloom ;
The flowers are my host
Tonight.

It is almost a miracle that from these simplest words the dramatist has constructed a work of such marked maturity and sophistication.

Yuya offers an instance of another play strictly focused on a very short poem, which is :

Alas ! I know not what to do ;
Reluctant though I be to leave behind
Miyako's spring, the flowers of the Eastland
May have scattered far and wide.

Unlike the vast majority of key-poems in Noh plays, this seems to have been constructed especially for the occasion, not to be a classical piece borrowed for the occasion. Its theme, however, is wholly conventional. Here the peculiar value lies in an inference. The heroine, a courtesan, is depicted as the author, inspired by her visit to a temple dedicated to Kwannon, the merciful. Her own reluctance is due to the selfish desire of the prince, her master, who wishes her to be only at his side. Her passionate desire is to visit in the far-away Eastland her dying mother, whose life is ebbing away like falling blossoms. On hearing her poem, the prince himself is moved as he has not been previously to grant her request. The inference of the poem proves more powerful than her direct and urgent appeal. The entire play obviously hinges on its lines.

The opening verses of a popular song supply the key to the remarkable play, *Yamamba*. They are simply :

The Mountain-Hag,
For ever dragging Good and Evil,
Must roam from hill to hill.

According to the play's symbolism, the rugged mountains are in the phenomenal world the signs of the vain and ceaseless struggle between Good and Evil. The Hag is depicted, when considered from a superficial view only, as ugly and uncouth, rough and forbidding as the mountain wilderness which she inhabits. But her dance reveals a deeper meaning, before which the ugliness vanishes and the vista opens upon a serene reality. The Hag is at heart far from vicious. Behind her ferocity lies a kindliness. She leads men through rough mountain passes to a religious peace. She is indeed a benign deity, which is to say that she is incomparably more wonderful and profound than her own devotees realize. A vigorously drawn scenery and supercillious outlook upon good and evil characterize this piece, representing some of the most astonishing features of Eastern imagination.

The difficult but clearly inspired play, *Sotoba-Komachi*, has long been recognized as a masterpiece of the Noh, though its precise theological meaning, not to mention the statement of this meaning, has proved somewhat baffling to discover. Broadly speaking, the doctrine seems thoroughly compatible with *Yamamba :* the thought that rude struggle and privation, even extreme wickedness and crime, may become a gateway to mystical realization. This doctrine is anti-rational, anti-scholastic, and essentially anti-social. According to this conviction, values entirely disparate to the eye of material thinking are obliterated before a dazzling light of mystical revelation ; philosophers and wise men do not possess the true and final word. A decaying log may become to the inspired mind a temple of truth, an impotent hag, a vehicle for supreme enlightenment. Distinctions of this world dissipate before mystical understanding. An impoverished, miserable old woman, subject to the frenzied hallucination that she is the lover whom years before she cruelly rejected, abruptly enters Buddhahood. Such revelation becomes instantaneous and without apparent cause. Its mysterious abruptness is implied by the truncated form in which the poetic capsule itself is quoted from the *Kegon-kyo :*

If man upon a stupa looks but once,
From evil states shall he be ever free.
If one aspires to Buddhahood
For but a single moment . . . . .

Although the quotation is broken as the limb of a lightning-blasted tree, the conclusion is sufficiently clear, insofar as any mystery can be. The play's essence is condensed not only into a short poem but into a fractured poem.

Much simpler and closer to folklore than *Sotoba-Komachi*, with its esoteric Buddhism, is *The Dwarf Trees*. This happy and innocent legend tells of an impoverished couple, of aristocratic origin, who grant hospitality to a priest waylaid by a fierce snowstorm. Later the priest turns out to have been the prince himself, disguised to go upon a pilgrimage. In the end the couple is restored to prosperity and showered with favors. The play's singular force lies not in its speciously romantic plot but in its wonderfully vivid picture of a storm-bound traveller. The drama itself may well have grown out of a tiny folksong, as some of Lope de Vega's finest dramas were germinated from brief popular ballads. The song catches not the play's idea but what is aesthetically far more important, its atmosphere. The scenes of the song and the play are literally identified :

At Sano Ferry
No shelter found we
To rest our horses,
Shake our jackets
In the snowy twilight.

Occasionally the catalytic poem seems all the more effective where it does not literally fit the play's main situation but nevertheless strikes the more effectively with a glancing blow. Such is the case with *Kinuta*, or "The Cloth-Beating Block." A woman maddened by longing for her absent lord attempts to recall him by the sound of cloth-beating on blocks stationed upon the roof of her house during a still, clear autumn night. The key-reference here is to a Chinese story of a wife who succeeded in recalling her warrior-husband from thousands of miles away. The tragic difference in this instance is that the device fails and the woman dies of her mad grief, though petitionary prayers gain salvation for her spirit. The Chinese legend was known to the playwright through a prose tale, apparently no fit poem especially devoted to it being available. The poem actually used is less direct in application but highly effective in its contribution to the play.

The Palace water-clock

Sounds louder with the northern wind,
The cloth-beaters' strokes outside
Quicken and then slow down
When the moon is in the west.

The very license in the application enhances the poetic force. One listens to the dying strokes of the cloth-beaters as a sad moon sinks below the western horizon. The poem captures both the play's main image and its essential mood.

On rare but memorable occasions the rubric poem is given a more or less elaborate setting. This proves the case in one of the finest plays, *Miidera*. Here, as will be recalled, the familiar story is of a maddened mother grieving for her lost son. She recovers both her sanity and her child at the same moment. Visiting a temple on the night of the full autumn moon, the marvellous beauty of moon and moonlit landscape propels her out of herself. In her mystic joy she seizes and tolls the temple bell. It is her hour of triumph.

A dozen or more poems praising the magic of moonlight are incorporated into the play's dialogue, fitted with consummate skill. Finally, we reach the crucial poem, introduced with considerable detail and for the first time joining the image of the bell with that of the moonlight. The piece itself, by Hsie Kuan, is typically brief :

The moon has left the hilltop full and round,
And through the clouds her tranquil way has found.
Perfect is the silver orb tonight ;
No corner of the earth without her light.

The story is that the poet wrote the first half of this little work first and was long perplexed as to how he should achieve the whole. Finally, the scene itself filled him with a great drunkenness. In a moment of ecstacy he recorded his inspiration in its final words. So great was his joy that in celebration he tolled the temple bell. The mother, the mad, unhappy woman, follows the same course, immediately recovering both her child and her spiritual equilibrium. The poem contains the crux of the dramatic situation. The play arises from it and is, strictly speaking, merely a manifestation of it.

In a few instances a poem achieves central meaning or comes close to it while expressing the play's thought or mood only in metaphor. Such is the case in one of the most powerful and skilfully composed of the plays, *Shunkan*. Early in this work, before the crucial elements of its dramatic situation have emerged, the monk Shunkan at the close of an eloquent speech depicts not so much what he is as what he will become. Quoting an anonymous poem, he says :

> At autumn's end
> The cicada hugs a leafless tree
> And sings his song of death
> And never turns his head.

He, Shunkan, is to be the cicada ; the leafless tree, the island of his solitary exile ; his song of death, his final despairing speech of the play ; and the frozen gesture of the insect, the impotence of his grief. The mood of this famous tragedy is transfixed upon a point of lyric metaphor, possible, perhaps, only in a culture devoutly believing in an animistic conception of the universe.

Sometimes in a decidedly less searching way the capsule epitomizes the play's story. *Funa Benkei*, for example, chiefly depicts a storm at sea during which a boat carrying exiles is thrown into imminent peril. Through prayer and magic the storm is allayed, the exiles proceeding smoothly to their destination. Although the poem quoted, in this instance composed by Fujiwara-no-Kinto, is relatively literal and prosaic, it none the less fulfils a central function in a play far more melodramatic than profound—in spirit, in fact, closer to the usual Kabuki than to the Noh. These are the lines :

> The wind has dropped,
> The ferry-boat leaves the haven ;
> As the skies clear
> The land of exiles looms across the waves.

In many cases, to be sure, even the most important quotation in the play colors only a part, not the whole. The capsule has strong artistic value but a less comprehensive affect than in the instances thus far cited. So is it in the First Part of the celebrated *Montome-Zuka*. The usual travelling monk stops to converse with women gathering herbs from fields in early spring, even before the snow has vanished. The poem is by Minamoto-no-Moroyori :

> To make a traveller linger on the road,
> They pick the tender herbs
> In Ono Field of Ikuta.

This picture gives a vignette of the early passages. Another poem summarizes the accelerated action. The heroine, caught in a love-predicament, drowns herself. From the same source an apt poem is quoted :

> Weary am I of life !
> I will seek my death
> In the waters of the river Ikuta
> Whose name proves false.

The last words point to the double meaning of the river's name, which suggests the verb 'to live.' Its waters in this instance afford an entrance to death. But the poem may more rightly be said to summarize an episode in the play than the play as a whole.

The central figure in *Kagekiyo* is blind, a fact of cardinal importance for the play. Words adapted from a poem by Fujiawara-no-Toshiyuki give a most sensitive and tragic image of his condition :

> Our eyes know not when autumn first comes in,
> Yet we know it from the murmur of the wind.

Subtler than this, perhaps, is a quotation in *Momiji-Gari* of part of a poem by Po-Chü-i. The play depicts a group of huntsmen entertained during an autumn hunt by a company of seductive women, finally unveiled as malignant enchantresses. The Mountain-Hag seemed ugly but was beautiful ; these women seem beautiful but are ugly. Before their seduc-

tion, the huntsmen are weakened by wine. The fiery autumn
and the wine in conjunction prove their undoing. Po-Chü-i's
words are these :

> The fallen leaves are burnt
> In autumn woods to warm the wine.

The quotation has a strong and strangely imaginative con-
gruence. In the blending of its images it closely resembles a
modern poetic style.

Of all Noh plays *Hagoromo* best represents the lyric spirit,
present to some degrees in all but here at its height. The work
is song, dance and poem before it is in the strictest definition
of the word a play. Being in a sense all lyric, there is less
demand for the lyric capsule. This could dissolve into the
play only to make it much that it already is and has ever been.
Hagoromo seems pure atmosphere, spring air, color, breeze,
sky and cloud. The inhuman, bird-like creature dominating it
at last vanishes into the heavens that have always been her
home. All this does not mean, however, that distinct lyric
elements are not incorporated into the poem, as lyric feathers
to deck Hagoromo's winged garment. But since hers is a
seamless robe, entirely of a piece, no one lyric element predominates. Nevertheless some quotations have a more comprehensive significance than others. Consider, for example, this,
from Ch'en Wen-hai :

> Far on a distant range of lovely hills
> Clouds suddenly climb ;
> And on a tower the bright moon shines
> From heavens cleansed of rain.

Hagoromo herself is an embodiment of this landscape or
better, cloudscape. Her longing is for the freedom of great
distances and expanses ; her movements in thought, if not of
body, are sudden and aspiring; she is the genius of the spring
moonlight, the mysterious spirit of the moon dancers ; also,
the play depicts a sudden, unwonted gust of sorrow, tears and
alarm, that rapidly passes off into brightness as a sky cleansed
by spring rain. Although the quotation does not determine

the play, it powerfully expresses it.

Yoroboshi stands among the noblest and most pathetic of the Noh. Like so many others, this is a metaphysical poem, celebrating inner or mental vision. A blind boy, inspired by great piety and devotion, overcomes his grief and is filled with ecstacy by what he only imagines that he sees : a wide panorama of Japanese islands and waters illumined by the spring moon. The play contains little external action or motion, even less than *Hagoromo*. It radiates not violence but peace. This is well expressed by a poem quoted from the *Shodoka* :

> The moon streams down,
> The breezes fan the pines ;
> On so serene a night
> How can one be troubled ?

Two plays of a strongly elegiac nature have very appropriately an autumnal setting : *Ikuta* and *Tsunemasa*. To the important and highly poetic autumnal coloring is added in *Tsunemasa* the theme of music. The love of music, as noted in another chapter, is the last infirmity of this warrior's noble mind, the strongest tie attaching him to this world and denying him the bliss of Buddhahood. His lute, "Green Hill", with him in the hour of death, haunts his ghost and his spirit beyond the grave. This is intimated in a key-quotation from *Royei Shu* :

> One note of the phoenix-flute
> Shakes the autumn clouds from the mountain-side.

So in this world music dispelled Tsunemasa's gloom.

Still more restricted in the scope of their reference are quotations in *Settai*, or "Hospitality", and in *Tomoe*. At the moving conclusion of the former occurs an episode regarding the young boy, Tsurawaka, son of a dead hero. The child displays the valor of his noble family in eagerness to carry the arms of a man into battle. His high courtesy also proves him true to his chivalrous traditions. The chorus, quoting a saying from the *Buddha-Contemplation Sutra*, declares :

> Sandalwood gives forth its scent
> When but a two-leaved shoot.

Although considerably less significant for a play as a whole than many poems previously given, the quotation still comes to much more than the average dramatic metaphor. It is at least central to one of the play's important and, indeed, concluding episodes.

The quotation in question in *Tomoe* concerns a young girl who turns out to be a manifestation or disguise of the Shite in Part Two. This capsule is singularly prophetic and rich in overtones. The immediate allusion is to one who knows nothing of what occurs within a temple's inner shrine yet feels a deep reverence that leads even to the shedding of tears.

> Nothing I know
> Of what goes on within,
> Yet reverence fills my heart
> And my tears flow.

The quotation goes far in establishing the tone held in the last incident in Part One and in leading up to the finale of Part Two.

In their briefer manifestations these minute capsules are occasionally poetic proverbs and thus, strictly speaking, belong rather to the category of aphoristic than of lyric poetry. Although the Noh is too poetic a type of drama to make persistent use of this more or less intellectual form, it does employ it and all things done in the ancient Noh were apparently done well. The celebrated *Aoi-no-Ue* depicts primarily the destructive force of the Princess Rokujo's jealously, even more venomous to her than to her enemies. This moralizing thought receives support from a proverb quoted from *Dai-Shogon-ron* :

> The flame of consuming anger
> Scorches only my own self.

Such a statement reads a little like an aphoristic couplet by

Alexander Pope. Of more direct importance for a play's central action is a proverb quoted in *Sanemori*. Here an aging warrior knowing his doom but fronting it bravely requests the honor of returning to his birth-place clad in formal red costume : "A man should go back to his birth-place in rich brocade." The plot of this exceedingly histrionic play depends for much of its effectiveness on the use of this robe and on the old warrior's permission to dye his white hairs black, as the hairs of a youth. The versified proverb is his justification for the first of these symbolical gestures.

Even one or two quotations by no means central in a play's main theme are sufficiently remarkable as poetic imagery to demand attention here. *The Damask Drum* deals with the futile love of an old gardener for a proud and cruel lady. In an adaptation from the *Gosenshu,* the playwright finds metaphorical expression for the old man's misery :

Though the waters parch in the fields,
Though the brooks run dry,
Never shall the place be shown
Of the spring that feeds my heart.

In many subtle ways this arid, wasteland image serves precisely the end of strengthening the poet's art.

At times the imagery becomes extremely modern, revealing what may be described as double exposures or poetry on two levels. Simple metaphor proves insufficient. A good instance occurs in *Toboku*. The image has, accordingly, a dream-like quality, one figure serving two purposes or substituting for another. The poem is ascribed to lady Izumi herself, whose ghost is the speaker. Its meaning can only be gathered from quotation of the entire speech in which the verse capsule lies embodied :

Blessed be the Sutra !

Your reading of the Book of Parables brings back to my mind an incident which took place while I was still in this world. When this was still the Shoto-mon-in, the Mido-no-Kwanpaku rode by the gate in his carriage, reciting aloud the Parables of the Lotus Sutra. Inside the gate, I, hearing it, composed the poem :

When without the gate
I hear the 'Wheels of the Law' rolling by,
From the 'Burning House'
I too am set free.—
Now your chanting of the Sutra
Brings that day back to me.

The 'Burning House' is, of course, an obsession with the things of this transitory world.

Finally, a metaphysical imagery adds further complexity to certain plays. An image in *Basho* is itself a convention of religious poetry. The quotation comes from Po-Chü-i :

Setting the lamp behind us, we gaze up at the moon,
To enjoy the beauty of advancing night.

The thought is, of course, that the wise man at times sets man and his artifacts aside to receive in contemplation the universal revelations coming to him from nature. The thought proves especially appropriate in a play written in part to support the animistic doctrine contained in the *Lotus Sutra*. The drama illustrates the thought that the basho tree itself possesses a soul. Although the quotation cannot be said to color or guide the play as a whole, it gives its doctrine eloquent support. Possibly the least widely operating of the lyric capsules quoted in these pages, it nevertheless supplies formidable aid to the play's dominant theme and idea.

It is indeed true that the English reader of the thirty or more "capsule" poems in translation on the foregoing pages may find them not only not lyrical but quite possibly not even poetic, the mere shavings or splinters of poetry, not live trees. Such a disillusioned reader may judge too hastily. All problems of aesthetic evaluation are difficult and this one especially so, owing to the somewhat peculiar standards of Japanese taste and the character of the Japanese language. After reading a play, we may, however, look back upon the capsule and find it far more significant than we had at first supposed. Does this mean that it is merely a part of the whole ? Quite obviously not to the Japanese, for in every instance the dramatist borrows a poem that by Japanese standards is itself a completed work of distinguished art. Our first conclusion, then, must be that by some extremely well established standards words that will unquestionably to some English readers seem to be trifles have in their true and original state considerable artistic value. Is the loss, then, wholly a matter of translation ? Rather, it would appear to be a matter of attitude, posing a problem for which such a study as the present should go at least a certain distance toward a solution. It would seem that the Japanese habit of reading poetry includes a more fervent application to detail, a more prolonged meditation or study of all possible inferences, a stricter attention to overtones than our own. The Japanese reader may, if sufficiently enlightened, virtually create an unwritten Noh play out of the seed of the capsule, as, in some cases, it appears almost certain that the Noh playwrights themselves actually did create their works of art. To the Western reader the discipline of studying the Noh capsules is, then, not only a discipline toward the enjoyment of the Noh itself but toward an enhanced understanding of Japanese style and poetry as a whole. By such application the value of these little poems will be vastly increased not through being illegitimately blown up or dilated but through being revealed as what they potentially are. The reader's understanding and the poem itself will be magnified to a position that, in this relative world, will be eminently tenable, especially since the world of art is admittedly beyond the stricter canons of material measurement. As millimeters become miles, the truth in this instance will not be falsified but will be revealed. Such are the ways of aesthetic comprehension in a culture trained by long-established tradition in aesthetic con-templation.

4 / *Conventions of Speech*

THE FIRST and last thought on unravelling the remarkable intricacy and contrivance in the Noh plays is the rigor whereby each formula of their art is drawn into the service of the play's single, dominating purpose, the emotional tone and spiritual goal by virtue of which the play exists. Nuances and details give it aesthetic distinction primarily because they stand in so strict a focus directed to the heart of each. To admire any part is insufficient without apprehending the weight of the whole. To express the case metaphorically, a Noh play is a statue within a shrine, intended to be examined from various angles of vision. Drama as commonly known in the West has another focus and goal. It resembles the same figure moving to a destination outside itself. The Noh play is of all types of art one of the most serenely and severely self-contained. Representing a climax of emotion, it dispenses with direct narrative or the sequences of suspenses and surprises constituting the line on which a typical Western play progresses. Motion in the Western play, or, for that matter, in the Chinese, is objective and without, in the Noh play, self-centered and within. The Kabuki has of late demonstrated its affinity with the motion picture ; the Noh survives only as a brilliantly decorated embodiment of the statuesque. Violent in the extreme in its interior motion, charged with the highest emotional tension, it conveys also an unsurpassed impression of stability. It is, in fact, the summation of classical stability, in no sense a paralysis of the limbs of art, a deathly or frozen form wanting vitality. It possesses a vivid life and beauty of its own ; charged with inner force, it tolerates not so much as a single gesture that fails to lead to the ultimate affect. All its nuances are devices to strengthen austere unity. The drama of the Hindus celebrates the equilibrium of spiritual repose ; the Noh celebrates only the integrity and poise of art itself.

The ensuing analysis deals with a few outstanding conventions of speech all of which serve as cords to bind the fabric as a whole. The nuances can scarcely be called ornaments, so thoroughly are they structural. They stand at the very antithesis from euphuistic or rhetorical embellishments. When subjected to analysis, they prove in no sense decorations. Their innate quality is not to adorn but to serve, being aids to bring the poet all the more promptly to his clearly conceived destination.

As works of strictly conscious artifice, these plays abound in formulas for which Japanese stylistic terms in some cases exist and, so far as the present writer is aware, in other cases do not exist. It will be more congruent with whatever utility the present project possesses, addressed as it is to the general reader, to disregard whatever terms Japanese criticism itself has devised and to start afresh with simple, descriptive words familiar in English though specially adopted for this study. Where the data is so specific, such words are clarifying and most convenient. Words coming the most readily to the English tongue serve even these exotic purposes best. Hence the following pages deal with such features as "interlacing," "overlapping," "repetition," "sequence," "interpolation," "dual speaking," "triple speaking," "multiple speaking," "choral speaking," "impersonal speaking," "identification," "dramatic paragraph," "travelogue," "formula of courtesy," "off-stage voice," etc. In each instance the word has, of course, new shades of meaning determined by the special character of the material to which it refers yet in each case enjoys the advantage of providing a term at least in general clear, descriptive and easily remembered.

Each of the terms represents a calculated artifice of dramatic speech. Although taken as a whole they give a fairly broad and summary account of speech in the Noh plays, they do not, of course, offer a comprehensive panorama of so vast and complex an organism. No matters rightly considered as linguistic are touched upon. It by no means follows that because the dramatists use so many artifices with such great persistence their texts are marred by redundant artificiality or affectation. The worth of the artifice depends in part upon a contrast with a neutral or negative background where communication becomes quite simple and direct, as in usual passages of social talk. Occasional passages are quite colloquial, in an easily flowing prose. With such the present inquiry is barely concerned. The most conspicuous quality of the Noh plays is their high degree of artificiality and, naturally, it is the element of artifice, not the occasional lapse into naturalism, that invites explanatory comment.

The most typical and easily explored usage, that termed "interlacing", is also the most immediately significant in revealing the sculpturesque nature of the plays and one of their most startlingly unique features. This is one of the several devices by which words are assigned to another person than the one who might be in normal conversation assumed to speak them. The play's actual text is deflected from following the natural line of speech, assuming instead a pattern for some reason more meaningful for the play's ultimate purpose. Dialogue is distorted with a purpose. The usage suggests the color pattern in the work of many modern painters, notably Leger, where colors create a design in juxtaposition to, not in accordance with, the drawing. Two levels are deliberately shown separately, not in easy conjunction. The first speaker is not allowed to finish his remarks. A second interrupts him, completing the statement in a manner that may or may not be in precise accord with the first speaker's intention. With relatively few exceptions, however, the full statement seems entirely of a piece. It is a statement required by the play. Who makes the statement, who begins it and who ends it, prove of minor importance. Often those elusive speakers, the chorus, take part in the statement and what identity, if any, the chorus possesses must be the subject of a later and somewhat extended inquiry. In any case, it readily appears that the character-delineation holds at most a secondary place in the value-scheme of the Noh. The speakers are scarcely ever delineated in terms of their own idiom. Incidentally, there seems small use of dialect in these eminently serious and poetic plays. As will later be observed in some detail, one speaker is often heard speaking overtly in the role of another. Interlacing is a relatively superficial verbal device leading up to the more drastic superimposition of one part upon another. In all such instances the result is to turn attention away from the casual image or passing moment and fasten it upon the play's essential meaning.

Illustration of such a peculiar device is virtually imperative. In the opening passage of *Sanemori* we read :

> *Priest.* Truly, who is there whom Buddha's Vow
> *Attendants.* Of Universal Salvation
> *Priest.* Does not embrace ?

Later in the same play occur these passages :

> *Sanemori.* 'Namu'
> *Chorus.* I surrender myself to Buddha ;
> *Sanemori.* 'Amida',
> *Chorus.* Good deeds.
> By virtue, therefore, of those words
> *Sanemori.* Never shall believer fail
> To win Amida's Paradise....
> *Priest.* The snows of yester-year still linger
> *Sanemori.* Upon the locks and beard of the old warrior,
> *Priest.* Attired in splendid robes.
> *Sanemori.* In the unclouded light
> *Priest.* Of the setting moon,
> *Sanemori.* In the light of the tapers,
> *Chorus.* Shimmers his rich brocade.

In *Kiyotsune* appears a passage somewhat less drastic in its artifice yet unmistakably within the limits of this convention :

> *Kiyotsune.* I cannot forgive your cruelty
> *Wife.* Nor I your wilful death.
> *Kiyotsune.* One taunts the other with reproaches,
> *Wife.* The other tauntingly replies.
> *Kiyotsune.* The keepsake is a source of woe.
> *Wife.* And a lock of hair

Chorus. Becomes for us a source of strife.

Here it will be noted that characters may speak not as normally speaking but with an objective voice, such as we commonly assume for a chorus. A character speaks not as himself but about himself. To Western readers these practices of the Noh may indeed at first appear confusing. The chorus may identify itself with an individual or an individual with the chorus. In the last line quoted the chorus assumes its privilege of speaking for two persons at the same time. In these ingenious usages there is much strategy and no binding rule.

In *Toboku* we read :

Chorus. Blossoms fall from branches,.
Like birds seeking again their ancient nests,
Maiden. Returning whence they once did come.
Chorus. Then your life's journey's ended ?
Maiden. Under the shadow of the flowers
Chorus. I seem to rest.

In that exquisite play, *Izutsu*, occur examples of the highly popular practice of dividing the quotation of a brief poem into two parts, the first and second parts spoken by different voices. This usage takes place in scenes of close mutual understanding. Far from violating the integrity of the quoted poem, the division in the voices actually enforces the poem's inner structure and fortifies the dialogue, each speech being, as it were, a stone in the same wall.

Chorus. The faithful-hearted youth
Sent her a letter with a poem
Telling his flower-like love
In words like sparkling dew-drops :
Maiden. "Standing against the well-curb,
As children we compared our heights,
Chorus. But I have grown much taller
Since last I saw you".

Here the maiden speaks as her lover and the chorus does the same. Later in the play substantially the same lines are arranged in another artificial pattern :

Daughter. "Standing against the well-curb
Chorus.   Standing against the well-curb,
          As children we compared our heights.
Daughter. But I
Chorus.   Have grown much taller".
Daughter. And much older.

Sumidagawa illustrates the formula thus :

Ferryman. 'Twas thoughtless of me
          Instead of Miyako-bird
Mother.   To call it a sea-gull.
Ferryman. So Narihira long ago
Mother.   Asked, "Is she still alive ?"
Ferryman. Remembering his lady of Miyako . . .
          To long for a sweetheart,
Mother.   To seek after a lost child,
Ferryman. Both spring
Mother.   From love.

The division of a quoted poem itself into two parts between
two speakers occurs likewise in the final passage of *Tadanori* :

Chorus.   "Belated
          I lodge beneath a cherry-tree in bloom.
Tadanori. The flowers are my host
          To-night".

In *Yuya* a poem is similarly treated :

Yuya.   "Mountains are now green, now white
          with passing veils of clouds.
Chorus.   Man finds himself now glad, now sad".

Kantan employs the formula thus :

Rosei.   How long will my glory last ?
          In vernal freshness

Chorus. That never fades but lives
    Like the moon still bright at dawn . . .
Rosei. Dancing I will sing a song of joy
    Again and once again while night endures.
Chorus. And yet while night endures,
    The sun is risen waxing bright.
    And while we think it is the night,
Rosei. It is already height of day.
Chorus. When we think it is the day,
Rosei. The moon is brightly shining still.
Chorus. Spring flowers are now in bloom,
Rosei. But leaves of trees are autumn-tinged.
Chorus. We think it is high summer,
Rosei. Yet we see the falling snow.

The abruptness and surprise in the transitions as described gain greatly in sharpness by the artful shifting from one voice to another.

The artificial breaking of the speeches aids also in the choreographic fitness of the dialogue :

Monk. Hardly have I spoken when flames come flying and
    hang above the tomb ;
Unai-Otome. Turning into hellish fiends
    That rack the afflicted souls,
Monk. They raise their rods and drive at her.
Unai-Otome. If I attempt to flee, before me lies the sea,
Monk. And flames are in the rear.
Unai-Otome. On left
Monk. And on the right,
Unai-Otome. Water and fire harass my feeble form.
Monk. Helpless,
Unai-Otome. To the pillar of the Burning House
Chorus. I reach my hands and try to cling.

A similar lyrical flow sweeping past the speakers and carrying them together on its irresistible wave is found in *Yamamba* :

Mountain-Hag. I must say farewell and go my endless
    rounds.

Chorus. In spring that prompts the trees to flower,
Mountain-Hag. I go my rounds of mountains viewing blooms.
Chorus. In autumn, following the moon serene,
Mountain-Hag. I go my rounds among the gleaming hills.
Chorus. In winter when the rain clouds turn to snow,
Mountain-Hag. I go my rounds, enraptured by the mountains
     white.
Chorus. Rounds upon rounds,
    Migrations without end . . .

Finally, one of the most artful instances of interlacing occurs in *Sanemori*, where the prolongation of a soul's misery in the after-life is emphasized by the monotonous exchange of phrases between an Old Man, who is the hero in his dramatic disguise, and a priest.

Old Man. Yes, I am Sanemori's ghost. While the ethereal
    part of my soul is in the world of gloom, the
    sensuous part lingers on earth,
Priest. And in this world of bondage
Old Man. Has lived more than two hundred years,
Priest. But still remains unsaved.
    As Shinowara Pond
Old Man. Day and night is stirred by ceaseless ripples,
Priest. So the darkened soul
Old Man. Is tossed by thoughts
Priest. Twixt dream
Old Man. And waking.
    Like hoar-frost on the withered grass
    My locks and beard are white with age,
Chorus. "My locks and beard are white with age" . . .

The device which we shall call "overlapping" resembles "interlacing" but with a difference of some importance. It is exemplified in the last two lines just quoted. In the case of overlapping one speaker starts his own remarks by repeating the last words of the preceding speaker. This is, incidentally, a device effectively employed in Middle English lyric verse, notably in the masterpiece, *Pearl*. In *Kantan* Rosei exclaims: "Let the cup go round from guest to guest". In keeping with this festive thought, the chorus begins a long harangue precisely with Rosei's words. The cup of language is passed from mouth to mouth. Later in the play the mock-hero declares : "Rosei awakes from his dream," and the chorus adds :

Rosei awakes from his dream
And rising looks bewildered,
Bereft of fifty years of glory.

Sometime the repetition has a minor variation. In *Shunkan* the tragic hero observes : " 'Wait with hope !' they shout," and the chorus rejoins, "Wait with hope and confidence," adding an emphasis to Shunkan's words.

In *Ama* occurs an unusually affective use of this form of repetition where the parts are divided between two speakers. The chorus concludes a long description of the exploits of a diver with the words : "Thus she came to the surface." The woman in question returns to the role of a speaker with precisely the same words. Thus she breaks the surface of her long silence as she rises from the water with an echo of the chorus. As always, the technical device aids in the unification both of the dramatic poem and its theatrical affect. Its parts are drawn so much the closer together.

A delicate variation of the device is played in the closing episode of *Eguchi*. The lady seems about to repeat the theme-poem of the play. Her words are : "I recall to mind." The chorus, its memory also stimulated, abruptly snatches the cue and recites the entire poem, of which the lady, precisely as if giving a cue, has spoken the first words only :

I recall to mind
I told one to take no thought
For a temporary lodging . . .

Similarly, "the Woman" in *Momiji-Gari* announces the theme for the exquisite last chorus in Part One : "O wonderous leaves on the green moss !" It is with these words that the chorus commences its lyrical passage. The formula is used repeatedly. Just before the chorus with which the play concludes, the hero, Koremochi, observes : "Koremochi, undisturbed and unconfused", and with these solemn words the chorus commences its own utterance. Twice in *Kagekiyo* the formula is also employed with powerful effect. The blind hero exclaims, "Here I must live," and "My eyes are darkened." Each utterance serves as the first line for a lyric address by the chorus in the passage immediately following.

Although never, perhaps, to excess, repetition is used for emphasis on many occasions when it does not flow from one speaker to another. So in the climax of the celebrated Noh play, *Ataka*, the chorus twice exclaims : "In awe and trembling let them pass." At the height of the forced gaiety in the drinking scene of the same play a convivial repetition occurs. Benkei shouts, "What a delight ! As at the feast of wandering water ;" the chorus begins its own ecstatic utterance with the same words. The chorus also enforces its final utterance with similar repetition of the words, "Ever roars the flowing stream". The weight of these phrases is increased by being reiterated.

The force of words in obvious rhetorical sequence gains not only when blunt repetition is used but when the strong rhythm of the phrases and echoing of key words also impel the movement onward. Repetition is the term best employed to denote precise duplication and sequence best used when a single rhetorical rhythm is pressed forward while accompanied with verbal variation. Instances are many ; their variations fascinating. The content determines the unique forms. In *Eguchi* words describing the wheel of material existence revolve in a pattern enforcing their own vitality :

Chorus. "The Law of the Twelve Causes is like unto a wheel
Endlessly rolling along a highway ;
Lady. Sentient creatures now sink, now rise,
Like birds that fly from branch to branch."
Chorus. Life after life into the past—
Lady. Whence the cycle first began is hidden from us.
Chorus. Life after life into the future—
Whither the cycle ends we cannot know.
Lady. Sometimes creatures are born into the happy state
Of men or heavenly beings,
Chorus. Yet by error overcast, their minds
Fail to sow the seed of salvation ;

> *Lady.* Sometimes they're reborn into the Three Worst States,
> Or fall prey to the Eight Evils,
> *Chorus.* And fettered by such misfortunes
> They know not how to enter the True Way.

Superbly affective is the passage in *Settai* where the victor and vanquished in the same battle are chivalrously associated in one movement, victims torn on the dark and malignant wheel of material existence.

> *Grandmother.* The slain foe was then his captain's page,
> *Benkei.* Tsuginobu was the trusted of our lord ;
> *Grandmother.* The one in the Heike's boat,
> *Benkei.* The other in the Genji's camp.
> *Grandmother.* The one was faithful to his lord,
> *Benkei.* And no less faithful the other.
> *Grandmother.* Both in the same grief suffered.
> *Benkei.* Be consoled in common sorrow.

A stirring passage of similar but not too similar nature appears in *Yamamba* during the dialogue between the Mountain-Hag and the chorus. The former exclaims :

> Mountains are but dust accumulated
> To rise ten thousand feet as peaks
> Girdled by the heavenly clouds ;

The latter varies the theme in a new strophe :

> Oceans are but drops of water gathered
> From mosses till they spread as seas,
> Whose billows ever rise and fall.

The Hag continues :

> Sounds of water from the caverned vale,
> Echoes from the wooded mountain-side—

And the chorus, as usual, completes the period with the final word :

Help man to bear the soundless voice.

In *Miidera* antiphonal verses artfully express the swinging of the temple bell :

Chorus. When the bell of early morning tolls,
Mother. It says, "Nought that is, e'er stays.
Chorus. When the bell of late night tolls,
Mother. It says, "All things are transient."
Chorus. What does the bell of early morning tell.
Mother. "When the transient ceases to be."
Chorus. What does the sunset bell proclaim ?
Mother. "Nirvana's bliss is then attained."

Probably the most moving and highly developed of all the sequences in the Noh occurs in the final episode of *Sumidagawa,* surely one of the most poignant passages in dramatic poetry. This is an antiphonal chorus in which the sacred words, "Namu Amida," are repeated for the salvation of a dead child's soul. First the chorus chants. With the final notes are heard the calls of the legendary Miyako-birds. Next, the child's voice is heard pronouncing the sacred syllables along with the chorus. Next, he pronounces them alone. Finally, he becomes visible and before disappearing forever from both sight and sound speaks a few frail words of his own asking whether it is really his mother's voice he has heard and whose power has summoned him from the grave. A similar supernatural voice occurs in the climax of Monteverdi's sublime opera, *The Combat of Tancred and Clorinda,* yet the Noh poet develops the theme with considerably more nuances than does the father of Italian opera. The mere words, unhappily in translation, follow :

Chorus. Namu Amida !
Mother. True to their name
    Miyako-birds join the choir.
Ghost and Chorus. Namu Amida ! Namu Amida !
    Namu Amida !
Mother. Surely just now among them I heard my child's
    voice. He seems to be praying inside this mound.
Ferryman. We, too, have heard your child. We shall keep

223

	silent ; say your prayer alone.
Mother.	O that I might hear his voice but once again !
	Namu Amida !
Ghost.	Namu Amida ! Namu Amida !
Chorus.	See, his voice and shape !
Mother.	Is it you, my child ?
Ghost.	Is it you, my mother ?

It would be impossible to imagine a style more consummately adapted to both lyrical and dramatic forms.

An overlong harangue or soliloquy is repugnant to a dramatic style, which almost by definition rejects the plain monologue and calls for dialogue. Yet extended speeches are frequently desirable in presenting a dramatic idea. Playwrights find devices for preventing them from becoming untheatrical. One formula often practised by the Noh dramatists, to which analogies in other forms of poetry might readily be cited, is the interrupting phrase, which may be termed an interpolation. This device allows a considerable expansiveness in the lyrical and the expository pattern while serving to maintain the passage in sound dramatic context. The usage is one of the commonest in the arsenal of Noh technique. Direct quotation would be cumbersome inasmuch as a fairly long passage is by definition concerned. The thoughtful student will be well repaid on examining such passages, a few of which should at least be mentioned without the burden of full quotation. These often, though by no means always, involve the chorus. Frequently the leading figure dances or mimes in rendering imaginatively a climax in his own career. The chorus describes the event in full, poetic and leisurely style, while the actor, maintaining visual focus upon himself, at appropriate intervals punctuates the choral narrative during a pause in his own actions with the utterance of a few words only. In the Second Part of *Tamura* no sooner has the hero been introduced than the drama becomes virtually a conjunction of recitation by the chorus and miming and dancing by the hero, with a few lines which he interpolates during the pauses in his action and in the chanting of the chorus. For this scene the English in the version of the Classical Translations Committee assigns the chorus seventy-two lines, the hero fifteen, disposed in four speeches of four lines, one, one, eight and one respectively. Especially typical of this device are the interpolations of one line each. Although these give direction to the choral narrative and reflections, in general affect they are little more than rivets holding the dramatic structure firmly in place, assuring a firm relation of what is heard to what is seen. Like all other devices in the Noh, their end is both poetic and theatrical unity.

The same principle obtains in *Kiyotsune*. Dramatic form leads by steady gradation to the condition where speech and spectacle ascend together to their climax. Again the problem is solved through the relations between protagonist and chorus. The fourth "dramatic paragraph" into which the drama falls consists in words shared almost equally between hero, wife and chorus. Three dramatic paragraphs complete the play, the second being unusually brief. Only in the second does the wife speak, a single utterance of but four lines. In all, the chorus speaks ninety lines, Kiyotsune, only nine, divided between four speeches. It will, accordingly, be seen that from the purely vocal point of view his words achieve little more than punctuation for the remarkably moving choral passages. Spiritually he is beyond the shadow of a doubt the central figure, the chorus merely speaking for him and unveiling his heart in a splendid flow of lyrical or narrative poetry while the actor accomplishes the same end through mime and dance. Few as his own words are, they acquire considerable weight. Their brevity illustrates the virtue of the extraordinary economy and concision at the essence of the Japanese practice of emotional expression.

The singularly beautiful climax of *Toboku* shows similar organization. Here again are three verse paragraphs; speech falls solely between the Lady and the chorus. The subject is the Lady's salvation through her art. Although a courtesan, she was also a poet and hence found a gateway to the spiritual life, culminating in ultimate Buddhahood. The emblem for this life is the beauty of a garden in spring, for which the "Plum-Tree-by-the-Eaves" serves as dominant symbol. Most of the lines are laden with garden fragrance, the beauty of the place being symbolic of the beauty of poetry, as that of poetry itself symbolizes the beauty of the soul. The essence of the play, as of all other Noh, is lyrical. Here the chorus chants fifty-nine lines, the Lady speaks, or sings, only twelve, disposed in five extremely brief utterances. The chorus has the first and last words. The Lady performs a dance symbolizing her poetic ecstasy.

In some lesser plays poetry in all its forms yields to the attraction of the spectacle. The congratulatory, mask-like work, *Tamanoi*, concludes with a Part whose entire text comes in English to only forty-three lines, of which all but seven fall to the chorus. The lines delivered from the stage itself fill in the intervals between the dances. These lines are doubtless impressive from the viewpoint of their relation to the strictly literary phase of the work.

Tadanori offers an excellent example of the orthodox technique of interpolation. Indeed all of Part Two cleaves close to convention. The first dramatic paragraph consists of a speech by the Monk, or Waki, followed by that of the Monk in unison with his attendants. The second paragraph is a monologue spoken by the ghost of the hero, or Shite. This substantial speech of twenty-one lines concludes the hero's main speaking part. With the exception of a single utterance by the Monk at its beginning, the remaining segments consist of a prolonged passage wherein the chorus does the bulk of the speaking, while Tadanori executes the dances and speaks only a minimum of words. Yet Tadanori's interpolation gives direction to the chorus. The hero exclaims: "Rokuyata looked and thought." What Rokuyata thought is the function of the all-knowing chorus to relate.

That this technique is used not only in the conclusions of plays but in their midstream appears in two memorable passages of *Yuya*, dramatic paragraphs seven and nine. Each exhibits the chorus in relation to the heroine. Yuya, a living woman, not a ghost, speaks tersely, the chorus chanting at length. The chorus delivers a descriptive song of twenty-eight lines, in the midst of which Yuya interpolates a poetic quotation of two lines. In the ninth dramatic paragraph the chorus chants for thirty-one lines interrupted by Yuya with a single line.

At the conclusion of *Tomoe* the device is pushed to its greatest extreme. First the chorus delivers itself of twenty-one lines, whereupon Tomoe deflects the narrative with four words. The chorus resumes with ten lines. Again, with a single line, Tomoe opens a new phase in the narrative. The chorus continues with fifty-six lines. Tomoe follows with a single crucial line, whereupon the chorus terminates the play with an effusion of twenty-five lines.

Finally, *Kinuta* contains two striking illustrations of the use of interpolation. In the first of these, in the fifth dramatic paragraph of Part One, the Lady mimes the action of cloth-beating while the chorus chants for over sixty lines, with the interruption of a single line only by the Lady. The second passage relevant here stands at the play's end, dramatic paragraphs three and four of Part Two. The chorus sings for twelve lines. The Lady interrupts with one, which is immediately repeated by the chorus with the opening of a chant of thirteen lines. The Lady interposes two lines ; the chorus, with twenty-three lines, continues to the conclusion.

In the eminently lyric technique of the Noh calculated use is made not only of the single speaker in opposition to the chorus, the latter a group removed from the acting area of the stage, but of dual, triple, and multiple speaking among the actors themselves. By far the most familiar formula for this simultaneous speaking or chanting occurs in the instance of the Waki and his attendant or attendants. Although the Shite may have his chorus of followers, he is more often a solitary figure, the protagonist, alone in his spiritual grandeur. The Waki represents the multiplicity of common mankind, striving, perhaps, for spiritual eminence but never for exalted position. The chief struggle lies in the heart of the Shite, who has no antagonist in the manner of the typical Western drama. He, or she, frequently finds in the Waki instead of an enemy an invaluable friend, inasmuch as the latter is so often a monk whose earnest prayers and recitations of the sutra assist in gaining the Shite's introduction into Buddhahood. The monk, in short, has his acolytes or attendant priests. Here there is strength in numbers. Talk takes place between them, especially at the beginning of a play.

First for simultaneous speaking in duet form, of which many striking instances occur. In *Kagekiyo* the dialogue develops along familiar lines ; the hero's daughter, Hitomaru, a poor girl, has only one attendant. They occasionally speak in unison. In the celebrated *Matsukaze* the two salt-makers beloved by Lord Yukihira and left in sadness by his departure from Suma Beach and by his death, are inseparable in their misery. Devoted friends, they frequently speak in unison. In *Shunkan* tragic irony depends on the unjust distinction made by the official order which pardons two exiles but leaves their fellow, Shunkan, undistinguished from the others in his deeds, to languish ain solitude on their island prison. Artfull the contrast between the happy generality of mankind and the unique misery of the tragic hero is achieved by pitting the hero in his solitude against the two men who are redeemed. The two lucky ones speak in unison. The Rosencrantz and Guildenstern of Japanese drama, they lack distinction. Their duet clearly attracts us less than the solo part of the victim of a destiny equally capricious and tragic.

Instances of multiple speaking are still more common as in a trio of voices in *Shunkan* itself, when the two pardoned men, departing in their boat, join the messenger in an ironic expression of good wishes to the unfortunate man.

As previously noted, the Waki has his supporters in his speeches, especially in the ceremonious commencement of the play. In *Takasago* we find Tomonari and his attendants speaking together; in *Tamura*, another monk and his attendants open the play with a unison of voices. In *Toboku* the scene is the same; first the monk and his attendants speak simultaneously; then the monk speaks alone; and this pattern is repeated. The fifth speech is of the attendants by themselves, the sixth, of the monk by himself. Thus the dramatist achieves both balance and variety within the firm order of his strictly contrived plans. The ritual of the travelogue, in which an account is given of the various places through which the Waki and his attendants pass before reaching the proper scene of the play, is almost invariably focused on a passage declaimed by both the Waki and his friends. A good example is found in *Eguchi*. Benkei, appearing in a considerable number of plays, is usually attended by his retainers who speak together and even at times in conjunction with him. In *Ataka*, where Benkei is conspicuous, a dozen warriors appear.

In *Momiji-Gari*, where the stage is also fuller than usual, are two typical groups, three attendant women who follow "the Beautiful Woman," later discovered as a manifestation of the Mountain-Hag, and four huntsmen accompanying the Waki, Koremochi, on his hunting and autumn sight-seeing visit into the hills and forests. Such groups as these clearly enlarge both the vocal and spectacular dimensions of the scene. They are treated all the more effectively for being handled with restraint, reminding us once more that the Noh is an aristocratic chamber music, whereas the Kabuki, with its extravagant and at times vulgar proportions, suggests occasionally inflated dimensions of the nineteenth-century symphony.

The chorus properly so called clearly differs vastly from the Greek chorus or any lyric and theatrical convention whatsoever on the Western stage. Although the Noh chorus merits the same name and performs some of the same functions as the Western forms, the Greek chorus, for example, did much which the Noh chorus does not do and left undone much which the latter achieves. The two are primarily alike in being a group of singers attached to the play in a more or less secondary capacity. But whereas in the Greek play the main actors perform almost all the acting and the chorus performs all the dancing, in the Noh the main actor performs most or all of the dancing, together with much of the acting as well, and the chorus remains solely musical and poetic. It is true that the purest lyric poetry in the Greek falls to the chorus and that much of the most lyric verse in the Noh is also rendered by the chorus. Yet the entire Noh play is much more clearly of a piece than the Greek. The protagonist speaks magnificent poetic lines, if not at the time of his dancing, at least in other parts of the play and the chorus enters more freely into the dialogue than in Western practice. Yet, as previously observed, the chorus neither acts nor dances. It fills the eye. Its costumes are rich. It lends appropriate ornament and elegance to the play as spectacle but little or nothing to the play as action. It describes actions both on and off the stage but does not perform them. Unlike the groups of attendants upon the Waki, at no time does it enter into the playing area. Its functions are many, ranging from the obvious to the most subtly contrived.

Sufficiently clear is its tendency to strengthen the play's organization by summarizing incidental speeches or sequences of speeches, the two, or on rare occasions, three Parts into which the work is divided, and, finally, the work as a whole. Thus it has the feminine propensity for having the last word. This is especially clear in the convention prescribing that the final words of the play itself and of the First Part as well shall fall to the chorus. In the thirty plays selected by the Society for Translations of the Classics, only one exception to the rule is found. Part One of *Miidera* fails to conclude with benefit of chorus. But this seems as much owing to a questionable description of the two Parts themselves as to a violation of the rule. No intermission or address by the Man of the Place is provided. It is true that the place of action shifts. But what is described by the editors as Part One more nearly resembles a fore-scene. It consists of less than fifty lines, with simple, forthright action and no interpolation of dance or miming. This is followed by an episode of the Chief Priest and his attendants completely in the manner of the typical Noh play Induction. Accordingly, it is not unreasonable to suggest that *Miidera* is a play in one Part and not in two. In other respects as well this work belongs to the simple and less liturgical type of Noh; it is a "Mad Woman Play;" it is without a ghost; there is a humorous episode introducing a temple servant. The chorus makes no appearance whatsoever in the section designated in the translation as "Part One."

Although by convention the chorus enjoys the last word, it is not permitted to have the first. This falls at times to the Waki, at other times to minor figures. But especially where the first speech is given by the Waki or at least rendered in a dignified manner, the chorus is likely to commence its own chanting by catching up and repeating the last words of the character introducing the stage-action. Thus in *Takasago* the play commences with words intoned by the Priest, Tomonari, and his attendants:

Today we don our travelling dress,
Today we don our travelling dress,
Long is the journey before us.

Thereupon the chorus picks up and repeats the second and third lines. In several instances, of which this play is one, the chorus will not be heard again for a considerable time. Its early appearance in the poetic and musical phase of the play establishes it, nevertheless, as an important factor, whose value is likely steadily to increase, mounting to its height in the last episode, where emotion is at its peak, where the musical and dance elements are strongest, and the poetry itself ascends to a climax. The chorus, of course, sings ; yet it must be noted that its words are considerably more emphasized than those of the usual chorus in such a form as grand opera. The words are intended to be firmly articulated and clearly heard, especially as the performances were originally given under relatively intimate circumstances, before a select audience, on a protruding stage, and in a comparatively small arena.

Here differences from the Greek are especially revealing. It is part of the history of Greek tragedy that as years advanced the chorus became not only less impressive or conspicuous but more detached and less intimately involved in the play's thought and action. In Aeschylus the chorus participates the most fully in the conduct of the action itself, has the longest part, and at times even holds much the position later filled by the hero, or central figure. In Sophocles the lyric perfection of the chorus reaches its height ; by no other dramatist is the choral ode as lyric so highly formalized or perfected. In Euripides the chorus as literature commonly shrinks in significance, becoming in a few plays little more than vestigial remains.

The Noh chorus is, perhaps, never as conspicuous as that of Aeschylus but is even more intimately woven into the fabric of the work. Even Aeschylus relished a contrast here. In the Noh each element has its own functions yet all are coordinated with the utmost smoothness. The seam between chorus and actors never attracts the eye. The intricacy and efficiency with which the Noh chorus is blended with the total context is remarkable beyond example, repaying almost infinite study. Only a few of the major features in this craftsmanship can be examined here.

The most obvious use for any dramatic chorus is exposition. The chorus relates the play's antecedent action, serving as background to its main figures. To use Japanese terms, in this regard it becomes a more poetic equivalent for the "Man of the Place", who during the intermission between Parts One and Two relates in comparatively colloquial language the legend on which the play is based. This Man of the Place is thus a comparatively prosaic character, better informed, perhaps, about the play's action than the audience but speaking their own familiar dialect or even appearing as the poet's serving-man, wholly without literary pretensions. Hence his words are not considered part of the play as literature ; they are program notes existing for the vulgar understanding ; or possibly we may regard them as an aid for those whose ears have not been acute enough to hear all the words that have been chanted or sung. In short, he is in a sense a choral figure but not a poetic figure. His functions were thought to be best served if his words were in large part impromptu. Stylistically they must have been at the antithesis from the chorus itself, whose utterances are likely to be even exceptionally elegant, cleanly chiselled and imaginative. The Man of the Place more than once serves as a convenient reference but is hardly an essential figure in the Noh. He appears in a considerable number of works but by no means in all.

A good instance of the expository role of the chorus occurs in *Takasago*, where it falls to the chorus in Part One to enlighten the audience on the legend of the twin pines of Takasago and Suminoye. The "Old Man" gives the more picturesque and personal account of their legend. The chorus enlightens the monk on its esoteric meaning : the pines are not only two lovers ; they are two anthologies, which are pillars that between them support the precious burden of Japanese poetry. The pine tree is symbol of poetry and art because it is unfading, lasting from age to age. For Western readers it may be worth noting that many Japanese trees are short lived ; evergreens accordingly stand forth more conspicuously than in other lands. Yet the idea of poetry's immortality and spiritual significance may be symbolized by other trees as well. As already noted, *Toboku* uses the symbol of a garden and in particular a "Plum-tree-by-the-Eaves" as signifying poetry ; the plum-tree is described as old and celebrated for its persistent annual bloom. This thought is expressed by the chorus in a long passage announced by the typical words :

> Poetry is indeed a sermon
> Preached by the 'Body of Law.'
> The memory of poets alone lives on for ever,
> So writes Ki-no-Tsurayuki . . . .

The philosophically-minded Greeks employ the chorus far more often for reflective purposes than do the aesthetically-minded Japanese. "What a piece of work is man ?" is a thought of Shakespeare and of Sophocles, not of Zeami. As already indicated, the Noh poets are the more inclined to use the chorus for descriptive or psychological purposes. Through the device of "identification" the chorus speaks for a character in the play, as a rule, its central figure. This is, of course, common in Western drama, yet with a difference. Western moralists delight in choruses that sympathize with the hero but still more in those advising him as to what he should do. Thus the appalling Puritan propensity for giving advice is seen faintly foreshadowed in the moralizing Greeks but exhibited the most violently by Milton. The chorus in *Samson Agonistes* moralizes on the unfortunate hero, informing him at length of his faults and telling him in no uncertain terms what he should do. From this didactic spirit the Japanese playwrights are, happily, free. A typical use of the gentler Noh chorus, with its descriptive and psychological aims, occurs in *Yoroboshi*. Here the chorus assists the blind child in a very different manner from Milton's chorus remonstrating with the blind Samson. It enters into the boy's heart, speaks for him a mature language which in real life he could not himself command, and renders his stumbling all the more moving for the audience by giving it verbal expression while the actor is free to concentrate upon the visual affect. The actor mimes his part while the chorus, assuming, as it were, his own mask, chants moving and tender words :

> Hither and thither do I walk.
> Alas ! My eyes are dead !
> I clash with people in the crowd,
> I stumble and fall down ;

233

O my faltering and uncertain steps,
How people scoff and laugh !
"Here comes the Blind Boy Stumbling,"
They say and I am filled with shame.—
No longer will I thus behave.

Then, after a short pause and silence, marking the end of one dramatic paragraph and the commencement of another, the chorus shifts its mask, figuratively speaking, and identifies itself with the boy's father :

Night is far advanced,
No one is abroad,
What were you before ?
What, tell me, is your name ?

The boy gives his name, while the actor presenting the father mimes his part. The chorus again speaks for the father :

To my heart your words bring joy,
I am your father.

Having said this, the chorus rapidly shifts ground, returning to identification with the son :

Then his heart begins to leap and bound.

A moment later the chorus once more speaks in behalf of the father, using the first person. Shortly thereafter the play ends with the chorus falling back into the third person and a comparatively calm, objective view of the concluding action. As forces of passion sweep through the play, the chorus responds with the sensitivity of a flag in high wind. Like the music which it sings, it expresses the successive shades of emotion. How much more aesthetic is this technique than the practices of the didactic or expository chorus familiar in Christian drama !

The Noh chorus expresses not only the waking thoughts of the characters ; it relates their innermost visions and dreams. Of this convention *Kantan* offers by far the most celebrated example. Rosei dreams that for fifty years—even for an infinity of years—he is emperor of the world. The pride of this world itself, concludes the poet, is such a dream. The actor playing Rosei places his head on a magic pillow and falls asleep. Part Two of the play consists of his dream. In it appear as figures on the stage an envoy, three ministers, and a court dancer, all of whom speak, though briefly. Much the longer section of the scene consists of lines recited by the chorus, ideally constituted to voice the thoughts of the deluded dreamer. This is the metaphysical theatre, attempted without aid of established stage conventions by Strindberg in his *Dream Play* and by O'Neill in *Strange Interlude*.

Representative of the more usual practice, even in the Noh, are choruses in such plays as *Kinuta* and *Momiji-Gari*. In the former the chanters describe the sounds of the cloth-beaters echoing through the stillness of the cold, autumn night. Throughout the Noh plays the chorus is the most accessible and affective vehicle for the projection of an inspired nature poetry upon a stage bare of even the least trace of naturalistic imagery. The descriptions as a rule fall more readily on the lips of the chorus than on those of the actors. In short, the chorus supplies the stage set. From it arises an imaginative creation of nature, a procession of sublime landscapes, almost as dramatically affective as the music which issues from its own mouths or from the instrumentalists supporting them. This is evidenced by the choral descriptions of mountain scenery in *Momiji-Gari*. It is, perhaps, best of all witnessed by *Miidera*. Emphasis falls on the spaciousness and peace of the scene.

"Above the hill the moon is resting,
The wind like a falling shower disturbs the lake."
Dreamy looms the Wood of Awaza
Before us in the darkening distance,
Across the vast unfolding sea
Lies the Mirror Mount
In moonlight swathed.
At Yamada and Yabase,
Unsought by passengers, the ferryman
Lured by the burnished moon,
Far out on the lake will row.

This, of course, is a Sung painting brought to new life in words. The play has a double focus, expressed in the autumn moon and the sacred bell tolled in ecstasy by the hand of the mad, bereaved mother. In each case the chorus expresses the emotion the most perfectly—although not impossibly the orchestra contributed importantly to the chorus's last words :

What has caused this happy union ?
It was the bell ;
It rang aloud to warn
The presence of a lunatic.
When dear lovers meet,
The bell their parting tolls,
But with parted child and mother
The bell their joyous meeting sings.

Devices used for the chorus take such a multiplicity of forms and meanings that a complete account is impossible and in addition to the foregoing observations only one minor convention will be noted here. Playwrights commonly take pains to distinguish what is read on the stage from what is spoken. Thus Shakespeare cultivates the convention that where letters are read even in scenes where the speech is couched in verse, the reading shall be prose. Documents on the Noh stage are, it seems, commonly committed to the chorus. So in *Ataka*, when Benkei pretends to read from his spurious scroll, the words are somewhat surprisingly recited not by him but by the chorus. Similarly, the reading of the pious scroll held in the hands of the Dragon Woman in *Yamamba* is transferred from her to the chorus, who chant the sacred text. The rendition of the text as a choral hymn confers upon it the greatest possible dignity and impressiveness. This episode brings the play to its moving conclusion.

A chorus or a character may not only project itself into the mind of a third person and even speak for him in full identification ; as witnessed in a quotation given earlier from *Kiyotsune*, one person may step out of himself not to be another but to become an entirely impersonal, external observer, so that he views himself in complete disassociation, as people do sometimes in dream. This is clearly a deliberate device, a careful, calculated convention, which nevertheless has its psychological validity. It appears in times of high tension and accordingly expresses the speaker's disturbance of mind. There is something strangely moving in this artifice, suggesting that much as it violates superficial actuality, in fact it truthfully expresses a profound actuality, the capacity of the aroused psyche to look down from a height coolly and objectively upon itself. In *Sumidagawa* the kind-hearted ferryman is profoundly moved by the mother's grief for her dead child. The mother is so prostrated by sorrow that she falls helplessly to the ground, unable even to pray for her son. The ferry man says:

This is not as it should be. However many people may gather together, it is a mother's prayers that will rejoice her dead child.
So saying he hands the gong to the mother.
Mother. You say true—
I'll take the gong
For my child's sake.
Ferryman. Ceasing her moan, in a clear voice
Mother. She prays with them under the shining moon.

This dialogue is clearly not literally but spiritually faithful to life. The Ferryman speaking of himself in the third person and later commencing a sentence to be completed by the mother herself is presented as moved and involved to an abnormal degree. Under the emotional pressure the normal avenues of communication are presented as completely broken down. It should be recalled that the mother is declared to be mad. The distortion of madness, or uncontrolled grief, is in turn reflected by her own objective view of herself, as she describes herself in the third person. This she has, indeed, done several times earlier in the play. One might suppose the following lines were spoken by the Ferryman, the chorus, or anyone save the mother. They are actually hers :

He was the child
This mad woman is seeking :
Is this a dream ?
O cruel fate !

The unity of all parts of the play, notably its words and actions, is further aided by the convention among the more tragic figures to give, as it were, their own stage directions. Stepping out of themselves, they depict themselves. Even the Japanese audience is quite possibly shocked by the transition but, since the playwright observes a well established convention, should not be disconcerted. Instead, a peculiar emphasis falls on both the words and actions and to their unified import. This convention is used in moments of especially strong tragic tension. So the priestly exorcist, Kohijiri, filled with the divine spirit, in performing his magic rite abruptly addresses himself in the third person :

> However evil the evil spirit,
> The mystic power of holy men will never fail.
> With these words he fingers once again his sacred beads.

One might suppose that the last line here would be given to the chorus, who indeed speak immediately thereafter. But not so. The playwright has more devious means for achieving his goal and enhancing the affect of astonishment. The artifice is psychologically sound.

The same affect is obtained in some of the last utterances of the miserable exile, Shunkan, who in acute self-pity steps out of his unbearable self to view his own distress and to express it. The exile exclaims :

> "Wait patiently !" they cry.
> Shunkan stops his bitter tears.
> Though like their distance voices now
> His hope is faint,
> He listens with a rapt intent
> Under the pine-trees on the shore.

In his moment of highest tension and greatest danger even the intrepid Benkei also steps out of himself. He has been challenged to read his non-existent subscription book.

> Out of the pannier he takes a scroll and calling it the subscription book

Loudly he reads. . .

In another play, *Settai*, in which Benkei appears, though he is not its central figure, tension produces in its final episode the same distortions. The grandmother, actually the central figure, describes herself :

The mother, filled with sorrow,
Knows not the night has run its course,
Holds the goblet and serves
Her guests with wine.

Her last words, referring to her orphaned grandson, fall into the same pattern : "The aged nun clasps Tsuruwaka in her arms." This tragic youth joins in the ironic joys of hospitality. He, too, leaps out of himself :

Tsuruwaka takes her place and serves
As though before his fallen father's face.

Oblique expression and what may be described as double entendre in action spring from various forms of transmigration and disguise affecting many parts of the Noh plays. The shite, or leading actor, is, of course, commonly manifested in Part One of a play as a humble person living in the locality of the hero's principal actions and in Part Two as his own ghost. Yet disguise in the more prosaic and familiar form, so common in Latin or in Shakespearean comedy, is by no means unknown to the Noh. The chief theatrical affects in one of the most famous of the plays, *Ataka*, derive from the Hogan's disguise as a baggage-man or common porter. The mad women are susceptible to much more serious transpositions, contrived with extraordinary theatrical ingenuity. On putting on her lover's headdress and looking into a well, Izutsu fancies from the reflection that she is herself her dead lover. Similarly, Komachi at one moment loses her philosophical calm and becomes the rude, vile beggar which she appears to be ; a moment later, with astonishing abruptness, she supposes herself to be the suitor whose petitions she had coldly and cruelly rejected. These transitions are generally made as drastic as

239

possible, presumably with an awareness that the more astonishing they are, the more theatrical. Thus Tamura, who
appears to be the aged, grey-haired warrior that he really was
in his ghostly manifestation in Part Two of *Tamura*, in Part
One is manifest as a youth, perhaps also with reference to the
eternal youthfulness in his poetry and song. Such transitions
are invariably reflected in the style or language. A typical
instance is offered in a choral passage in *Sumidagawa*. The
chorus at first achieves full identification with the mother
but before we are barely aware of the change shifts to its
more usual position of full objectivity.

> O you people there,
> Dig up the sod
> So that I may once again
> Gaze on his mortal form.
> He whose life was full of promise is gone,
> And she whose life is worthless is left behind.
> Before the mother's eyes the son appears
> And fades away
> As does the phantom broom-tree.

On a lower level of poetic importance but none the less of
much consequence in the spirit and execution of these ritualistic plays are what may be termed the formulas of courtesy
used far too frequently to be enumerated. They fall most
naturally into place in the opening scenes, before the action
passes into a world too intense to exist for long on the plane
of manners and etiquette. The travellers proceed on their
ritualistic journeys. In time they encounter some "Man of
the Place, " some fisherman, husbandman or other typical
and undistinguished person. The exchange of words between
the monks and the common people is invariably courteous
and cordial. Frequently if a person is summoned or confronted with a request, he at first declines with the excuse
that his customary duties call him elsewhere. On being urged
more earnestly, he invariably grants the request. Often
when he has given all the desired information, he leaves with
the polite remark that should it be possible for him to be of
any future service, it will be agreeable to him. Such expres-

sions are repeated in identical words from play to play. They contribute much to setting the key of the plays in a decorous, aristocratic, grave and gracious vein. The plays that begin with grace end with passion that is still controlled. Shakespeare observed that actors should always be graceful and never yield to mere melodramatic violence or extravagance. Zeami, expressing the same thought with a more profound conviction and a more poetic language, declared that even the most tragic actors should always move as though wearing flowers in their hair. The decorous style is never forced until it becomes affected, formalistic or cold ; it remains one of the most characteristic and strongly attractive features of the Noh. Passions are the more authentic and forceful in never being torn to tatters. This tone, of course, appears no less in language and speech than in action and gestures.

Most conventions of importance known anywhere in the theatres of the world are either present in the Noh or have their equivalents in this remarkably stylized theatre. Yet in some instances a device, though known, is husbanded and used infrequently. Such is the case with off-stage voices. A particularly affective use of this contrivance occurs in *Eguchi*. The young woman who will later be revealed as a manifestation of the Lady Eguchi speaks from behind the curtain to the Monk, addressing him as "Oh! Reverend sir!" She has been evoked from her ghostly existence by the force of poetry that she had herself written long before during her earthly life. On entering, her first words, evidently abruptly spoken, are : "Oh! What prompted you to recite that poem ?" The Sanskrit dramatists employed this device not only more often but with more ingenuity. In the Noh it is used so infrequently as barely to warrant description as a convention. An audience might conceivably have experienced it as a touch of apt realism.

As final item in this exposition of Noh technique, it is noteworthy that silence no less than speech characterizes the productions. Even the musicians were allowed to pause. The silences on the stage in fact constitute an important part of the entire conception, affording an analogy to the wide, empty spaces used persistently in early Chinese and Japanese pictures. The device was pursued with much deliberation. This is unfortunately indicated slightly or not at all in most translations of the Noh issued before the Second World War. In the volumes of the Noh presented by the Japanese Classics Translation Committee the defect is as far as possible removed. References in these pages have several times been made to "dramatic paragraphs." The translators have marked with numerals these major sections into which the plays fall. The typical Noh play falls into two Parts, marked by an exodus from the stage of the chief actors and at times by the impromptu, colloquial explanation of the play's story or background by the Man of the Place, whose expository words are pure commentary. They are not given in written form. Each Part of the play itself has its sections, two or three at the least and a dozen or so at the most. No fixed verse forms are used in the least comparable to the strophes of the Greek chorus or to the romantic stanzas in which were composed the religious dramas of medieval Europe written synchronously with most of the great Noh. To the cursory reader the divisions may seem arbitrary, like divisions in a classical text, made with pedagogical intention and merely for convenience of reference. Closer inspection shows them to have aesthetic value—to use a seemingly far-fetched analogy, resembling the sections into which are divided the free verse of Walt Whitman's *Song of Myself*. Like almost all conventions of the Noh, they are both genuine and elusive. Their significance is principally for the theatrical imagination, either as guides to the producer or aids to the reader who reads, as he should, with the spirit of the theatre at heart. Pauses help to permit the profound but occasionally recondite meaning to sink more deeply into our consciousness.

From the observations on the patterns of dialogue described in this chapter some generalizations on the art emerge. The Noh drama if not actually eclectic is elaborately compounded. Almost every conceivable feature of the presentational arts is employed. Not only are poetry, acting, miming, dance, music and spectacle presented but virtually all devices and inflections known to theatrical art are used. The many forms of vocal art, as song, chant, formal and colloquial speech, verse and prose, quotation and direct utterance, are found. Much more remarkable even than the multiplicity of elements entering into the Noh play is the manner of their conjugation. And here what may without too bold a conjecture be described as the spirit of Japanese art enters the most strikingly into the picture. The distinct elements, like serpentine segments, are placed in the total design with the most extraordinary firmness while the elements themselves remain remarkably distinct. Where another culture welcomes a chemical fusion of parts, the Japanese, placing a phenomenal value on clarity of outline and form, prefers a pattern of well divided parts. If one character speaks for another, it is clear that he does so. As dancing is sharply distinguished from miming, so is verse from prose and song from speech. It is this manner of composition that above all distinguishes the formal aspects of art in Japan from those, say, in Elizabethan England, the drama for the Sanskrit or even for the Chinese stage. On the stylized stages of other lands the actor merges the elements of his art more completely than is the practice of the Japanese actor. Ultimately, form is achieved with equal success with the use of the two methods. But the methods differ widely.

A revealing analogy may even be discovered in customs of cuisine. In serving meals the Chinese conspicuously excel in dishes which combine many ingredients with a harmony at once aesthetic and gustatory, whereas in the service of Japanese meals the ingredients are the more often in separate dishes. The Japanese possess an unsurpassed facility in the various arts of inlay. In this regard few crafts are more significant than their lacquer work. Their art is remarkably self-conscious, with relatively diminished scope provided for spontaneous inspiration. Similarly, the Noh stage is laid out in patterns along which the actors move with the regularity and decorum of chessmen. This is the manner of both their speech and their action. It is a world of imagination in which form becomes formula, seen by friendly eyes as the perfection of art and by less cordial eyes as a possibly over-severe regimentation, where spirituality and vitality are sacrificed to contour and design. Whether one prefers or even relishes such art is a matter of taste and training but to fail at least to admire it would be gross insensibility, for the Noh play is incontestably one of the most meticulous achievements of the creative mind.

5 / *The Power of Symbols*

ANY DRAMA as clearly stylized and artificial as the Noh, standing at the antithesis from a representational mirror of life, must seem even at first glance symbolical. Although its narrative and its ideas may appear simple, straightforward and clear, its manner of presentation is according to our normal habits of communication indirect. The playwright and his performers present a highly contrived lens through which life may be examined with aid of an art difficult to reconstruct and to some extent difficult to grasp. Especially the observer foreign to the tradition—and this will certainly include most educated Japanese of today—must adjust his thoughts to a distinctly unusual experience. In such circumstances criticism must begin with fundamentals. This type of drama is essentially symbolic.

A symbol, as the word is broadly used, may be a term in science, in logic, in a mystical treatise, or in a poem. All language is symbolical but poetry in a particularly gratifying manner of its own. In the more explicitly literary sense of the word, symbol is employed in distinction from metaphor. A symbol is commonly thought of as a substantive, a metaphor as an adjective ; one presents an equivalent for a subject, the other, a description of one of its aspects. Although this distinction undoubtedly has use, it should not be distorted by exaggeration. All entities are defined by qualities and any part or phase of an entity is itself an entity viewed from a lesser distance. The chief distinction here lies in the superior power of the symbol to delimit or isolate an idea, the superior power of the metaphor to qualify it. The symbol is a favorable medium for a classical discourse, the metaphor for a romantic context. One belongs to the power of language to achieve organic form, the other, to achieve colour. Emotion may be a leading feature in either type of expression. The symbol is designed for repetitive use, the metaphor chiefly for its passing utility.

The complexities of figurative language are, of course, by no means confined to these two features. Plays upon words, for example, extremely common in Japanese literature, generally share in symbolic or metaphorical expression yet in themselves possess a distinct and a third quality, a peculiarity of their own. The "figures" of rhetoric, as that word was commonly employed by writers of the traditional school, were by no means all contained in the figurative aspects of language as now usually understood, signifying images, symbols, similes and metaphors. All deliberate formulas of language, all artful and conscious arrangements of words, may be constituent parts in the body of poetry. Yet accepting the universally received meaning of metaphor and the specialized meaning of symbol, it will be acknowledged that these figures are among the most conspicuous features of the poetic style, conferring on it a large part of its vitality.

That metaphor is strictly a language-form and the symbol even in its most specialized meaning a term applicable to all the arts is of special importance in a consideration of the Noh. This venerable form of Japanese dramatic poetry exists as an art combining the heard and the seen with an expressive symbolism through music and a spectacle rich in all manner of significant visual images. Its symbolism also has close affinity with that of painting, sculpture, architecture and the decorative arts. These are facts of much importance. A poem especially remarkable for its metaphors, as *Hamlet*, has far less share in the domain of symbolism than one having more affinity with the fine arts, as *The Divine Comedy*. Shakespeare, living in the England of the sixteenth century, flourished in a land and a times unexcelled in the arts of speech and somewhat deficient in the fine arts. As an Italian of the thirteenth century, Dante worked in a language that as yet had no acknowledged prestige as an art-medium but in a culture scarcely surpassed in dynamic expressions in sculpture, architecture, painting and decoration. Both Shakespeare and Dante are more palpably artificial though in the opinion of the present writer not on that account better artists than such a poet as Chaucer; in the present context it is worth noting that Chaucer possesses neither the metaphorical richness of Shakespeare nor the symbolical richness of Dante. England of Chaucer's century was far less dynamic in language than Shakespeare's England or in art than Dante's Italy. Possessing less sensational powers in these respects, Chaucer is not necessarily in the end less moving or even less artful. It is only clear that he is less the virtuoso.

Japanese culture of the creative period of the Noh more nearly resembled Dante's culture than Shakespeare's or Chaucer's. Its literary language was far less metaphorical than Shakespeare's and much more ingenious than Chaucer's. Some metaphor naturally appears in it and at times it must be confessed that the dividing line between metaphor and symbol is less than wholly clear. Nevertheless its imaginative force springs far more from its use of symbol than of the less sculpturesque figure of speech.

A symbol readily becomes a convention, belonging in this case not only to one work but to many. True, metaphors and similes are known to be unimaginatively reiterated until they become clichés. That cheeks resemble roses and lilies is, for example, a conventional and shallow metaphor in Renaissance verse. An outstanding quality of the truly live metaphor is its freshness and informality; it is less likely than the symbol to be repeated. It finds itself at home in the lush garden of a young culture and an expanding society; the symbol flourishes best when removed from the high winds of change, firmly established in the quieter walled-in enclosure of a static society. The spiritual revolution experienced in the century of Rabelais and Shakespeare provided an ideal climate for metaphor, which is the efflorescence of language; the closed society, as in the Christian Middle Ages or the same period in isolated Japan, favored the development of the symbol. These conditions have validity for the most elementary appraisal of the poetry of the Noh. Its images tend to the generality of the symbol and as a rule avoid the specific reference of the metaphor. Its dramatic language assumes a garment of ritual.

The treatment of symbols will be fresh in each major work yet the basic form of the images will be pre-established in the social mind. The symbols are neither those of science nor philosophy. They are close to religion yet not to a scholastic theology. Moving and sincere as their propaganda for Buddhism proves to be, they are not doctrinaire. There are few allegories in the Noh. Much of their beauty lies in their power to convey the vital spirit of religion without the intrusion of the harsh and hardening technicalities of dogma. Although it would obviously be absurd to call *The Divine Comedy* academic (one is not so sure of the *De Monarchia*), Dante's scholastic poem is clearly more intellectual than any Asian drama except the debased allegories of the latest period of the Sanskrit. Whatever symbols are found in the Noh—and they are legion—are pure poetry.

Although the Noh, unlike *The Divine Comedy*, is by no means scholastic, it is, like Dante's poem, indisputably close to the arts that lie outside the bounds of pure literature but adjacent to it. Its actors are statuesque, their priestly robes decorative or pictorial. Its profuse nature imagery is not employed, as imagery in Shakespeare, to express the passing moods or "humours" of the characters but to express their organic relation to eternal forces in the universe. The sky, the mountains and the sea exhibit the conflicts of the *yang* and *yin*, as do the least motions within the human mind. The images of nature witness a universal condition : no dry schematized plan, but an eternally live conflict. The dragons of cloud and wave are also the forces at war for domination of man's heart. The sensuous world does not, as in metaphor, merely resemble man's heart. The two are understood as being in a profound and poetic sense one. This climate of thought makes the nature poetry of Asia and the great painting of classical China and Japan what they essentially are. When this is not grasped, the poetic meaning of the Noh itself inevitably slips through the fingers.

A poetic symbol always shares at least something with metaphor in that it connotes a resemblance. It is not a mere sign, in an arbitrary shorthand, by which thought is efficiently communicated in a short-cut, as when the correct button is pressed on an IBM machine. It establishes likenesses or kinships. It is not an act of convenience but a victory for the imagination ; not merely physical but an act of love.

Viewed in this light, it will be seen that the basic form of the Noh play rests on symbolism, which is also analogy. There are as a rule two Parts, Part Two containing a primary manifestation of the hero or heroine, Part One containing what may be regarded as a symbol for this dominant figure. Of course, since in the mystical systems of Asia all physical creatures and their mental images are manifestations of spiritual realities, there is no one true, basic manifestation ; the essential can never be manifest, art providing only the closest approximations. The projection of the shite in Part One is, then, broadly speaking, a symbol for the shite in Part Two. Such a likeness is not properly verbal and hence not metaphorical. It betrays the depth to which a symbolic habit of thought sustains the entire fabric of the Noh.

The modern world has all but forgotten one of the greatest sources for dramatic affects that the world has known : the god in disguise. Although no type of drama exploits this conception as persistently as the Noh, it must assist the student of the Noh to recall how widely it has appeared both in literature of an essentially dramatic quality and in the actual theatre. Small sympathy as Jewish thought has with this conception, it will be recalled that Jehovah frequently appeared in disguise to the patriarchs, though becoming more wary of such manifestation as time advanced. It is often said that a god must be seen in disguise ; to look on his, true face would be a consuming fire. Jesus found small use for disguise, for his manhood itself was a mask to divinity, but immediately on his resurrection conditions totally changed. He appeared to Mary Magdalene as a gardener and to his disciples as a stranger. The Trinity itself looks suspiciously like three disguises for One God. And the pagan gods are in these respects obviously still more mercurial. Pallas appears in many forms to Ulysses, the goddess of wisdom being a genius of dark corners. Hermes in disguise guides Priam to the tent of Achilles. Euripides depicts Dionysus in one of his many disguises or, if one prefers, manifestations. Ovid's most celebrated poem treats the disguises of the gods as one of its chief themes. "Baucis and Philemon" is an analogue to

Takasago. The Scandinavian gods, with Woton as chief, were equally found of masking. Most Hindu gods are manifestations of other gods standing behind them. Hindu mythology is a tree hung with masks. Even the heroes, as Rama, are incarnations of gods. In the oldest Sanskrit plays the most powerful scenes depict gods disguised. Krishna, for example, appears as an ambassador in *Broken Thighs*, and Indra in the still finer play, *Karna's Task*, as a brahmana. The Tibetan and Tamil dramas are heavily stocked with gods in disguise. Their final scenes are unmaskings. One of the greatest contributions of religion to imaginative literature and poetic drama is the conception of the disguised god. The Noh itself supplies the most persistent evidence for this contention.

It is well to ask in what sense the faithful lovers and the two deities in *Takasago* are related to the two trees figuring so conspicuously in the mythology of the play ? The trees are certainly symbolical of the two lovers and the two gods yet they are also something more. No simile is used to tell us that the persons are merely "like" the trees or the trees "like" the people. The monk observes the trees and the people at the same time. We should not be oversimplifying too grossly to regard the two old people as a higher manifestation of the basic conceptions represented by the trees, as the deity of Sumiyoshi is a higher manifestation than the Old Man appearing as his symbol in Part One. In the transmigrations whose eternal movements comprise the universe, a single soul may be imagined as passing through thousands of such manifestations.

Behind all the images lies a complex and primitive world of animistic thought. One and the same invisible spirit becomes manifest in the old man, and the Deity of the Shrine. Properly to grasp the play's unity of form, its integrity and its forceful meaning, one must perceive that a single spirit moves through tree, man and god, more nobly manifest as god and hence appearing in the play's calculated climax in a form endowed with superior force and dignity. Yet, ideally speaking, he is always one. This is not the cloudy pantheism of Wordsworth's cosmic vision ; it is the primitive belief that all forms in nature and even in art are instinct with life as man is instinct with life and that the spirit may enter into an infinite number of bodily forms, even appearing simultaneously in several forms. How can man be so stupid, the Calvinist asked, as to believe that on creating a graven image he has made a god, a being that lives as he, the creator, lives? But to a primitive, as to a Pirandello, it is clear that man's creations may be even more alive than he. All things, say the Buddhists, fade; but they also observe that the pine-tree or the image carved from it may long outlast the man who sleeps within the shadow of the pine and that the image carved from it may long outlast the worshipper at the shrine. Existence signifies life. What is not alive is in the religious sense non-existent. Existence implies relation, since, according to the mystical belief, nothing absolute can be comprehended; we arrive at knowledge by threading a way through a network of symbolical or metaphorical relationships, each manifestation standing in relation to what goes before and after. The structure of the Noh play rests on this doctrine of symbolism. The word symbol derives, of course, from the same root giving us "similarity." The Noh playwright is devoted to a study of similarities.

This belief in the reality overshadowing the manifestations is poignantly expressed in *Shunkan*. In this play three exiles set up home-made shrines to contain the gods whom they cannot worship in their rightful homes; yet the gods are truly present even in their humble shrines and, after all, the priestly mind realizes that all shrines are symbolic of the invisible.

> While in Miyako we still lived,
> We vowed to make a pilgrimage
> Three and thirty times to Kumano's holy shrines.
> Before we had fulfilled our vow,
> This banishment befell us
> And our vow was unfulfilled.
> Now we have asked the gods of Kumano
> To deign to dwell upon this isle.
> We have set up images
> Of the nine and ninety shrines
> Between Miyako and the Mountains Three . . .
> Though distant from the hills of Kumano,
> Our shrines are sacred to their gods.
> Our hempen garments

Old and soiled, must serve
As pilgrims holy robes ;
White sands in place of rice we throw
And so dispel all evil ;
Instead of sacred stuffs
We take the snowy flowers of *hamayu.*

The speakers discourse of symbols of symbols, in all of which power resides.

An exceptionally clear instance of the symbolic method in the Noh occurs in *Funa-Benkei.* Here the exiles on taking to their boats encounter a storm, raging with utmost fury of wind and wave. At an earlier period in their lives the exiles had overcome and drowned their enemies in a sea-battle. Now they recognize in the waves the ghosts of those whom they have so ruthlessly killed returning to work vengeance upon them. The waves and the warriors become one. The same magic spell calms the seas and allays the vengeful ghosts. "To take up arms against a sea of troubles" is metaphorical expression. To image Benkei and his companions struggling against the waves and their ghostly foes is to inhabit a world whose imagery passes beyond metaphor (though through it) into symbolism. The latter is the chief highway of the Noh.

A clear view of the matter must shun a doctrinaire or an excessively rigorous one. Metaphor and the spirit of metaphor are, of course, present in the Noh. Thus the chorus in *Matsukaze*, speaking for the heroine and her sisterly companion, observes :

Yet is our destiny like a stagnant pool
Left on the low-tide beach . . .
We are unwonted weeds
Cast on shore by the fisherman.

This type of verbal ornament that passes as rapidly as the sounds of the voice pass is not on the whole typical of the Noh, whose images are as a rule built on a more clearly structural plan. So even in this scene, the two women are in fact "Women of the Place," or the spirits of the shore, bearing a symbolical relation to the entire scene. The Noh poet does not affect the typical Shakespearean metaphor. Still less does he affect that most logical and self-conscious rhetorical development of the incidental image, the extended Homeric simile. The Noh style, already packed, would possibly have been overcrowded had it added to its gift for symbol the gift for profuse metaphor. The austere Noh is imaginative enough without the addition of baroque luxuriance. The Noh does not paint the lily; it suggests it.

The figurative use of names supplies one of the least advanced types of imagery in the Noh, a usage where symbolism has progressed only a short way beyond metaphor. The plays abound in such figures, which often lie quite beyond the possibility of idiomatic translation. They contain as a rule a species of pun. So in *Matsukaze* it is in time made explicit —what the hearer should, ideally speaking, have recognized from the beginning—that the heroine's name suggests 'Pine-Breeze,' and her companion's name, Murasam, 'Passing-Shower.' At the play's climax the full force of Matsukaze's name is brought home, since in her mad infatuation she mistakes a pine-tree for her dead lover. He, in fact, loved both girls. They were to him as gracious as the breeze in the pine or the light shower nourishing it. The play's action is thus contained in the kernel of the girls' names. This is not metaphor, which is legitimate decoration. It is, on the contrary, symbolism, a structural quality. Similarly structural in its affect is the extended picture of a cold season of the year, symbolical of the girls' sexual coldness.

A more forced and less poetic manifestation of the same type of name-symbolism occurs in *Miidera*. Here a dream-reader discovers good reason for dispatching the bereaved mother to Miidera. The editors of the Classical Translation Committee's version observe that the first syllable of "Miidera" is homonymous with the root of the Japanese verb meaning "to see," and that the temple is located in the province of Omi, the first syllable of this name being homonymous with the verb meaning "to meet." Consequently, the mother will at Miidera meet and see her lost child. This play upon words may, to use the Elizabethan term, be regarded as a "conceit;" it is to be noted, however, that here again the conceit is no embellishment but a necessity in the story. The play's action hangs on the word-play upon the two place-names.

Although it would be untimely here to enlarge on a subject so peculiarly a province for Japanese textual scholarship, the conspicuousness of the usage leads to additional comment. Especially in passages of secondary importance, lines that threaten to have a barren, prosaic, or matter-of-fact quality, take on poetic meaning through overtones implicit in word-play. This is the case with the place-names listed in the protracted accounts of the Waki's journey or of any other descriptions of travel. One of the more brilliant instances of this convention of travel through a picturesque forest of metaphor raised to symbolism occurs in *Yuya*. The unfortunate heroine, who longs to visit her dying mother but is instead forced to accompany her princely lover on a blossom-viewing party, passes along a road where all the place-names remind her of her distant parent. A temple located at "The Meeting of Six Ways" suggests the six regions of the after-life ; another suggests cremation ; another monument is called "The Easy Child-Birth Tower." This type of imagery was passed along by the poets of the Noh to the younger school of dramatists, where it came to enjoy an even greater vogue.

Another among the less ambitious types of symbolism intimately concerns stage-business, though it invariably leaves its imprint also upon the language. This is the use of keep-sakes, as headdresses or costumes, where the shadow that is the object recreates the image and even the presence of a character absent from the scene. A striking instance may again be drawn from *Matsukaze*. The princely lover, before his departure from Matsukaze and his own death soon thereafter, left with her as keepsakes his headdress and cloak. Madly longing for him, on putting on these keepsakes she imagines herself transformed into him. Clad in this disguise, the heroine performs her mad and harrowing dance. Such symbolic use of stage-properties, entirely typical of the Noh, possesses great dramatic power. The part symbolizes the whole. The instance just cited gives the play its climax.

The Far East in general and Japan in particular take delight in the puzzle of boxes inside boxes, the search, symbol within symbol, for the innermost box and its contents encased within layers of decorated mystery. The Noh plays well exhibit this orientation. So far as a play's action presents an advance,

it is an advance inward, not outward, an advance in penetration, not a horizontal movement in a free, open space. The
play is, accordingly, the flower, the observer, the bee intent
on making his way into its heart. One envelope is the container for another. As the play progresses, the coverings are
removed. An analogy descriptive of the aesthetics of the
Noh is the principle of construction in space employed in
paintings of the baroque school. The eye enters the picture
on a broad and relatively superficial plane. As in a baroque
stage-set, the revealed space as the eye explores the canvas
passes progressively further into the background. The picture's
essential meaning is disclosed in this background, not in the
foreground. An arch or doorway frames an inner space. In
the background occurs, perhaps, the apotheosis of a god.
The technique belongs conspicuously to Tintoretto and to
his great follower, El Greco. It belongs also to the artist who
so remarkably assimilated the meaning of the baroque style
without being overcome by its excesses, Velasquez. In the
foreground of his "Maids of Honor" is the painter's easel
itself ; in the rear, in a mirror, are reflected images of the
king and queen. Likewise in his "Tapestry Weavers," the
labors of the factory occupy the foreground, the finished
masterpiece shines in a lighted alcove in the extreme rear.
The eye moves slowly to this culminating point of attraction.

The Noh are short plays with a severely delimited content
to which the dramatist, nevertheless, brings great scope.
The importance of the climax is immeasurably enhanced by
planes of allusion that lie far outside the restricted area of
ultimate attention. By this means the largeness of the conception is established even within a small frame. Hero or
heroine of the Noh is an Atlas on whom the world is placed.
The playwright must first construct this world before balancing
it on the predestined shoulders. The process becomes essentially
symbolical if, as seems reasonable, analogues may be considered
symbols. These analogues fall, roughly speaking, into two
categories, though to distinguish them drastically would
argue a misconception. They may be called the historical
and the literary. Much the same impulse inspires each. In
one instance no text is quoted and no specific source insisted
upon. We merely learn that on another occasion than the

play's main action—as doubtless on many occasions—the essential features of the present acute dramatic situation have manifested themselves. By this means the play's action is seen in a much larger context than could have otherwise been the case. By inference, too, the audience itself is suggested as the scene in whose hearts, properly speaking, the imagined action occurs. In a religious world of interminable rotation nothing occurs for the first time. The playwrights, like the great mystics, delight in the image of the ceaselessly revolving wheel. Their ideas are disclosed through repetitions whose affect is to remove the tyranny of time. It is the discipline of the enlightened to realize that whatever is painful or enjoyable is in its essence transitory, since it has been manifest countless times before and will be so as many times in the future. The poet's originality lies in the depth to which he can penetrate the mystery of universality which teaches that inasmuch as all things are eternal, the unique or original exists only as an illusion in the world of art. Each incident in reality is endlessly multiplied.

More convincing emotionally and imaginatively than the evidence of history is the testimony of poetry. Hence the Noh play elevates quotation to a ritual. This manner of composition was also part of the ritual of the literary art throughout the Far East. Actual quotation was employed the most assiduously by poets in China and Japan, where education itself was largely a matter of memory. The technique of the Noh masters was borrowed directly from the Chinese though developed with nuances peculiar to the Japanese stage. Though in Sanskrit literature in general the formula is even more studiously employed and sacred texts freely quoted, the usage in Sanskrit drama does not favor the degree of direct verbal quotation cultivated in the Noh. It may be useful to recall here that European poetry of the neo-classical period entertained a somewhat similar practice ; the "learned poet" was esteemed most highly who could employ both patent quotation and silent theft with the most frequency. At least in pedantic circles, the more he quoted or paraphrased, the better, whether from the bible or from Virgil. The result was, naturally, a pastiche, clever work wanting in vigor of creative imagination. When carried by motives of literary vanity to excess, such a style indicates degeneracy. Proceeding from different motives from those of the Eastern poets, it leads to far different results. In the one case virtuosity is the primary concern ; in the other, a philosophical and an imaginative incentive becomes dominant. One exploits a verbal surface, the other postulates an idealized conception of man's universe. One ends in parody or travesty, the other in heroic verse drama. The Noh drama never declined into a rococo period. There is no Noh equivalent to *The Rape of the Lock*.

Sometimes the quotation is deliberately altered to fit its new context. Especially where such is the case, the audience is expected to recognize both the original and its amendment. Whatever may have been the roots of the Noh play in popular folk entertainment or in ritual, by the time it became, with Zeami, a thoroughly mature literary form, it was clearly addressed to a specially qualified and learned audience. It is frequently observed today that reading of a Noh play calls for extensive annotation ; especially where quotation from the classics is used, some editorial notes are distinctly desirable. Without such aid, most readers must remain deaf to overtones of considerable importance. Yet even to its first audiences, Noh plays cannot be held as learned a poetry as *The Divine Comedy*, nor so crammed with allusion as *The Waste Land*, and even today the Noh style seems immeasurably less esoteric than typical work of Ezra Pound or James Joyce. Allusions are not excessively numerous nor are they either meaningless or obstructive to readers largely uniformed. The place-names, so conspicuous in the descriptions of travel, are doubtless the more meaningful to persons well acquainted with Japanese culture and geography yet have some worth to almost anyone of reasonably warm and supple imagination. Most of the theology enters the plays on a distinctly elementary level. A few texts, as the *Lotus Sutra*, are favorites, with a few passages quoted in play after play. Just as in the singularly impersonal style of Noh poetry it often makes small difference who is speaking, for all is ultimately centered in the shite, it makes little difference what poet is quoted, whether Japanese or Chinese, more ancient or more modern. Sometimes the name of the poet quoted is actually given in the text ; more often not. Either way makes small difference. Although on certain occasions it is helpful to know the entire myth or the entire chapter in Japanese history on which a play is based, these occasions are surprisingly few. William Butler Yeats, for example, in such a play as *The Death of Cuchulain*, with its profuse allusions to Celtic lore, makes far more demands on the erudition of his reader or audience than do the Noh poets. With the possible exception of the place-names, remarkably few direct allusions occur. Quotations are worked with the utmost smoothness into the text. We are not overburdened with an immense pantheon, as in Bhavabhuti's *Rama's History ;* Milton is considerably more recondite than Zeami. So far as the English reader is concerned, the annotated versions in the volumes by the Classical Translation Committee argue strongly in behalf of the reader's confidence. One can hardly avoid the suspicion that the first European scholars at work on the Noh found their meaning hard to unkernel partly because they were themselves clearing ground in the strenuous spirit of pioneers. The radically new poetic and dramatic form, the archaic language itself, and the portentous, almost inhuman-looking figures on the stage promoted some unfounded fears. Of course to the Japanese the stage figures can never have seemed quite as strange as to the Westerners and the same holds true for the figures of speech. It can never be too strongly urged that the Noh plays are more remarkable for their simplicity than for their complexity. Each focuses in the end upon a comparatively simple emotion, clarified alike by music, dance and words.

The three features of the imagery just outlined, the common symbol from nature, the historical analogy, and the literary analogy, may be examined further for the great variety of their inflections.

Teaching, as they do, the transiency of life, the Noh plays concentrate attention on the melancholy fading of autumn and on the still more poignant falling of the spring blossoms. To establish and sustain this sufficiently accessible emotion, almost innumerable poets are quoted, a large proportion being Chinese. Quotation and context alike have so clear a meaning that no affectation of learning intrudes. The poet is cited not so much to give venerable and classical authority to the familiar thought, as Christian churchmen might quote the bible or the Church Fathers in support of a belligerent argument, as to give an additional poetic richness and dimension. In a conservative society truth, even if a truth of the heart, is a line stretched between past and present. By virtue of quotation the force rather than the fact is asserted. Need for clarification does not at any time become an issue. So many are these poignant images drawn from the seasons that quotation here would be complete redundance.

Again and again mutability is further symbolized by the wind, with a meaning impossible to miss. To the Japanese poet the movement of the moon, on the contrary, means less than the sheer fact of the moon. The moon as a rule becomes symbol of constancy, much as the stars conventionally hold this value for Westerners. The ability of the human being to participate in the universal reality symbolized by the moon is represented by the many Noh images of the reflection of the moon in water. Two women drudging at their toil on a beach capture the moon in the troubled water of their pails, an act symbolizing their common relation to eternity.

Often Noh images have great subtlety yet are at the same time forceful and clear. These are typical achievements of the Noh, as they are of all major poetry. The dramatists succeed by avoiding insistence. An instance considered in these pages from more angles than one occurs in *Sumidagawa*, a play on a mad mother in search of her lost son. The boy came from Miyako. He was stolen by kidnappers but fell ill and died in the presence of kindly strangers. As he is about to die, lonely and homesick, he begs that he be buried beside the road to Miyako, where shadows of travellers coming from his home city may fall with some measure of consolation upon his grave. The grave is the site of the play's final scene. A more delicate or moving image would be hard to imagine.

The reality of the poetic experience ever depends on a seemingly frail meshwork creating in fact a form of high stability. That there is a fragrance in good deeds is a biblical commonplace which in turn gives significance to the ritualistic use of incense. The connection here between the abstract and the sensuous remains as a prose statement unconvincing and banal. When, however, the poet utilizes it with all the delicacy of his art, the commonplace is transfigured ; the water of prose becoming the wine of art. This metempsychosis occurs in *Yoroboshi*, one of the most sensitive and mysteriously lovely of Noh plays. The play's religious thought centers on the worship of Kwannon, beneficent god of mercy. Charity performed in his name is expressed as an act of beauty, comparable to the action by which the cherry-tree puts forth its blossoms. This is symbol, not metaphor, and a symbolism whose elegance and charm no mere description can capture. The passage is too extended for quotation ; in fact, it encompasses the entire play. Magical as the art may be, its beauty is instantly compelling. Not in a spirit of explication but merely of commentary, it should be recalled that the shite of this play is a blind boy whose sensations of touch, hearing, and smell are unusually acute. The audience has been drawn into full participation with the child's experience. His condition is, I believe, much more intimately, tenderly, and poignantly imagined than that of Milton's Samson. The force of the entire play is focused upon such sensations. Its climax, however, is not an episode dealing with smell but with the more dramatically viable sensation of touch. The blind boy stumbles into his father's arms. The play's every image supports its every other image. A profound simplicity provides the base for its stylistic sophistication. The same type of imagery appears in *Tamura*, likewise a work dedicated to Kwannon, and in many other plays.

From Western standards it might well be supposed that the most unlikely subject for a play would be a garden. A garden as subject-matter presumably suggests to us first of all a lyric poem. But every Noh play *is* a lyric poem. *Toboku* employs the symbolism of a garden, to say the very least, in a dual capacity. That the garden's beauty is evanescent as its falling petals affords one of its meanings. The plum-tree-by-the-eaves, cherished by the poetess, is still alive long after her death, providing the symbol of her art's immortality. Her life vanished like the leaves of the tree. As the petals of the flowers were scattered over the earth, so were her flower-like poems over the whole world. Through the transitory flesh she fashioned a bridge not merely to art but to Buddhahood. The garden is, accordingly, much more than the scene of the play ; it is its essence, its fragrance, the very air the spectators breathe. The play's symbolism is a garden-maze of the highest delicacy, firmness and beauty. At the same time it manifests the peculiar perfection of style in the Noh plays and the antithetical position of this style so far as dramatic poetry in the West is concerned.

Networks of symbolism, whereby different levels are established for the same image, are often less subtle or convincing than more spontaneous images yet have for Western readers the advantage of sharing in the intellectual type of imagery favored in the Middle Ages and supremely exhibited in *The Divine Comedy*. This is the method of complex allegory, the symbolism computed in compound interest, which according to scholastic theory is best exhibited when manifest on four distinct planes. In short, in the perfect scholastic allegory each image carries four distinct meanings. (The usury which the scholastics denied in economics they practiced in symbolism.) Although Japanese practice hardly favored such mathematical ingenuity, at times a multiplicity of meanings is eloquently achieved. *Takasago*, already examined in this chapter, affords a good instance. The two pines stand for two old people, man and wife ; for the gods of two bays in widely different locations ; for the arts that, like the pines, are unfading ; and for two famous anthologies of verse compiled on two distinct occasions in Japanese history, the *Manyoshu* and the *Kokinshu*. Although it might seem that the virtuosity required to keep these diverse ideas consistently suspended before the attention of audience or reader was more a contrivance than an act of powerful imagination, even the most casual consideration of the play reveals how artfully and seemingly with ease this is accomplished. The play in question is "a god play," peculiarly devoid of narrative line, melodramatic climax, or struggle between opposites. It is serenely itself. Any sense of monotony is removed for the thoughtful observer by the intricacy with which its essential fibres are interwoven. A more essentially symbolical work can scarcely be discovered.

In virtually all the Noh's symbolism considered in this chapter an expansion of imaginative dimension proves the predominating feature. This is most vividly exhibited in the quotations from classical poets and in references to or recollections of time past. The imaginative problem, as previously stated, is that the poetry shall demonstrate that no man at any time stands alone. The fathers of poetry have described man's condition, no matter what this may be. Someone before us has always stood where we stand. Upon this belief rest the wisdom of the Eastern sages and their faith in the unfading relevance of art.

When, in *Kinuta*, the wife whose husband has long been absent devises her mad plan of making of the nocturnal noise of her servants and herself beating cloth a message to reach his ears, she recalls a wife long ago in China who achieved this airy telegraph. That in the end the older wife won her husband back and the woman in the play gains no such good fortune in no way invalidates the image. In fact, the variant has in itself a hook of poignancy fastening the imagination still more tightly.

In *Miidera*, it will be recalled, a mad mother, bereft of her child, is suddenly and miraculously lifted out of herself by the splendor of the full autumn moon. As the calm permeates her entire being, uplifting her heart and purifying her distraught soul, she abruptly recalls that on similar occasions sages had written poems in praise of the moon, poems that she and the chorus quote copiously. At last she recalls, too, that a devotee, intoxicated by the beauty of moonlight, seized and madly tolled a temple bell. She does the same, thus at last dramatizing her revelation. The bell becomes symbol of her redemption. But the thought came to her as she recalled a person who long before had traversed the same path. The moonlit valley was to her far more than her senses or her unaided mind apprehended at the moment. It led her to a culmination of the experiences of a myriad of the saved who had long preceded her. Her moment of ecstasy was the topmost blossom on a tree of the most venerable age, its roots in the ultimate past. She recovered her lost son only after recovering the wisdom of poets and sages who long before either were born had from the terraces of temples contemplated the moon. Her experience was entirely analogous with theirs. To borrow the Japanese image previously mentioned, holding her bucket steadily in hand, she captured the perfect image of the moon which they, too, had adored. A symbol becomes a thread on which to hang a universe.

Again, in *Sumidagawa*, throughout the greater part of the play runs the image of "the Miyako-bird." A bird's name suggests to the mother the name of the town from which she and her son have come. Flying in a strange region, the birds come to her as a good augury. In the play's last scene they are imagined as uttering a Buddhistic cry, which first turns the tide of fortune favorably toward the ghostly meeting of mother and son. The bird is symbol of home and hence of reunion. But the thought comes to the mother as she recalls a passage by the celebrated poet, Narihira, to whom the bird also gave promise of the recovery of a beloved one :

Ferryman. 'Twas thoughtless of me,
　　　　　 Instead of Miyako-bird,
Mother.　 To call it sea-gull.
Ferryman. So Narihira long ago
Mother.　 Asked, "Is she still alive ?"
Ferryman. Remembering his lady in Miyako.

A typical image of much psychological veracity and poetic force occurs in the famous play, *Aoi-No-Ue*. Here in her madness the jealous heroine, as ghost, confuses the remembered incident of her rude assault upon the chariot of her rival in love with the vehicle standing outside the burning house in the famous parable in the *Lotus Sutra* expounding the perishable world of mortality, ever in flames, while the chariot of the law waits at the gate to rescue the enlightened. Rokujo comes as a spirit possessed by a fiend to work her vengeance on Lady Aoi. In her madness she confuses her fury in the mortal world that is past with her agony in the immortal world that is present. This symbol, with its affect of montage, is startlingly convincing, with the frenzied quality of a nightmare.

The Noh's basic structure, as so often described in these pages, is a double exposure. This commonly takes the form of the present related to the past or of the Japanese world to what is acknowledged as the more venerable and classical world of China. Clearly, a symbolical manner of thinking is implicit in this dualism. It accounts for much of the great power and beauty in the poetry of the Noh, which happily establishes an imagery stationed safely between extremes of the pedantic allegories of our own Middle Ages and the flaccid improvisations of Western nineteenth-century romantic and sentimental verse. In the West only the great baroque poets hold firm aesthetic grasp over the treacherous and tempestuous world of metaphor. In Western terms, poetry in the Middle Ages was too often chained in the pedantries of metallic allegory, in the Romantic Age, lost in a jungle of watery metaphor. Shakespeare's baroque extravagance could be enjoyed but not imitated. Japanese poetry of the Noh plays, viewed in terms of its symbolism, is controlled without pedantry and forceful without anarchy. Its symbolism is a high-point in the architecture of both dramatic and lyric form.

6 / *Vespers of the Moon*

SIZABLE OBJECTS often have small but useful handles. The handle in itself no doubt appears diminutive yet enables us to manipulate the entire object and even to bring it to its full utility. One such handle to that singularly difficult theatrical form, the Japanese Noh Play, is provided by its extensive use of the image of the moon. This image is often largely, though never wholly, descriptive and at times becomes eminently symbolical. In other words, it may be of relatively secondary or of primary importance. When seriously considered, this convention illuminates not only the greater part of the Noh drama itself but much of the aesthetics not only of Japan but of the Far East as a whole. It further aids the elucidation of the Noh by a fruitful and an almost inevitable analogy with painting. The bearing upon sculpture, architecture and the other arts is real though of considerably less interest or importance.

The Noh Plays as a form are drenched in moonlight. Herein lies a part of their mystery, of their peculiar type of beauty and their fragrance as art. In the moon and its light the dramatists clearly found a vehicle to express much in life and thought which they treasured most. The key word here and the most commonly found on the lips of the Japanese critics themselves is the untranslatable one, *yūgen* whose literal connotation is "obscure and dark," by which is meant, among much else, "suggested or partly-concealed beauty." English words, all in one way or another importantly relevant, are : understatement, intimation, elegance, aristocratic grace, composure, equilibrium, serenity, quietism. The conception

264

owes much to all the mystic systems of the East, notably Buddhism, Taoism, and their multifarious sects. The moon assists the contemplative mind to gain and hold its focus. Although there is no moon goddess in the East comparable to Artemis, the moon becomes in itself a symbol of the way, while around it cluster a circle of bodhisattvas, one of whom is heroine of the celebrated drama, *Hagoromo*.

It is best to begin any literary investigation with palpable facts and in as modest and unphilosophical a way as possible, reserving generalization and serious interpretation to a conclusion. For purposes of ready reference, thirty plays will be used, those selected and to some extent annotated in the three-volume work by the Classical Translation Committee. These versions, with their annotations, carry authority. Though we must walk in the moonlight, there is at least a certain degree of security here and a reasonable assurance that most, though certainly not all, varieties of the Noh come within view.

In all thirty plays the moon is specifically mentioned and more or less conspicuous in the sky. That the dramatists tend to direct or focus attention on the moon image is further indicated by the custom of having the latter, or climatic, Part of the play enacted in moonlight. The convention proves, in fact, even more restrictive than this. Seventeen of the thirty plays are divided into two Parts. In thirteen of these the first passage in Part Two specifically sets the scene with reference to the moon. In two of the remaining four the Second Part is introduced as an action occurring at night, where the moon is almost certainly to be inferred though not actually mentioned. Even though the thirteen plays in one Part perforce dispense with this precise formula, the moon in them becomes, if possible, even more prominent, especially in the closing or culminating passage. *Hagoromo*, for example, is a play about a moon spirit. Its heroine vanishes into the moonlight. *Miidera* is strictly focused upon moonlight; its heroine is moon-struck; worship of the moon affords the key to its entire dramatic action. As will presently be shown, the imagery in *Matzukaze* is most artfully centered on the moon. Generally, though not invariably, the autumn moon is preferred. The closing passage in *Sumidagawa* proves typical. It is said of the heroine : "She prays with them under the shining moon." There is a perceptible tendency in plays whose shites are feminine to be especially rich in such symbolism.

It would be a superficial though by no means negligible observation that this practice fitted the custom of introducing in Part Two a ghost, a god, or a supernatural revelation. In Japan, no less than elsewhere, a ghost or spirit walks most comfortably at night and more particularly by moonlight. A Halloween moon is perhaps best of all. A further explanation may be that being as a rule benign the ghost is not to be presented as a spirit of total darkness. He—or she—is merely a noble being comfortably removed from the garish light of day.

There is special occasion for calling critical attention to these facts. On the actual stage no symbol for the moon and no artificial lighting is employed. Color, of course, is muted by moonlight and no artificial and sensational lighting is employed. "This lantern doth the hornéd moon present," is the pedestrian image used by the mechanicals in *A Midsummer-Night's Dream*. No such prosaic pseudo-naturalism occurs in the highly poetic, aristocratic and essentially mental drama of the Noh. Even on reading, the Noh text, here, as always, tends to be elusive. Especially in view of the sparsity of discussion of this subject, it may safely be held that some excellent scholars of the Noh literature have to a large extent overlooked or at least underestimated the prevalence and importance of the moon symbol. Although the reader does not at first find it forced upon his attention, the more he ponders and meditates on the texts, the more revealing and vital a feature this is shown to be.

The subject, of course, must be seen in proportion. In some extremely fine and impressive plays this lyric imagery proves distinctly secondary. Among these are, for example, *Ataka, Shunkan*, and *Kagekiyo*, all with men as their central figures. *Sotoba-Komachi* at least ends with a nocturnal scene. Oddly enough, moonlight is most conspicuous in the three One-Part plays just cited, above all, in *Miidera*. Yet the formula for the Two-Part play lent itself ideally to the convention. In several of the plays Part One ends with a sunset or a moonrise. Part Two is conceived as the Waki's dream. The monk dreams the action by night and dreams that it is night and the night's magic is ruled by the moon. Or if he does not actually dream, he spends the night under the moon in prayer for the hero's soul. Presumably we should assume a full moon in all these plays. As previously noted, in only two of the thirty works is there no specific evidence of a nighttime action.

The most casual inspection of the Noh must warn the reader resolutely to resist whatever temptation he may have to impose Western moon-symbolism on the Japanese poet-playwrights, for it should be recalled that the moon-symbolism of the West differs radically from that of the Far East. Thus the moon has to volatile Western poets, because of its alteration from night to night, become symbol of inconsistency or change. The phases of the moon, for example, fascinated the restless William Butler Yeats. To the East, on the contrary, it is a traditional symbol for constancy. Also, in the West the moon is likely to be regarded as cold. Not so in the East, as *Hagoromo* may suggest. Again, the moon-goddess of the Greeks is not only cold but virginal, in contrast to the amorous Sun God, Apollo. No such view of the moon exists in the Far East. Although the moon as a sex symbol is well known in the West, in the Orient the moon was visited and captured many centuries ago by mystic Buddhism. In Western mythology the moon almost ceases to be the moon. Thus Artemis is an eminently feminine deity who merely operates the moon, which in itself constitutes merely her chariot. Such a conception is highly anthropomorphic. In Japan, on the contrary, the moon is less important than the moonlight, less an object in itself than is the peaceful radiance that it pours over a wide and romantic landscape, in which water and reflections in water generally prove conspicuous. Thus the moon becomes an index for the totality of nature and so for contemplative immersion in the entire natural scene. Its dry battery supplies the emotional charge linking man with the universe. The moon, if a god at all, is a bodhisattva, a serene and heavenly spirit at once free from attachment and by the very virtue of this freedom, or detachment from a stem, a lotus floating in heaven. All irksome details of nature blotted out, it achieves union with the all. Especially appealing is the ease and grace with which the dramatist's mind passes from the plain, descriptive image to a profoundly natural though philosophical symbol. The primary cause for this ease will be examined at the conclusion of this chapter.

The moon-struck stage of the Noh is, perhaps, most clearly exemplified in *Miidera*, one of the so-called "mad-women plays." A mother is driven insane by the loss of her son, kidnapped by bandits. He in turn has become a young assistant in a far-away monastery at Miidera. An interpreter of dreams informs the mother that she has had a prophetic vision foretelling her recovery of her child if she visits the monastery. This she does; yet immediately before recovering the boy she regains her own sanity through a traumatic experience, actually forgetting him and casting her entire heart and soul on the beauty of the full harvest moon. Signifying her ecstasy, she rashly tolls the famous monastery bell. Her religious experience cures her of her mad fixation; her union with the supernatural delivers her from her natural but yet mad attachment to the world of normality. Her action and her words and especially her copious quotations from the classical poets confirm the moon's healing power. This is, in fact, symbol of the serenity and vision which to Eastern thinking signify enlightenment. This conception of the moon becomes the crux of the entire play.

The organic complex of imagery of which *Hagoromo* is comprised is palpably focused on the moon cult. Here the heroine is herself one of the thirty spirits attendant on the moon, representing in turn its monthly phases. The spirits are literally dancers. Each is designated as a bodhisattva. The play is brilliantly musical and choreographic, a hymn—resembling at least in these respects a Pindaric ode—danced as a ritual in the moon's honor. As the Maiden sings :

Thee do I adore,
O Prince of the Moon,
Thine be glory and praise,
O Bodhisattva Seishi.

The editors of the Classical Noh Play Translations observe : "Seishi is a major bodhisattva, who together with Kwannon is a satellite in the trio of the Buddha Amida in Western

Paradise. . . . The Prince of the Moon is an incarnation of Seishi."
The play is thus in celebration of the fully achieved serenity
and detachment of the transcendent spirit, whose icon is
the moon.

> In many dances of the East,
> The beauteous Maiden of the Moon,
> In bright beams of the Perfect Truth,
> Through the mid-September night
> Upon the land of mortals showers
> The glories of the wondrous land.

More personal but no less artistically perfect is the moon-
image pervading that exquisite play, *Matsukaze.* Here the
statement is considerably less perspicuous and might in a
superficial glance at the work even be overlooked altogether.
Profound symbols must not be mistaken for casual metaphors.
The two women, the Shite and her friend, upon whom the
work is focused, repeatedly turn to the moon-image. They
observe that in each of their pails carried in their salt-making
the moon's sphere is reflected. Later on they sing in a culminating duet:

> Thus to the company of this noble lord
> Who ever stood exalted like the moon
> The Suma humble maidens grew attached.

No glancing phrase has ever had a more primary or significant
meaning. The noble prince, whom the two girls loved, was
in truth an incarnation of the ideal realization of "Truth" so
commonly symbolized by the moon.

The religious and metaphysical aspect of the symbol is
clarified and conjugated through many plays. So in *Kinuta*
we read of "the autumn moon of truth." This, as the translators beautifully rendered the Japanese, is "the unprejudiced
moon." Its all-embracing significance appears in the image
of "the moon imaged in a dewdrop." In that much
agitated play, *Yamamba,* there is a similar reading of the
sky:

269

> Where like the light of Truth
> The moon sheds its beams.

In *Sumidagawa* it is said :

> The clouds of mutability
> O'ercast the shining moon
> That should light up the endless
> Night of life and death.

A note by the editors of the English versions of the plays already referred to remarks: "The full moon is likened to Sakyamuni, who dispels the darkness of ignorance and enlightens mortal minds."

It is to be noted that deities are frequently compared to the moon. Thus in *Tamura*, Kwannon is "like the autumn moon." In *Toboku* we read :

> The moon, mirrored in the waters of the pond,
> Images the Buddha.

An enlightened hero is also likely to be so associated. Thus Kagekiyo "shone like the moon." It should be noted that the moon's cool reflection is clearer in its outline than the sun's. The moon is associated also with temples. So the temple in *Tamura* is blessed with "moon-blanched portals." In *Izutsu* it is said : "Above the temple hangs the moon." It leads the way to the ultimately serene. In *Kiyotsune* it is declared :

> The moon descends the western sky.
> I'll follow him to the Western Paradise.

This association with religion and contemplation is further intimated in such a phrase as "A monk knocks at the moon-light gate" (*Toboku*). The moon is, of course, indicative of peace of mind. Again, in *Tamura* we hear that "The moon takes her unfaltering way." And the poet in *Tamanoi* celebrates "beauty clear as the moon in a cloudless sky."

The autumn moon, as we have seen, is by far the most

favored. This appears to be because the sentiment of autumn touches even the moon itself with a type of melancholy or sadness which Japanese thinking finds not only rich in pathos but in the quiet pathos that connotes also elegance. Here above all is *yūgen*, the tone marking the ideal goal of art in general and of the Noh in particular, since drama enjoys an almost unique advantage in cultivation of all sentiment, mood, and emotion.

Of course in many pages of the literature of the Noh the highest degree of symbolic meaning, as already observed, is by no means consistently maintained and yet it can confidently be said that symbolism is never wholly out of sight. Here there are differences in both episodes and characters. A monk or a hero is more likely to employ the image seriously than is a commonplace character—though ideally speaking there should be no commonplace person in the audience. Dramatic speakers who are neither theological nor for the time being converted to metaphysics are likely to regard the heavens more sensuously. In *Eguchi*, for example, a group of courtesans sails in a pleasure-barge on a "moon-viewing party." The heroine is herself one of the cult of the moon and an inspired poetess. Yet the moon of the episode in question is more erotic and epicurean than philosophical or mystical. The courtesans, for the most part passing unenlightened days in the sensuous world, go blithely on their pleasure-trip: "A pleasure boat . . . appeared floating in the moonlight." In this spirit the girls reflect :

If the moon is an old friend,
How can one flee the world ?

Perhaps by "an old friend" the courtesans were thinking of their former lovers. But the poetess herself did flee the transitory world, inspired by the moon's all-powerful spell. Only slighter spirits accept the appellation of "the fickle moon," for the sky is not marred by such heresy.

In short, no sharp distinction exists between this pleasure-loving faculty and the contemplative or the religious mind. It should be recalled that even the most thoughtful poetry of China and Japan avoids the categorical, intellectual type of symbolism and allegory found in late and decadent Sanskrit writers, in the literatures of the Near East, and throughout the European Middle Ages. Almost imperceptibly we pass in the Noh from romantic description to words of profound spiritual content. Sometimes the transition in a play tends to be between the lighter touch of Part One and the graver meaning or revelation of Part Two. But in general the moon is clearly understood as a religious symbol superior by far to the hard counters of intellectual discourse. It signifies not a particular doctrine but a manner of envisaging life in its entirety. The moon means enlightenment itself.

In *Basho* we find that the moon both is and is not associated with learning. First we read :

As the autumn moon climbs the sky,
In the stillness of my cell
Buried in the heart of the hills
I read aloud the sacred book.

Here the monk is conscious of an isolation favorable to his contemplation but even though the moon is radiant in the sky, he perforce reads his book by lamplight. To the mystic all learning is sophistical and suspect. A little later in the play the monk has laid his book aside, as the stage-direction shows. "The Hermit rolls up his *sutra* and slips it back in his kimono." The meaning here is that the worship of the pure moon itself is far to be preferred to studies, no matter how brightly illuminated, beneath the scholar's lamp. At this point the chorus chants a philosophical poem by Po-Chü-i, adding significant reflections upon it :

"Setting the lamp behind us, we gaze up at the moon,
To enjoy the beauty of advancing night."
With obedient heart
From the master's lips
I learn the inmost meaning of the holy words.

The chief explanation for the great force of this imagery is its firm foundation upon a long and glorious tradition. The moon-cult in the Noh descends directly from the profound

thinkers and artists of China. This is a deep and clear well
from which the dramatists drew their refreshment. The
poetry of the Noh is much closer to the Chinese than is the
theatre. One recalls in much the same spirit as the Noh the
many poems, muted in tone but of great beauty, by Tu Fu
dealing philosophically with the autumn moon. More celebrated still and astonishing in its subtleties is Li Po's lyric
with its imaginary conversation between the drunken poet,
the moon, and his moonlight shadow on the water. Sung
paintings with their silken landscapes and seascapes drenched
in moonlight are too celebrated and numerous to be parti-
cularized. Historically considered, in their nocturnal and
moonlit imagery the Noh Plays, then, represent the moons
of China reflected in the Sea of Japan. But surely their reflections come but little, if at all, behind the fascination of their
inspired and luminous originals.

7 / Play into Poem: Poetry and Magic

TWO MAJOR obstacles that may to some degree be overcome stand between the Noh plays and their admirers in the twentieth century, especially those in the Western world. The first springs from the unique degree to which the Noh plays are lyrical, not as including music but as having the lyric's concentration of emotion and form, the second, from their strong preoccupation with the supernatural and, to a less degree, the particular character of this supernaturalism. The main stem of European thinking and tradition divorces the purely lyrical experience from the dramatic and has cast behind it as culturally outworn a serious regard for the supernatural and for the peculiar aesthetic and emotional coloration characterizing the world of magic. Western thought, accordingly, inclines to a skeptical or supercilious view of these qualities as exhibited in the Noh. A play, the West feels, needs a plot or at least an argument to be a play. It is assumed to unfold not as a flower but as an action. Although historical scholarship encourages the view that drama may arise from song and a view that in another age than our own man's thought was engrossed in supernaturalism, magic, and, to use the prejudicial word of the Enlightenment, superstition, mature drama appears to us to follow upon other directions. A play still deeply lyrical at its core and inspired by supernatural thinking looks in some way primitive. The West, unlike the East, flatters itself that it has graduated from the earlier stages in spiritual and aesthetic evolution. So ambitious an appraisal of culture, perhaps, hardly submits to either proof or refutation. Yet in the instance of the Noh

Plays it leads to prejudice. Be the general rule what it may, a moderate effort enables almost any sensitive and imaginative mind to find in the Noh work of much power and strong attraction.

Paradoxically, for most Westerners, at least, it is not the very real intricacy of the Noh play but its simplicity that presents the initial hindrance to a warm reception. With intricate construction and design in almost all forms of art the civilized world everywhere is acquainted. We are familiar with major art works of great subtlety. Western literature and drama abound in magnificent evocations of irony and conscious artistry, of elaborated technique and sophisticated thinking. In drama the West has developed comparatively long works with well established usages grown into conventions. Plays as a rule tell artfully contrived stories, have a multiplicity of characters and scenes, exhibit at least some of the leading qualities of fiction. Similar plays, of course, arose also in the East. The chief Sanskrit dramas are of this description. Although the practice has long been prevalent in China to produce short scenes from plays, so that a day's program will include parts of many plays, Chinese dramas themselves are as a rule long and, from European standards, rambling constructions, where the audience's attention takes in the parts as they flow past. Similarly, Chikamatsu's romantic plays in their essential qualities as a rule follow after the Chinese theatrical tradition. They offer broad panoramas, scene unfolding after scene, the audience's attention following the action as though on a boat sailing down a long, sinuously winding stream. Beside these works a Noh play is a circular pond whose full extent is taken in almost at a glance. Frequently, without realizing clearly from what source his discomfort springs, the Western reader of a Noh plays feels uneasy and dissatisfied. He is simply not accustomed to drama where so many attributes that long tradition has taught him to assume essential to the theatre are so clearly lacking. The critical problem is not whether the Noh lacks these qualities. It most certainly lacks them. Perhaps the Noh should not be termed drama but instead some eccentric conjunction of dance, song and spectacle. It will hardly be drama according to the definition formulated by Aristotle.

The question would still remain, is it art and art for the theatre? As we have already seen, the plays are without notable dramatic characterization, without plot, without an antagonist, without imitation of manners, without dramatic dialogue or conversation in the accepted meaning of the words. Lacking so much, what do they actually possess? The first answer is much and almost too much.

As Western thought has developed, the readiest defense of the Noh is that it realizes on the stage an experience in vital respects agreeing with what the West customarily regards as lyrical. Alone among theatrical forms, it combines suspense with the statuesque. Here it will be well to reiterate our definition and to forestall a possible misunderstanding. Especially in recent usage, the term "lyric theatre" or "lyrical drama" has come to mean any theatrical production in which music and singing predominate, as in opera or musical comedy. Reference to the Noh in these terms would be largely justified but comparatively unimportant. The word "lyric" is used here not in this well-known connotation but with an equally familiar though certainly more elusive meaning. The lyrical experience is the experience of lyric poetry, evoked by a poem that has at least the potentiality of being sung, a poem with extreme concentration of image and emotion, evocation of life characterized above all by its emotional and unitary nature. It may or may not be personal in the biographical sense. The description of the lyric as a personal poem, a "lyric cry," a soliloquy of the soul, belongs to romantic criticism. All agree that the ideal lyric rises warm from the heart. Whether this heart is explicitly that of a private person chanting his own confessional, giving an entry in the diary of his own emotions, or explicitly the cry of the universal heart does not apply to the definition of the lyric as such. Viewed in historical terms, the foregoing distinction lies merely between the lyric poetry of a romantic or a classical age. If the Noh plays do indeed, as here proposed, resemble the generally received conception of the lyric, it is clear that they resemble not the romantic lyric of self-expression but the classical lyric with its bolder and more overt universality. Their themes are general, not particular. Even if each play is conceived as having been originally performed for a single temple, at a single feast, the meaning is clearly conceived in the broadest possible terms. The chief Noh plays fail to bear the signatures of particular men ; they have instead the universality of the stars.

The typical Western play presents a sequence of contrasted emotions. The orthodox Noh play, like the Western lyric, voices an emotion which, regardless of its possible complexity, is sharply focused and powerfully concentrated. The emotion rises to a climax, in most instances a decisive propulsion of the hero on the way to Buddhahood. Each play is a spiritual discipline, a step towards the divine. The predominant emotion is usually itself tragic in the sense that extreme grief is expressed. A lover longs for his or her beloved, as in *Takasago* or *Izutsu* ; a parent longs for a missing child, as in *Miidera*, or a child for the parent, as in *Kagekiyo* ; a hero thirsts for fame, possibly for poetic fame, as in *Tadanori* ; or a fallen angel, as in *Hagoromo*, longs for her lost dancing-place in the skies. A single hero or heroine is presented, dominated, as in *Eguchi*, even obsessed by a single passion.

The goal of the play, after building up the image of this emotion, is to present its relief. Occasionally the emotion is gratified in earthly or human terms. In *Miidera* the mother recovers her child, though in the more representative *Sumidagawa* she does not, beholding him in that instance only as a ghost. But Miidera is purged of her madness, as are all the many mad women of the Noh stage. The essence of the action, if action it may be called, is almost invariably the freeing of the soul from its obsession with mundane reality. Only the love of the arts is commonly represented as spiritual and, in *Tadanori*, even that, when contaminated by love of fame, is presented as a blemish on the soul.

The utmost economy is further maintained by the disposition of the characters. Of the principal figures in the typical Noh play, the shite and waki, the former is the focus of attention from the dramatic point of view, the latter, usually a monk or priest, neutral in himself, is frequently a counsellor and friend through whose prayers the central figure is redeemed. Nothing more clearly represents the focus of the Noh plays than this subordination of one of these figures to the other. The waki dominates only the induction to the scene, which contains as a rule the poetic travelogue and is in substance a descriptive background. The play exists for the sake of its most vital figure and incident. It moves but moves forward only to a single event, essentially of a mental, not an active nature. No such austere focus has established itself on the Western stage.

The customary, though by no means invariable, division into two Parts actually constitutes another phase of the ideal of monolithic form, for the entire First Part is introductory. Here in the most familiar form the hero, who is dead, appears in transformation as someone in a lower walk of life, whose words are as a rule characterized by marked modesty, although, especially at the conclusion of Part One, they intimate the truth that greater things are yet to come. The waki, like the audience, either suspects or knows that something super-natural has been experienced. In the Second Part, as the mist dissolves, the hero's ghost appears, but almost invariably with the splendor befitting his noble position in times past. His stature is all the greater and more impressive because to his well established grandeur as an heroic person is added the mystery of supernatural power. To Westerners this condition is familiar in part through the ghost of the elder Hamlet. Comparable ghosts, of course, appear in classical drama, especially in Euripides and Seneca, yet as a rule in a position such as that of the *deus ex machina,* important but briefly seen figures in the play's progress. In the Noh, on the contrary, the ghost's role far exceeds all others in importance. This role obviously becomes much more impressive than the mystifying manifestation of hero or heroine in humble disguise in the play's First Part. The ghost is not a shadow but a heightened reality. In classical mythology ghosts are, of course, very literally "shades," dim images cast by a power and a glory that has flourished in the real world. It is the singularly revealing property of the Greco-Roman world that the active, mundane life seemed real and any other existence, an image or airy projection of the superior reality of this world. Their art is, perhaps, better described as plastic than as essentially creative. In cultures more cordial to the creative imagination, imagined figures may well be more theatrically real than those held real from the European point of view. To the East the supernatural world is not a pale world but one of augmented and intensified reality.

The dramatist of the Noh play resembles a sculptor who revolves a model until the model reaches precisely the point from which he wishes his image to leave its deepest impression. Movement in the more usual play, either of East or West, is forward. But in the Noh it is a revolving movement upon a fixed axis. There is, to repeat, no narrative, only a development with suspense to a calculated crisis. The very thought of plot, so attractive to the restless mind of Aristotle, would seem meaningless to a master of the Noh.

An emotion is a motion of the soul, a movement within the heart. That emotions are not static, the Noh dramatist profoundly understands. They exist in time ; like thunderstorms, they come and go. Hence a presentational art such as drama, peculiarly tied to the emotional life and to the coordinate of time, must move on one plane even if stationary upon another. The Noh playwright builds up his emotion with extreme calculation, from the singularly leisurely and ritualistic opening to the climax of dramatic action, music and dance. Suspense without action becomes his paradoxical formula. The typical Noh play is a mystery without a plot. From the very first entrance of the hero in disguise we feel instinctively that we are in the presence of an unmeasured force. The First Part ends with a singularly deft turn, with the audience aware that much is impending which cannot at the moment be revealed.

Three or four examples are required to illustrate the variations upon this theme. With an unusual but logical turn of imagery, the emanation of the elderly Tamura in the play bearing his name is a youth. Only a few delicate hints can lead us to suspect his real identity. The entire dramatic paragraph must be considered :

Chorus.   From your noble looks
              You seem no common mortal.
              What may your name be?
Youth.   Though I be nameless,
              If you would learn who I am,
              Watch as to the temple I return

Chorus. Where is your home ? Is it as close
           As are laced reeds in a wattle fence,
           "Or far from here
Youth.   Lost among the pathless mountains ?"
Chorus. If you are in doubt
           Watch where I go—so saying
           He leaves the Gishu Gongen.
           Look, he seems moving down the hill,
           No, he's climbing upwards
           To where Tamura Shrine tops the slope,
           And throwing wide its moon-blanched portals,
           He glides across the hall
           And vanishes into the sanctuary.

The unfolding of the poet's theme in *Basho* involves awareness that a woman is in fact a tree merely appearing as a
woman. Much unlike the romantics, who envisaged an anthropomorphic universe, the pessimistic Noh poet, who imagines
an animistic universe, depicts the Spirit of the Tree as hesi-
tant when it consents to assume human form and speech :

Woman. That you should think me human
Chorus. Makes me feel ashamed.
           The full-orbed moon is shining bright
           Upon my homeward path ;
           The garden is white as driven snow.
           If you would pierce this vain form of mine
           Unreal as *basho* leaves in snow,
           How could I hide my shame ?
           While thus she voices her uneasy thoughts,
           A distant temple bell tolls,
           "All is ephemeral,
           All is ephemeral,"
           And she fades away.

Here the truth is indicated, not stated. The audience presumes
but does not know. The technique is intriguing or even tan-
talizing.

In *Izutsu*, with another plan, the shite's identity is clearly
stated but no sooner is this revealed than the figure fades

from view. One stage of the development is concluded, still leaving the continuation an aesthetic and emotional necessity.

> *Chorus.* Scarce has she revealed the name
> Of her who tied the nuptial knot
> When but nineteen
> And made her vow before the gods,
> Than she fades away behind the well-curb,
> Than she fades away behind the well-curb.

Part One of *Toboku* has a comparable conclusion. The poetess who loved her garden and her plum-tree has spoken.

> *Maiden.* I still dwell within this flowering tree.
> *Chorus.* You say, you dwell among these flowers.
> But blossoms fall from branches,
> Like birds seeking again their ancient nests,
> *Maiden.* Returning whence they once did come.
> *Chorus.* Then your life's journey's ended?
> *Maiden* Under the shadow of the flowers
> *Chorus.* "I seem to rest. I am
> The mistress of the plum-tree."
> Then in the sunset glow
> She melts into the shadow of the tree,
> She melts into the shadow of the tree.

Surely, words as delicate as these have seldom been written! A like atmosphere of mystery and passion for anonymity characterizes the conclusion of Part One of *Sanemori*.

> *Chorus.* "My locks and beard are white with age,
> And since this shape is temporarily assumed,
> I would not others see them,
> Nor that my name be noised abroad,
> Lest rumour's tongue again put me to shame"—
> Thus leaving the holy presence,
> He moves away, but as he nears
> The pond of Shinowara
> See! Phantom-like he fades from sight,
> See! Phantom-like he fades from sight.

The repetition of the final lines in the four passages just quoted illustrates a convention by no means uncommon. Clearly, all four passages in question serve the same purpose yet no two are closely alike. The distinctions indicate the profound imaginative skill with which the playwrights vary a fruitful theme. The humble human figures in the first half of the play are indeed ghostly ; only the ghosts in Part Two achieve an emphatic and even italicized humanity. To use quite another imagery, the figures in Part One are ornaments on the base of the pedestal leading the eye upward to the fully revealed figure for whom the entire movement primarily exists. Each play is a revelation.

Though most of the plays are in two Parts, many are in one and a few are in three. The Part would in general be defined by the scarcely profound consideration of the emptying of the stage. To be precise, in the plays offered as representative by the Classical Translation Committee, seventeen are in two Parts, twelve in one Part, and one in three Parts. Yet in keeping with what is now the generally accepted definition in the West, all are One Act Plays and certainly all are brief, none exceeding more than a few hundred words. All are concentric. This pressure to integrity of form is intense and clearly the dominating quality in this tradition of playwriting. There are, for example, no such divisions as represented in the Kabuki plays, or in the typical Chinese and Sanskrit dramas. There are no such distinctions in mood from one Part of the play to another as exist in the sonata form in Western music. Each play has the setting of a particular season of the year and generally after the waki's imagined journey is accomplished in the Induction, also a unity of place. But it is the deeper unity of thought which gives the whole its lyrical quality. No song, or, for example, no *lieder*, can be more rigidly orientated. Frequently there is, in substance, but one character, the shite, appearing in two manifestations and supported by the waki, who is little more than the priest attendant upon his soul and the chorus that speaks of him and often even for him. In this regard *Aoi-No-Ue* offers the most interesting test case. The shite is in Part One the ghost of the Princess Rokujo in the form of a Noble Woman, that in Part Two, Princess Rokujo as possessed by an Evil

Spirit. But the play is named for the Lady Aoi, who, as the bitter rival of Princess Rokujo, may be regarded in Western terms as the antagonist. Noh practice admits the protagonist but not the antagonist. Hence Lady Aoi, who is supposed to be on a sick-bed, is represented by an embroidered cloth, thus preserving the focus of attention on her rival. In the light of Western aesthetics of the drama such a practice would be unthinkable but no less unthinkable was it for the Noh dramatist to risk diffusion in the attention or the sympathies of the audience. It is as though neither King Duncan nor Macduff had appeared in Shakespeare's *Macbeth*.

Once this simple formula is understood—and the playwrights exercise the greatest pains that it shall be understood—much of the aesthetics of the Noh play becomes clear. Each play is the song of a single character, as a rule his swan-song before passing over the bridgeway into Buddhahood. His last exit is his entrance unto the "Western Path," the gorgeous going-down of the sun into infinity. His mental vision will presumably be the summation of the greater part of his life-time. Nothing is spiritually frozen or static in the spirit of the plays. But the law of art as the Noh dramatists understood it is sharp as a spearhead, demanding skilfull handling and the most expert touch. The West envisions a similar ideal but realizes it not in drama and certainly not in lyric drama but in the lyric poem as commonly understood.

This statement concerning Western practice requires further consideration. The true lyric, the lyric in its purest forms, not merely the short poem, casts a revealing light on the Japanese practice and offers the most attractive analogy. Here reflections in the field of comparative literature are useful. Literary forms indeed seem capricious and easily misguide us. The West has no form comparable to the Haiku ; the Greek epigram is quite another matter. Neither the pure song nor any literary form in Japan closely resembles the lyric ideal as realized in the West. In form and spirit Chikamatsu's domestic plays come close to ideals of fiction, both East and West. Occasionally an Act in one of Chikamatsu's romantic plays, as the remarkable scene of the ancient, go-playing philosophers in his *Battles of Coxinga*, bears a strong resemblance to the Noh. The spirit may thus pass dexterously from form to form. What the West considers as strictly lyrical enters into and possesses the soul of the Noh, as a spirit, according to mythology, manifests itself in an alien body.

The lyric, or potential song, is, like the Noh, characterized by its acutely sensitive emotional core. Hence the reflective ode in the manner of Horace, the casual verse epistle, the poetry of wit, though all may be brief, only speciously resemble the lyric. Even incipient dramatic elements in a poem do not as a rule bring any close approximation to the Noh. Most of Browning's dramatic monologues or dialogues, for example, have little or nothing in common with the aesthetic formula of the Japanese plays. Unlike the Noh dramatists. Browning concerned himself with traits of character, the interaction of people, social problems and intellectual or moral issues. His speciously dramatic writing tends to be a commentary on society, whereas the Noh plays probe only the primary features of the heart and soul. In the Noh the literary idea has just emerged from the sentiment of the dance, the music and the mime. Moving and even sufficient as the poetry is in its own right, its quality is very unlike any strictly literary or purely dramatic work in the West. We should do both it and ourselves a serious wrong to consider it in any terms removed from a profoundly realized lyricism.

A rapid survey of Western usage assists a commentary on the Noh. In early classical tradition was the convention that poetry was never merely spoken. It was of two sorts, that chanted and that sung. The poetry of Homer was given a recitational form of chant, that the Pindar, attended with both song and dance. The conception of a poetry primarily to be either read or rendered in a spoken voice seems to have developed only in the later and declining period of Greek civilization and first to have become dominant with Rome. The singular beauty of Roman inscriptions symbolizes a new conception of the word. Poetry readings rather than poetry concerts dominated the Roman literary scene. Their odes were to be read, not sung and danced. The Romans also lost a hold upon the dramatic chorus, which played so large a part in both Greek tragedy and comedy. Plautus and Terence possessed none of the lyric power of Aristophanes. Song the Romans certainly enjoyed, though it is notable that many of their singers were foreigners, especially Egyptians and Greeks. Moreover, in songs the virtuosity of the singing voice was more valued than the words, while the more serious poetry became increasingly verse to be read. In a world essentially political, the orator's voice drowned out the true lyric. The music-loving philosophers of the early Greek world became a legend of the past.

An illustrious age of song at once literary and musical gradually arose with the Christian Middle Ages and may be said to have persisted, though with waning force, through the activity of the fathers of Christian hymnology and the troubadours even to approximately the times of Goethe, after which the divorce drastically widened between the arts of music and verse. The chief drama of the Middle Ages at least was in lyric verse; that of the Renaissance, in more declamatory forms. The extraordinary developments in Western baroque and romantic music itself, producing large orchestras and elaborate ensembles and an opera usually devoid of literary merit, hastened this development. The German *lieder* appear to have preserved the earlier tradition longest. This, in time, yielded to the art-song, which has proved only a minor feature in the culture of our own century. Hence some particular effort is required to reconstruct in thought the quality of a completely composite art in which the finest poetry, music and even dance are united. Only with such an effort will the synthesis in the Noh be realized.

The song itself as a form should be re-examined in this regard. Many of the *lieder* are in reality ballads and ballads as a form of Western poetry stand remarkably close to the Western conception of drama. Some of the famous German and Scottish ballads are virtually drama and one only wonders that in the vaguely defined period between the Middle Ages and the Renaissance so few ballads were transposed for the stage. A few, certainly, gave their stories and characters to the contemporary theatre, as in the popular balladry on the theme of Faust. But no narrative poem affords a fruitful comparison with the classical Japanese theatre, to which the spirit of narrative itself proves repugnant. The ballads are rangy poems, secular in spirit, tales of adventure, dwelling on real persons in sequences of events. The Noh plays, on the contrary, are rounded smooth as globes, religious in spirit, introspective in view-point and are impersonal meditations on the condition of the soul. The ballads are simplicity itself ; the Noh are, to be sure, completely simple at their core but highly sophisticated upon the surface. Except for the conjunction of music and words, the two forms stand worlds apart, as far apart from the viewpoints of literature as from those of music and choreography.

No close parallel exists to the Noh, either in East or West. But likenesses sufficient to cast considerable light upon the riddles of the Noh do exist. The abstract conception of lyric poetry by no means exhausts the values of comparison. Some provocative considerations arise where they are, perhaps, least expected. So far is this true that to relieve the shock of incredulity the second generalization proposed at the beginning of this chapter may now be put to further examination. The Noh play is inspired by supernaturalism. It lives in a veritable mist of supernaturalism. This is not the mythology of the Indian drama nor the popular magic of the Chinese but a profound mystery of its own creation, a region of unearthly beings breathing terror and astonishment. At the heart of the Noh is a profoundly supernatural conception of existence. How far this reflects Japanese thinking at large and how far it was itself a convention of literature or the stage raise historical questions which the present writer, with perhaps the present generation as well, is incapable of resolving.

The centrifugal human mind is capable of throwing off whole universes and peopling them with beings either highly similar to or in various ways widely dissimilar from itself. The most striking instance of a mythological world intimately resembling in body and soul the human world is the Greek pantheon. The Oriental mind is capable of more audacious conceptions. It has given the world an infinite variety of angels and fiends, of strange birds and beasts, dragons, centaurs and chimaeras dire, inextricably involving all life with an invasion of the supernatural. Yet some distinction, even when made popularly and without benefit of philosophy or conscious effort, always exists between the natural and supernatural. Magic is distinguished from non-magic, most of all by cultures that employ witch-doctors ; the worlds of the soul before birth and after death are distinguished from this "middle earth" that we know so well, angels and demons distinguished from members of one's family. Nevertheless good and evil spirits may according to folklore possess a mortal man at any time. Man is surrounded by mystery and lives within mystery, as conscious thought is surrounded by dreams ; the world of Latin comedy standing at one extreme represents the real world, the world of the Noh standing at the opposite extreme is dominated by the supernatural. Its heroes are saved by the magic of prayers offered as a rule by the priestly waki. Its principal characters are almost as far removed as possible from being common mortals. They are ghosts, emanations, vestiges of mortals, spirits, once men, who have come from the hells of an after-life, or airy bodies that were once mortals but are seen as bodies possessed by fiends. There are also a few minor gods and in at least one celebrated play, *Basho*, as previously observed, the leading figure is the spirit of a tree. As consequence of this complex and mysterious world, events occur with the utmost caprice. In *Tamanoi* a prince who loses his brother's fishhook visits the sea-god's palace at the bottom of the ocean to recover it. In the course of his exploit he marries the sea-god's daughter. In *Yamamba* a Mountain-Hag turns day into night, raises a thunderstorm, and performs a magic dance. The world is altogether irrational. Priests, ghosts and gods possess it wholly. It is true that the poetry of the Noh presents a strikingly convincing picture of the sensuous world. But the world of men is reflected almost entirely in symbolical terms and even here it is man's uncontrollable emotions, not his society or his laws, that are chiefly depicted. That princes reign, warriors fight, and laborers toil is sufficiently clear and merely assumed. Such considerations are no more than scaffolds to display a drama of spiritual intensity. The magic of ancient sacred music and dance is enlisted, together with the magic of a ritualized poetry to evoke a world of astonishment. No drama rivals this in the full measure of its supernaturalism. The medieval Mystery Plays reflect far more of Jewish history as contained in the Bible than do the Noh plays of Japanese history. The medieval characters are closer to tangible reality. Doubting Thomas plunges his hand into the wound of the risen Christ and in testimony of the validity of resurrection shakes it dripping with blood in the faces of the audience. Christ's resurrection is as material an event in the plays as it is in the hard, earthy woodcuts by Dürer. Western plays about ghosts, to be sure, are fairly numerous in the eighteenth century and after, yet are merely parlor magic when placed besides the convincing supernaturalism of the Noh. Brazenly founded on man's delight to have his sense of horror titillated, the Western works fulfill a purely histrionic function. No one is convinced. But the supernaturalism of the Noh, arising from their sincere effort in religious propaganda, is at least founded on well-remembered superstitions and deeply stamped with imaginative sincerity. Plays carrying such powerful emotional impact cannot present a universe superficially conceived. The supernaturalism carries a deep conviction which no sensitive mind can escape. It by no means depends on isolated miracles or mere tricks of destiny. The mystery of the plays is the air which the audience breathes from the moment that the first actor enters the stage, or even from the moment that the first note of the music, representing the symbolic cry of the cock, casts its spell upon the theatre. In producing this effect, the force of the music and the magic of the dance can scarcely be exaggerated. But the strange, unnatural movements of the actors, the always unnatural gestures, the rich priestly costumes, strained voices, and elliptical poetry contribute much. The world as unveiled by the Noh is studiously and consistently supernatural.

II

The Noh is lyrical both in the special sense favored here of being close to the true lyric and in the broader and less abstract consideration that it embraces song and dance; and it is also a world of pure magic. These, however, are sweeping generalizations. Is there a body of lyric poetry in English which the scholar of the Noh in quest of analogies may consider with peculiar profit? There is indeed, though at first sight the suggestion may appear almost wildly perverse. This is an impressive segment in the work of one of the most remarkable lyric poets of the Western world, Robert Burns.

To clear the road in this regard for useful exchanges, it is well to acknowledge first of all at least some of the important qualities of Burns' thinking standing in complete antithesis to the Noh and in most instances to almost all Asian thought. The Noh is steeped in tradition on all sides and in tradition of all kinds, aesthetic, popular, religious, philosophical. It reflects a remarkable instance of a closed society, insular Japan, of the Middle Ages. The Scottish poet composed many aphorisms that fling defiance against such a society, one of which is the memorable

The man of independent mind,
He looks and laughs at a' that.

Burns, though keenly intelligent, is also comparatively naive ; in this championship of the peasant and the common man he is completely sincere. Also unlike the authors of the aristocratic Noh, in much—though by no means in all—of his verse, he writes as a fervent moralist and reformer, a rustic successor to Horace and to Juvenal. At least in one of his moods he accepts the importance of sin and, at least where political criticism is concerned, this he never forgets. The amoral position of the Noh philosophy would certainly have shocked him. Where the Noh is antiaphrodisiac, he is frankly erotic. Where he often jests, the Noh usually grieves. He celebrates a village life where the Noh envisages an unlimited universe. He can be sentimental and vulgar where the Noh is always dignified, aristocratic and austere. He glories in an effect of improvization whereas the Noh delights in ritualistic forms and a high measure of art consciousness. He exploits self-consciousness in the most romantic manner, whereas the Noh poet as an individual remains severely retiring and conscious only of two elements : art and the universal, which two he is inclined at times to regard as virtually one. Burns at his best acknowledged his art to be "fun," Zeami found art to constitute at least a large part of religion. How, then, can the Ayrshire country bard resemble the suave master of the Noh ?

He does resemble him in highly revealing regards and more deeply than does any other English poet, not excluding William Butler Yeats, who intuitively grasped so much of the Noh's thought and projected his understanding of the plays in the unpopular dramas written in the later years of his life. In a word, Burns occupies territory adjacent to the Noh because of his profound grasp of lyrical thinking and writing and his sincere participation in a world of primitive supernaturalism totally unlike the sophisticated "Gothic" world of his contemporary, Horace Walpole. Moreover, Burns' extraordinary superiority in the pure lyric and in a grasp of the supernatural derive alike from the common springs of a deep traditionalism, as venerable, perhaps, as the traditionalism behind the Noh plays themselves. His songs, both in musical and literary form, were the final flower of centuries of Scottish music and rhyme, his supernaturalism, the direct heritage of centuries of Scottish superstition. He spoke in reality not for a class but for a country stubbornly proud of its intensely local heritage. There is much in common between peninsular Scotland and insular Japan. Burns' achievement accordingly bears a surprising treasure for any thoughtful student of the essence of the Noh plays. Such a study is as truly rewarding as, on first glance, it may appear to be irrelevant. Only with a firm grasp of the true nature of lyricism can one begin to penetrate the meaning of the mysterious Noh. In theoretical and descriptive literature one may ponder forever-and-a-day on the themes of both the lyric and superstition. But what these conceptions signify, especially for the poetic mind wherever it may be found, is best ascertained by close consideration of the type of poetry of which Burns is the crowning ornament. The discipline of the appreciation of this element in Burns' work is therefore one of the most rewarding disciplines for the modern or English-speaking student of the Japanese works. It strikingly exemplifies the validity of the concept of comparative literature.

Behind Burns lyricism lies the peculiar affinity which he discovered between words and music, a fusion duplicated merely on different terms in the Noh. Burns described the genesis of many of his songs as residing in the music itself. When in a creative mood, he would sing to himself some Scottish tune suggested by his emotional state until words commenced to flow. In this respect his practice was at the time highly exceptional. A strong tendency in England for music and the short poem to become divorced commenced at least a century before Burns wrote, or approximately with the death of Milton. The words of true songs grew increasingly neutral or even insipid ; the best music was either wholly separated from the voice or clung to words regarded as relatively unimportant ; serious poetry tended to be purely literary. Between Doctor Johnson and Burns yawned this deep chasm. Johnson wrote poetry to be read, Burns, at least a great part of his poetry to be sung. This condition determined many distinctions in the quality of the verse and the feeling which it conveyed. Burns' true songs are primarily emotional, Johnson's typical verse is proportionally intellectual. Johnson wrote verse essays, which criticism might without injurious misrepresentation describe as rhymed prose. Such poems expatiate over wide areas of thought. From Scotland to England came, at least in the same century, James Thomson, whose masterpiece of didactic poetry, *The Seasons*, also illustrates the opposite pole from Burns' lyricism. It became a prize poem for school declamation. That its words were several times set to music does not alter the fact that as a poem it is emphatically un-lyrical.

A lyric by Burns is concentrated upon its own mood. The best of his songs are also deeply emotional and many of them, like the Noh, tragic. They place us in a relation to experience in this respect similar to the Japanese dramas. The themes are simple and of universal significance. A woman mourns her lover lost in battle. A man mourns the death of his beloved. Friends and lovers are parted. Children lament their parents or parents their children. Life is depicted as cruel and intensely ironical. The poems deal with the universal trials and triumphs of the heart, each work being rigorously contained within itself.

Most of Burns' thoughts so lyrically expressed are highly familiar to readers of the Noh. Typical of both is the awareness of life's contradictions as symbolized by the seasons of the year. Like the Noh poets, Burns is in the most intimate touch with nature, knowing it in its most varied moods and contrasted seasons. His relation to nature is imaginative and spiritual, not, as James Thomson's, material and utilitarian.

Following the ancient tradition of Scottish poetry, he turns to the seasons equally, notably to the winter, fall and spring. He knows nature's harshness, its imperviousness, its betrayals. The Japanese poets similarly dwell on the withering of spring blossoms as evidence of the transitoriness of life ; the theme is repeated often in Burns' finest songs, as in *Highland Mary*, where the sorrows of parting are rendered more poignant by the spring scene. With the Noh poets, Burns is aware of imaginative meanings in the atmosphere. The heroine of *Kinuta* bids the wind blow gently in a favorable direction to carry the sound of her cloth-beating to the ears of her distant lover. Similarly, Burns evokes the West Wind to carry imagined messages between his love and him. The wrench of parting, so poignant in the Noh, appears movingly in such a poem as *Farewell*. Basic themes in life, as the contrast of youth and age, give undying validity to Burns' work, just as to the Noh. His singers remember youth in their age and foresee age while in their youth. There is a grandeur in his lyricism :

> As fair thou art, my bonie lass,
>   So deep in luv am I,
> And I will luve the still, my dear,
>   Till a' the seas gang dry.
> Till a' the seas gang dry, my dear
>   and the rocks melt wi' the sun . . .

There are similar hyperboles in the Noh.

The intense love of place, so typical of the Noh, is voiced with most moving sincerity in Burns' songs. Each nock and cranny of Ayrshire has for him poetic significance. The tragic note is struck with great conviction as he is threatened with leaving his homeland ; *The Author's Farewell to his Native Country*, has a stern pathos to which parallels in the Noh are readily educed. Some readers will recall further that this Celtic and poetic feeling for place is similarly reflected in Yeats' account of the meaning of Western Ireland for its native inhabitants.

Burns' tenderness and solicitude for the lesser creatures in nature suggests the Buddhistic thought in such plays as *Basho* where, as it will be recalled, a storm-tossed tree finds itself temporarily transformed into a woman. In Burns' *On Scaring Some Waterfowl* the poet laments the molestation of nature by man. The birds are pictured as fleeing from human contamination. Burns, in other words, reveres nature for itself ; he does not construe it as an allegory of man or God. His animism is also more primitive and closer by far to the Noh dogma than is the romanticism or pantheism in Wordsworth.

The meaning and subject-matter of Burns' verse, however, approaches the Noh the most strikingly as it explores the supernatural. The strained, pseudo-gothic affectations of the supernatural in Ossian and the innumerable architects of Nightmare Abbeys scarcely touch him. Scotland may have fathered much of the "revival" of the primitive and supernatural in English and European literature but with Burns this domain was in no way borrowed, imported or traduced. To him it came as direct and lawful heritage. No major poet surpasses him in the realization of the supernatural. There are indeed goulish figures in Ibsen's *Peer Gynt* and in Strindberg's *Lucky Phar* and *Snowwhite*, but in no case is the magic conveyed so convincingly as in Burns' lyric art. Whether as a man he believed the popular superstitions or not, is a matter of no particular relevance for his poetry. He was close enough to them in spirit to believe them poetically and to cause them to live completely in such poems as *Halloween, Address to the Diel, Death and Doctor Hornbook, Tam O'Shanter,* and many others. The legends reported are for the most part the black, diabolical, and macabre fantasies of northern, Protestant superstition and of superstitions older and even grimmer than those of Christianity itself. The beliefs share in the world of universal folklore. Terror and astonishment lie in general at their root. His beliefs are, indeed, considerably more primitive and less philosophical than the thought creating such typical images as The Mountain-Hag in *Yamamba,* or the seductive Hag in *Momiji-Gari*, the Cutty Sark of Oriental theology. Yet the Japanese thought also has its roots in both folklore and primitivism. True it is that when, with dilated eyes filled with astonishment and terror, poor Tam saw Cutty Sark, the girl was half naked and when the audience at *Yam-*

amba witnessed the Mountain-Hag she wore a mask and garments stiff with decorated brocade. Nevertheless, the two illustrate Kipling's words on the kinship of the Captain's lady and Molly O'Grady. An important likeness should not be lost because of comparatively superficial distinctions.

The prominence of the dark spirits or demons in the Noh plays can scarcely be exaggerated. If no other evidence were required, the many masks still in existence used in early productions would attest the fact. One hardly need recall the prevalence and power of such imagery in the sculpture, painting and poetry of the Orient, and especially of China and Japan. These terrifying spirits possess the highest measure of reality, flourishing in the most serious, keenly imagined and aesthetically distinguished art and poetry. Reflecting an essential element in Japanese thinking of the Middle Ages, they have every historical and aesthetic right to their conspicuous position upon the stage. In the rural Scotland of Burns such masks of evil were no less common, even though no sophisticated philosophy in exposition of them existed.

Behind all such images stands the fundamental attitude toward good and evil entertained by Burns and by Zeami. Certainly Burns was no systematic thinker, though the sharpness of his intellect should not be doubted. He had strong convictions at certain hours of the day and possibly even stronger at certain hours of the night. He could easily imagine superstitions in which he can hardly have shared. He could wear a Scottish mask or an English mask, be royalist or republican, for or against King George, for or against human passion. He could also be for or against sin or the devil. His philosophical ambiguity by no means indicates a lack of mental power ; rather, it indicates a breadth of mind and in particular a depth of humor. At the same time he feared the devil and loved him, dreaded him and laughed at him. The fiend cropped Magi's tail but left Tam free, after granting him a fine show for his pains. Burns rather liked Cutty Sark after all. No poem better shows this attitude than his *Address to the Diel*, which appeared in his first volume of poems and is the last of an illustrious series of addresses to the devil stemming, as one of Burns' editors somewhat broadly declares, "from the thirteenth, fourteenth, and fifteenth centuries."

An' now, Auld Coots, I ken ye're thinkin
A certain Bardie's rantin, drinkin,
Some luckless hour will send him linkin
  To your black Pitt ;
But faith ! he'll turn a corner jinkin
  An' cheat you yet.

But far-you-well, Auld Nickie-Ben !
O, wad ye tak a thought an' men !
Ye aiblins might—I denna ken—
  Still hae a stake ;
I'm wae to think upo' yon den,
  Ev'n for your sake !

In *Death and Doctor Hornbook* the poet is seen on even more
congenial terms with man's second inveterate enemy, Death.
A stanza is sufficient to convey the general sentiment :

"Weel, weel ! says I, "a bargain be't ;
Come, gie's your hand, an' say we're gree't ;
We'll ease our shanks, an tak a seat ;
  Come, gie's your news ;
This while ye hae been monie a gate,
  At monie a house."

Many of Burns' poems are banners flauntingly flown against
conventional morality and the orthodox conception of sin.
Of such pieces a fair representative is *A Poet's Welcome to
His Love-Begotten Daughter* :

What tho' they ca' me fornicator,
An' tease my name in kintra clatter ?
The mair they talk, I'm kend the better,
  E'en let them clash !
An auld wife's tongue's a feeckless matter
  To gie ane fash.

To hold that Burns stood beyond good and evil, as the
Mountain-Hag declares that she does, would be to speak
loosely. A helpful contrast is invited. Blake stood while

Burns danced. Blake dreaded a chaos of ideas without a system, while Burns shunned the tyranny of ideas as he shunned all other shackles on mankind which he regarded as tyrannous. Certainly Byron had a more deep-seated conviction of Calvinism than the rustic Burns, who winced at life's pains but only in moments of sentimental despair dreaded the pains of hell or submitted to a clearcut conviction of good and evil. His special inclination was to discover good in evil and evil in good. It is true that the Mountain-Hag of Zeami preached to the art-dancer in search of wisdom a sermon in mysticism whose theological technicalities Burns might not have understood. Yet their fundamental positions often draw close together. One can hardly avoid the conclusion that Burns cultivated an appetite for the macabre because he felt somehow an affection for it, because at heart he loved not only all frail things, as field-mice, hares and flowers, but all evil things as well. He himself defied most of the orthodoxies of life and at one time or another thought himself justified in so doing. He accepted the human world much as he accepted the world of nature, for he greeted the savagery of winter almost as heartily as the delights of summer and spring. This attitude is, of course, in agreement with the Buddhism from which the thought of the Noh derives. The mature mysticism of the *Lotus Sutra*, especially dear to the Japanese dramatists, contained in it not only sophisticated mysticism but animism and was grounded on basic conceptions close to many of Burns' own intuitions. He at least vaguely felt what the sutras learnedly expounded. Burns actually stood closer to these works than to the apologies for Calvinism, a creed which he detested.

Whether or not he accepted the doctrine of evil, or sin, he certainly accepted the belief in the tragic, the dark, the sinister and the macabre. This acceptance in itself inspires much of his finest poetry. It springs from profound experiences close in many respects to the experiences of life reflected in the philosophic dramas of the Noh. The sincerity, the imagination, even the essentially dramatic elements, are in Burns' songs. Like Goya, he is most dramatic where black is boldly thrown upon his canvas. The poems already mentioned in connection with his macabre imagination for the supernatural,

Halloween, Address to the Diel, Death and Doctor Hornbook,
and *Tam o' Shanter,* clearly have a strong dramatic flavor.
The literary form of the Noh they certainly do not share yet
something of the linguistic purity of the Japanese poetry they
do share and much more of its view of life and its poetic
imagery.

To repeat : two elements in poetic imagination, strong
lyrical feeling and vivid imagination for the supernatural,
are basic factors in both Burns' poems and the Noh dramas.
Although it may seem a long stride from Ayrshire to Japan,
such a step is singularly well directed for an English-speaking
student desiring a warm and just appreciation of the poetry
of the Noh.

SCHOLARS OF the Noh continually face the question as to the precise aspect of these complex works which they are viewing. Although in important respects the plays resemble pure poetry, or the pure lyric, it is obvious that they are not strictly this ; to imagine them to some extent as presentational art, as already remarked in these pages, is inevitable. This is, in general, the viewpoint of the reader of any play, no matter how literary his predilections may be. By virtue of the dialogue form, with gestures and movements understood and the scene given a local habitation and a name, the playwright inevitably demands such a reception. Perhaps scarcely aware of what he is doing, the reader follows the path that leads to the making of drama, even though he is still content to regard himself simply as reader. He may still be on the side of the book as opposed to that of the presentational art, the spectacle, the living voice and the theatrical music. In the foregoing chapter the plays have been regarded primarily though not exclusively as poems. In the present chapter they will be viewed as performances of one sort or another.

The Noh can be performed in any number of ways and its strictly theatrical features taken apart, even for detached inspection. Since its costumes stand among the most gorgeous and beautiful fabrics imaginable, they have formed a conspicuous part of countless exhibitions of Japanese textiles. Its masks can without hesitation be placed among outstanding works of Japanese sculpture. Its fans and other stage properties are masterpieces of decorative art. The world of the Noh is a classical treasure-chest. Many of its finest byproducts are in the Emperial collections and other great repositories, both in the East and West. Numberless museums are the richer for these. Thanks chiefly to the generosity of old and noble Japanese families, the present-day Noh companies possess many pieces of precious stage equipment. If equipment for a production is collected, it is either borrowed from existing treasures or, when made anew, executed with good taste and scrupulous pains. The basic integrity of Noh calls forth good workmanship by all hands. Even the particles of the Noh stage exemplify the purity of the whole and frequently shine brightly in their own light.

Detached fragments of the Noh are not necessarily properties used on the stage. The Noh casts forth many satellites. Films and recordings represent at least continuous charts or maps of performances. Each in its own way is of value, though never remotely equivalent to the sum of the whole. The more intimate art of the actor, with its singularly magical affect in the instance of the Noh, cannot be duplicated on the screen. Obviously, the sound film comes closer than any other projection of the performance to a comprehensive image of the whole yet this very inclusiveness begets an element of superficiality ; filmings of the Noh possess attractions especially treacherous and specious. A film audience, if unwary, is led to imagine that it has seen the play when such is far from the truth. Nothing presented in two dimensions can ever intimately resemble anything in three. It must lack the full conviction of the more sculpturesque or more flesh-and-blood art. The pictured actor will always be more an abstraction than the live actor. The pictorial form may well become more subjective but must always lack the illusion of the theatrical figure as an item in the real world. Moreover, the film is an art in itself ; the simple filming of a play is not an art; it proves, paradoxically, both too close to its original and too removed from it. Within there lurks the fallacy of naturalism which never in its severer forms accords with creative imagination. The ideal filming of a Noh play would be much unlike anything as yet seen, for it would have to accord with the principles of the film, not those of the stage. The literally faithful film has its value and even its charm ; sound, words, color, and image are present ; but the sensitive spectator still feels a want difficult to analyze fully but too vital to overlook.

Because of this concealed want within the total affect of the customary documentary film of the theatre, the final affect of such a film, its profuse pretensions notwithstanding, is often less gratifying than projections from the play far less comprehensive. A single stage property that is real may weigh more than a total image that is shadowy. An analogy is seen in reproductions of painting. The black and white reproduction always shows less than the color print but also at times reveals more and misrepresents less. The simple sound tracks of Asiatic plays prove especially rewarding. The record cannot in its own terms be absolutely faithful but will certainly come closer to the original than any visual reproduction. In the Western World today Asian drama is known almost as well through films and records as through books. Records have, perhaps, most of all to teach the world outside Asia, for they simplify the auditory aspect of the stage, disclosing the peculiar solutions of speech, song, sound affects, and instrumental music. Much of value may confidently be expected in the next few years in these media expressing Asian theatrical culture. Transportation of theatrical companies is difficult. Among other problems, the Noh groups are almost exclusively amateur. But by films and recordings their presentational art may at least be partially understood. All progressive theatre schools and music schools should be equipped with sets of films and records representing the Asian stage.

Are the Noh plays as performing art bound to be at home only in Japan and to what extent are they at home even there? In Japan they constitute a cult, in this respect even comparable to that other ritualistic cult whose activities center upon tea, the tea being transportable but not so the cult. As the critic and novelist, Donald Richie, has convincingly conjectured, the style of the Noh plays as commonly seen today would probably be easily recognized by the great-grand-fathers of the present actors and possibly not recognized by Zeami himself. Some strong evidence has been educed pointing to an uninterrupted flow of tradition and yet to prove slow but by no means unimportant changes through the centuries. The excellent scholar, P. G. O'Neill, for example, is of the opinion that the original productions were less mannered than those today, were given at a less retarded pace and consequently in less time. It is possible that artifice has seemed to the actors the very essence of the plays and that the long, continuous development in their production has brought about this slow-moving but steady increase in stylization. If the absolute Noh is considered to be what its founders either saw or desired, it is within reason to doubt that it is anywhere to be seen at the present time. At least from an antiquarian viewpoint, all present productions should be honored well short of idolatry, remarkably moving as they may be.

Certain of the most vigorously minded Japanese masters of the theatre have themselves exhibited a degree of restlessness in the presence of the tradition. Must the Noh plays receive the traditional performances? Are they, perhaps, conveyed to us better in something like modern dress? The question has been asked with entire seriousness of Shakespeare and why not of Zeami? Even in view of Japanese veneration of tradition, experimentation has been less than might reasonably have been expected. Especially as Westerners become, through improved translations and accumulated knowledge, better acquainted with the plays, some novel and fairly successful undertakings may be realized. No works of art as clearly powerful as the Noh have ever been confined to a single type of interpretation, nor is any miraculous exception to be expected in this case. Variations cannot afford to be vast, for then not only the surface but the core of the original would be lost and common sense argue that a totally new effort from the beginning should have been made. But classics remain alive by virtue of a succession of ever-fresh interpretations, or, to use a term from mythology, manifestations. Not even the Noh can be expected to escape this historic principle. Extreme conservatism is mere timidity, whereas art itself is the audacity of the soul. It is not always necessary to give *Peer Gynt* with Grieg's music and far less *A Midsummer-Night's Dream* with Mendelsohn's.

In the instance of the Noh performed outside Japan the text is basic; the best translation is urgently required; the ideal of economy so brilliantly achieved in the original writing argues that little or nothing shall be omitted and obese additions at all costs avoided. The idiom of any play being produced must be tested with the speaking voice. Some amendments in any printed text are permissible. Yet the poet's words, even when reflected vaguely, as they must be, in translation, constitute the core about which all else develops. Costumes, gestures, music, dance, even though none of these undergoes the indignity of translation, may be adapted much more freely than words to the imaginative dictates of a new age and a fresh mind. The basic incident, myth, thought, must remain. Where this is sacrificed we may possibly have a better play but certainly neither a better nor a worse version of the old one. And where a sincere conviction exists that the old work is a masterpiece, this should and will survive. Whenever the rewriters pass off upon the public their own works with counterfeit laurels of the masters still on their own brows, they do the theatre no service. Judicious procedure rejects extremes, either to left or right, reveres the masterpiece, accepts its power to throw out new suggestions for new interpretations and even for totally new works, but above all, rather than insist upon a radical, liberal or conservative stand, requires that a clear and intelligent view shall be held as to what is actually being done. The last issue is well illustrated in the instance of the so-called "Noh Plays" written by Yukio Mishima, and recently translated with his usual felicity by Donald Keene in *Five Modern Noh Plays*. The truth of the matter is that these are vastly more modern than Noh.

All these works by Mishima are "based", as the translator states, on well-known Noh plays, three of which may be read in English in the volumes of the Classics Translation Committee: *Sotoba Komachi*, *Kantan*, and *The Lady Aoi*. *The Damask Drum* has been translated by Arthur Waley. All the plays by Mishima are spirited works of unusual merit, in many ways reflecting the classical works on which they are in a sense founded. As in the instance of the classical Noh, they are prevailingly serious or tragic ; one, *Kantan*, follows its original in being lighter in tone. But the transposition has been so great that essentially new works are produced. This is not an art of putting the Noh plays into modern dress, as *Hamlet* has several times been successfully performed in

modern dress. The frequent practice of modernizing Shakespearean productions has touched primarily the decor. The
audience has often given extraordinary attention to Shakespeare's words precisely because no shop-worn costumes in the
Tudor style have stood between them and the poet's language.
With the Noh plays in Mishima's hands quite the contrary
course is followed. Except for ingeniously planned echoes that
prove in the end to be incidental rather than fundamental,
the material is almost wholly new. The ornaments are old,
the heart is new. It is true that something of the initial
situation remains, even when the spirit has wholly changed.
So in Mishima's *Sotoba Komachi*, one of life's most irksome
wounds, the split between age and youth, is successfully drama-
tized, as in Zeami's play. The discerning psychological insights, especially in *The Lady Aoi*, testify to Mishima's appreciation of at least a broadly similar intention in the classical
work. Active fancy enlivens both plays named *Kantan*.
Yet the basic styles of acting, the imagery, and, above all, the
philosophy and religion are vastly different. In one group the
style is mannered, in the other, largely naturalistic ; in one
the imagery springs from a nature-worship meditating on the
seasons of the year and shrines set among mountains and by
rivers and bays ; in the other, from the nervosities of indus-
trialized urban life ; in one the outlook on life is that of Buddhistic mysticism, in the other, that of an emancipated and an
uncommitted hedonistic wit. Although disillusionment with
the social and material world lies in both views, beyond the
disillusionment of the one stands an essentially idealistic
religion, beyond the other, a blank. To anyone familiar with
the classical works, the complete disappearance of the religious
outlook is on the face of it astounding. That this difference
should exist is both obvious and readily explained in historical
terms. Nevertheless, when one work, as here, is placed beside
another, the mind is almost stunned by the discrepancy.
This distinction alone overwhelms whatever minor ties
exist between the ancient and the modern works. These
"Modern Noh" are more a semi-serious parody of their originals
than a direct continuation of the Noh tradition.

Only a morose mind would wish that Mishima had done
other than he has done ; yet to Western eyes his wit and his

outlook will seem more Gallic than traditionally Japanese. He "modernizes" Zeami even more fully than Anouilh and Giraudoux have modernized the Greek tragic dramatists. The power of the Noh is strikingly exhibited by its long shadow cast across the centuries, as visible in the acknowledged indebtedness of Mishima for his situations and certain of his conceptions of playwriting. Yet in the end his is a twentieth-century art, not a fresh interpretation of an old one. His work testifies to the spell of the ancient masterpieces ; it shows enterprise, courage, imagination ; it fails even to suggest any specific means for maintaining the original works themselves on the stage with an ever-changing and a fresh vitality.

This force inherent in the Noh encourages at least some faith in its power to emerge with a considerable degree of integrity, even outside the country of its birth. That it may never achieve the conquest of a large popular audience is highly plausible. Especially in Communist countries it is difficult to foresee within the near future any perceptible popularity for a drama so metaphysical and introspective. The modest proportions of its stage fail to invite sizeable audiences. It has sometimes been called the chamber music of the theatre and as such appears in both a favorable and an aristocratic position. One is reminded of Strindberg's "Intimate Theatre". In Japan it is cultivated, as we have seen, by amateurs and where it is cultivated abroad, it will presumably appear first under similar auspices. The movement toward the open stage favors its own entrance, indeed seems hospitably to prepare the way for it. Some equivalent for the bridgeway, or passageway unto the stage, used for the protracted entrances and exits, aids greatly in performance. Architectural difficulties appear by no means unsurmountable. The audiences will presumably be among the cosmopolitan-minded and the students. Academic auspices offer considerable promise. In the more active theatrical centers the public is beginning to recognize what rich potentialities are in store for a theatrical consciousness embracing the most widely dispersed areas of the globe.

One of the more striking instances is afforded by the Institute for Advanced Study of the Theatre Arts, in New York City, a school for actors directed by John Mitchell. Here, enjoying the luxury of eminent directors coming for relatively short periods from abroad, a company of student-actors has produced plays, to mention a few, in the Kabuki, Noh, Chinese, and the Indian manner. Where so much has been done with, at least in many respects, such meagre physical facilities, good promise is given for how much more can readily be accomplished on a larger scale. It is by no means inconceivable that before the end of the present century most of the major Noh plays will have received moving and by no means infrequent performances in the Western World. They can safely be regarded as a rare but sturdy species capable of blooming in widely dispersed localities. The logic of the theatre itself suggests this. The Noh are the ultimate word in stylized drama and one of the most powerful manifestations of the lyric and the metaphysical theatre. Although known to the world to some extent for half a century, only recently have the channels been fairly opened for successful stage renderings outside Japan. The general progress along already established lines in modern theatrical music, dance and decor offers considerable hope for the lifting of the curtain now largely concealing from the eyes of the West the varied theatrical triumphs of the Asian stage, among which the Noh plays must hold a peculiarly high place. Of this, more in a succeeding chapter.

Some of the earlier impact of the Noh upon the West is typified by the work of Ezra Pound, a pioneer and in so many respects a herald for new awareness in the arts. Yet of all the arts drama has been one of the least to interest Pound. For some personal reason unnecessary to investigate here— possibly because of an inveterate egoism—Pound has never really warmed to the theatre. Poetry itself and the poetic symbol have focused his thoughts. Hence when he and his friend, Fenellosa, first encountered the Noh, they thought of it essentially as part of Japanese or Oriental poetry, not as a monument in the theatre. The austerity of its style, its overtones and its system of symbolism, its intensely artificial and superlatively mannered idiom, quickly won their enthusiasm. The essential orientation of the works they at once grasped surprisingly well; their effort now seems virtually heroic; but at first it fertilized the general stream of imaginative literature in the West rather than the drama itself. Ampler research in the theories and in the theatres of both East and West was required to focus a searching light upon the complicated surface of the Noh literature and stage. Neither as theatre nor as dramatic literature was the Noh drama until extremely recent times sufficiently revealed to acquire any direct currency in the West. During the earlier decades of the present century it suggested much ; reports of it were stirring ; but the thing itself was held in a precarious grasp.

In all such cases some initial distortion of vision seems inevitable. The reception of the Chinese drama throws some light on that of the Japanese. If the Noh plays at first meant more to the West as poetry than as theatre, the Chinese plays meant vastly more as theatre than as literature. In fact, as literature they meant almost nothing. When the modern European stage first discovered the attraction of the open stage, the Chinese theatre exercised the chief generative force. The Chinese had in these respects many advantages. The Kabuki had never been exported and even to this day has been very seldom and somewhat unsatisfactorily witnessed abroad. The Noh has remained austerely in its homeland. But most European visitors to China were attracted by its musical and spectacular stage, by the generous Chinese enthusiasm for the actor's art, the hospitality of the Chinese theatres, and a warmth of humanity felt even where the subject-matter was often grasped with much imprecision. Moreover, fairly good Chinese theatres flourished in many quarters of the world, wherever any considerable Chinese community existed. The present writer found his eyes first opened to the spell of the theatre not by E. H. Sothern's productions of Shakespeare but by the Chinese theatre in the New York Bowery. The obvious fluency of the Chinese stage and its feminine, rococo charm were much more accessible to the Western romantic imagination than the angular astringencies of the Noh, even had they been available. It was typical of the early years of the present century that from a childhood and youth in China came Thornton Wilder to bring liberation from the naturalistic stage and the proscenium arch. The early history of the impact of the Noh upon the West is a story of its influence on poetic style, on closet drama and on playwriting that adopted only those features of the Noh which at once promised to please Westerners. It came as a blessed influence upon closet drama and verse drama, which in the earliest years of the twentieth century had sunk to an extraordinary condition of both poetic and theatrical impotence.

To realize the value of the Noh at the present juncture in English and American literary history it is helpful to recall the dark screen against which it has been thrown. It is hardly too sweeping or supercilious a statement to declare that in the early years of our century an almost incredible mass of tedious verse dramas was being written, a surprisingly large proportion of which even reached the stage. These dismal and remote echoes of the voices of Shakespeare and Milton reverberated a hollow blank verse linked to romantic posturing and footless abstraction. Words were loose, images vague or overprecious, ideas fantastic, and vigor lost. Meaning vanished before an advancing vacuum of dreamy idealism. The times awaited the sharp line and the precise word to rouse drama from its unaesthetic lethargy. It demanded short plays with fresh and vigorous symbolic statement. Pound's studies in European poetry encouraged T. S. Eliot's innovations in pure poetry ; his studies in the Noh and material aid from other fertilizing associations encouraged W. |B. Yeats' pseudo-Noh plays, which stand among his most brilliant creations. What Noh plays have already signified and may signify still more fully for the creative mind of the Western stage is best indicated by Yeats' work.

II

In the last chapter it was argued that Burns' lyricism and attachment to the supernatural present important common ground with the basic lyricism and magnetic supernaturalism of the Noh. Here the situation is similar though by no means identical. Yeats deliberately follows—imitate would be too strong and too injurious a word—works with which he had at least some acquaintance, whereas the relationship of Burns to the East is clearly no more than coincidental. In each case the dissimilarities must be recognized as almost more

striking than the likenesses. No need to list again the pronounced Western qualities of the obstreperous Scotchman.
The redoubtable Irishman was in many respects no less typical
a Westerner and a Celt. Far more than the austere and emotionally taught masters of the Noh, he loved violence, romantic
extravagance and abandon, the neo-primitive, the anarchic, the
untamable. His wide reading and mental sophistication notwithstanding, the inflammable and truculent Yeats remained
half-barbarian at heart. Disliking the civilization of his own
times, his attachment to civilization itself was more literary,
theoretical and abstract than even he himself realized. Decadent Byzantium, at least in theory, he loved ; but he
lived in a superficially civilized Ireland. His position comes
remarkably close to the mental and spiritual condition of the
Irish scholastic theologians of the heroic age of Ireland's
culture in the Middle Ages. He combined a highly masculine
capacity for intricate intellectual schematization with a feminine impulsiveness and a vagabond's emotionalism. As
intellectual as the neo-scholastic Blake, whom he knew well,
and as lyrical as the downright Burns, whom he did not know
well, he reached out to two typical extremes of Western
thought, northern impulsiveness and Mediterranean logicality.
In each case he departed to a sensational distance from the
mind of Zeami, a genius severely disciplined in his emotional
life and pious, not philosophical, in his profound religious
life. Each is a master craftsman, though the Japanese master
is the more eminent, if less versatile, since he holds the firmer
hand over his favorite art form. Yeats, with his own extraordinary and intuitive reading of the heart and his instinct
for artistic form, grasped, even through the ponderous veils of
translation, many of the leading principles of Noh style and
incorporated them as elements of greater or lesser importance
in some nine or ten of his most brilliant works.

Further preliminary observations are required to arrive at
anything approaching precise definitions of Yeats' indebtedness
to the Noh, a subject, curiously enough, that has not as yet
been carefully explored by his critics. Especially on the
basis of the information about the Noh available to him, he
must have realized the plays to be inadequate to satisfy his
appetite in the essentially theological subtleties which he so

keenly relished. The Noh plays are, indeed, metaphysical, religious and contemplative but in these matters provide no reasoned or systematic statements. For such Yeats turned to the Chinese philosophers, still more to the Sanskrit or Hindi masters, and most of all to the neo-platonic or Christian sages of Byzantium. One of the most moving passages in one of his finest poems, *Lapis Lazuli*, recreates the image of the Chinese humorous sages, presumably Taoists, with a manner close to Chikamatsu in his famous scene of the mystic go players as given in the philosophical interlude in *The Battles of Coxinga*. At the center of Yeats' mystical system was the worship of an egg as center for spheres of endless rotation. The classical expressions for this belief he discovered in Indian mysticism. His philosophical ideas he derived to a considerable degree from India, his ideals of style, from Japan. Indian poetry and drama appealed to him less than the Japanese. The Japanese vogue, supported by the French Impressionist painters and promoted by Whistler and Clive Bell, arrived in timely fashion to Yeats' hand. The aesthetic gospel according to Japan he also learned virtually at first hand from Japanese friends. The sharp but delicately ornamented Japanese sword supplied him with a symbol for his own favorite weapon, the pure, imaginative word. Equipped with a Japanese aesthetic to wage spiritual or, as Blake would have said, mental war in behalf of a Hindu philosophy, he possessed what his soul chiefly desired. Yeats was born with the gift for major poetry but still more was he instilled with an irresistible passion for the drama and even for the stage. He rightly perceived, more, perhaps, by instinct than by learning, that the finest flower of Japanese poetry resides in the Noh. To the Noh he turned not in a prolonged study of the thing itself, imperfectly revealed through the available translations and commentaries, but in quest of the beauty of its artistic design and poetic symbolism. Much too inspired an artist to venture on direct imitation of an object seen, as he must well have known, through a glass darkly, he visited the Noh not for the sake of transporting its art bodily to the West or to follow piously in its footsteps, to dress Noh plays in Irish costume or attempt their presentation on an Irish stage, but to derive as much and no more of what they might give him for his own highly original and creative work. The results appear in a series of short plays of extraordinary power in various degrees indebted to the Noh. The pattern is singularly simple and clear. The nearest to the Japanese is the first written, *At the Hawk's Well* (1917), with *The Only Jealousy of Emer* (1919) a close second. The influence is seen in gradually decreasing measure in *The Dreaming of the Bones* (1919), *Calvary* (1920), *The Resurrection* (1931), *A Full Moon in March* (1935), and *The King of the Great Clock Tower* (1935). The impact of the Noh was never forgotten ; traces of it are still visible in his last plays, *Purgatory* and *The Death of Cuchulain*, both appearing in 1939. None of the short plays written after 1917 is entirely without marks of the lessons which first and most strikingly bear fruit in *At the Hawk's Well*. This even holds true for those primarily romantic extravaganzas, *The Herne's Egg*, and *The Cat and the Moon*. Closer scrutiny shows also the ground preparing for the reception of the Noh even in such early plays as *On Baile's Strand* (1904), and *The Shadowy Waters* (1911), more than once revised. In his earliest and most romantic years he was as yet unripe for a warm reception of the Noh, even had it been available. That he never pressed forward to greater indebtedness than shown in *At the Hawk's Well*, but instead step by step diminished his borrowings, is chiefly owing to his fervent quest for individuality in art, his desire to create a form truly his own. Besides, even Yeats was to some measure a practical playwright, catering to a public. He knew that the romantic dish spiced with broad philosophical farce was more favorably received on the Irish stage than the austere stylization which he rightly recognized as the body and soul of Noh. In his eyes, which saw with so much clarity, the pseudo-Japanese manner called for specially trained dancers and actors. Ninette de Valois, as few others, appeared to him capable of carrying off the more stylized scenes and thus he wrote a few plays with her in mind. Yet *The King of the Great Clock Tower* he thoughtfully dedicated to her with the words : "to Ninette de Valois, asking pardon for covering her expressive face with a mask." The judgment of the poet did not surrender to the chivalry of the man ; the chivalry merely found a path to expression through the gesture of the dedication and in itself indicated the various obstacles that Yeats recognized as standing between himself and a complete acceptance of exotic technique which his ideal self may have envied.

At the Hawk's Well best illustrates what the Noh plays meant or failed to mean to Yeats. It cannot properly be called an imitation. Yeats, for example, bears witness to the typically Western conception of drama as conflict between individuals and ideas. The Guardian of the Well has perhaps the chief role. It is she, at least, who performs the culminating dance and holds the other two important figures at bay. Yet she by no means dominates the piece as the shite dominates the typical Noh. The rivalry between the Old and the Young Man has a strong Western ring. Furthermore, the play lacks the tragic climax of the Noh and falls considerably short of the intensity of the Japanese style. Yeats' well is comparatively cold ; the abstraction of the symbolism contrasts with the Noh's simple humanity. Yet like the Noh this is an essentially lyrical drama with important conventions obviously borrowed from the Japanese. Before this play no English play came remotely as near to the Oriental.

It is unnecessary to dwell on some of the more obvious borrowings, which speak loudly for themselves. There is an almost naked stage, with no curtain and no scenery. Throughout the series of plays to which this belongs Yeats employs a device oriental in spirit though not drawn directly from any Eastern source. The musicians on entering perform a ceremony of unfolding and then folding up a cloth, a ritual repeated at the play's end. During the unrolling and rolling up the chorus chant lyrical verses. On the cloth is inscribed a highly stylized symbol relevant to the play, in this instance "a gold pattern suggesting a hawk." One recalls Oriental textiles similarly ornamented.

Yeats' play is on an even more restricted scale than the succinct Noh. There chorus and musicians are separate and consist of at least four for the orchestra and usually eight for the chorus. Here there are only three, who perform both functions. As in the Noh—or for that matter, the early Greek drama—the chorus enters into conversation with the actors. In traditional manner they both sing and speak. Like the Japanese chorus, they serve in introducing and in terminating the play; during its course they habitually describe the actors' pantomime. The Old Man in Yeats' work is certainly suggested by both "The Man of the Place" and the Waki but takes a somewhat more active part than is usual with the parallel figures in the Japanese works. Both usages stress the basic contrast between old age and youth. The two men in Yeats' play further signify two other aspects of life, one the passive and contemplative, the other, the active and creative. Like the Japanese masters, Yeats is secretive. Only after the play has run most of its course do we discover, what even the cast of characters fails to inform the reader, that the Young Man is the hero of the chief sequence of Yeats' lyrical dramas, Cuchulain. For conclusive evidence that the Guardian of the Well is actually Aoife, his former wife and mother of the son whom he is destined unknowingly to kill, we must patiently wait until later plays of the series. This persistence of disguise is a feature of myth which Yeats could have derived from no source so readily as from the Noh but he signally failed to treat it with the practiced hand of the Japanese playwrights.

The use of stage properties and the pantomiming without properties are both drawn from Oriental sources and stand closer to the Noh than to the Chinese drama. Here the central feature is "a square blue cloth" which represents the well. This suggests the much stylized and modest constructions on the Noh stage representing imaginary mounds or monuments of various kinds. The well in *Izutsu* (*The Well-Curb*) offers the closest parallel. This object is in Yeats' drama the focal point of the entire action. The hawk-woman guards the well; the two men, one young, the other old, vainly attempt to drink from it. It is the peculiarity of the well to remain dry for long periods of time and when it does flow, to do so only in meagre quantity and at such unforeseen moments that it virtually escapes ministering to human needs. Austere in their mood as the tragic Noh plays are, the general purport of Yeats' symbolism is thus decidedly more pessimistic than the Japanese. Basically, his play, like *Waiting for Godot* and so much of the avant-garde symbolical drama of the mid-twentieth century, is an image of frustration. Nobody succeeds in drinking from the well, just as nobody arrives to greet Godot. The typical Noh play ends with an introduction to Buddhahood. Mortal man himself, as with Yeats, is doomed but in the Oriental work salvation lies beyond the mortal veil.

Of all parts in Yeats' play the Guardian of the Well comes closest to the Noh, yet with important differences. Thus she has no speaking part, though she utters the cry of a hawk. Her first appearance is pure pantomime, her second, pure dance. The division itself into two parts, the two incarnations, a mysterious old crone with faintly hawk-like gestures, and a gorgeous young spirit, half woman and half bird, is obviously inspired by the Noh. In Yeats' play, however, the heroine does not go out for a change of costume. She merely casts her black cloak, the old woman's garment, aside and arises as the fierce bird-dancer. Like so many of the Japanese supernatural enchantresses, she is a half-sinister figure. If the well signifies salvation, she signifies also a tragic error. The hero goes off-stage in vain pursuit of her. The most plausible explanation of the symbolism is that the well represents salvation that lies behind the material world ; the Guardian is the sensuous world ; the hero, or the complete man, must possess both body and soul to become whole. He is seduced through an heroic preference for the passionate or earthly life. Elsewhere Yeats employs symbols to express the reconciliation of opposites and the fulfillment through imagination of the desires of soul and body. This is signified, for example, in his vision of Byzantium. *At the Hawk's Well*, however, an early play in his sequence, merely presents the problem without its solution. Any such train of thought is, of course, philosophical in content and allegorical in form. The images and figures stand for abstractions. The play is actually a poem much in the manner of Blake's Prophetic Books. Its cast of thought is a romantic scholasticism. Thus while its imagery strongly suggests the Japanese and is suggested by the Japanese, its heart is with the scholastic divines, with Duns Scotus and Dionysius the Areopagite. While much of its technique is with Zeami, its soul is with Dante.

One of the most striking and least compromising resemblances between Yeats' lyric drama and the Noh consists in the singularly vivid nature imagery. The description of the rugged scene about the woodland well has great beauty. The images are brilliantly woven out of both the speakers' dialogue and the lyrics of the chorus. Similar address to the mind's eye where the landscape is paramount occurs in *The Dreaming of the Bones*, especially in a passage of imaginary travel much in the manner of the Noh travelogues. The characters ascend a mountain to view the coast of Ireland in magnificent panorama from its summit. This is a close approximation to like passages in the Noh.

Certainly Yeats cannot be said to fumble in his manipulation of the Noh style; he simply employs what he needs and rejects or alters as he wishes. Throughout his pseudo-Noh plays the masks have an important place. Especially in the later plays his usage comes even closer to the Japanese than in *At the Hawk's Well*. Still, he never strays far from Oriental precedent. In other words, he at no time composed a play in which all characters wear masks and seldom composed a lyrical drama in which a mask does not appear. The general rule for Yeats, as for Zeami, follows the eminently reasonable plan that the more naturalistically conceived characters, those existing in what we call real life, do not wear masks, whereas ghosts and supernatural beings do wear them. Yeats apparently came in a short time to realize the logic of this distinction and to make use of it. In *At the Hawk's Well*, however, the Old Man and the Young Man wear masks but not the obviously supernatural Guardian of the Well. Quite probably Yeats felt that a mask would impair the dancer's freedom. In almost all his lyric dramas he prescribes that the persons not wearing masks shall have their faces "made up to resemble masks." Such is the case here not only with the Guardian of the Well but with the three musicians. It is further noteworthy that the instrumental music is clearly intended to be closer to the oriental than to the occidental style. The three musicians play respectively a drum, a gong, and a zither, admirable for accompaniment of the singing, the pantomime and the dance. Such music performs an ideal function in the theatre without obscuring the beauty of the verse. If it fails to promise fulfillment of the Western ideal of pure music, at least it reminds the speculative critic that pure music in the West itself has of late changed its character in part through Oriental influences. Compositions by Stravinsky, Bartok and Prokofiev, like the dances of Martha Graham, Ted Shawn, and Ruth St. Denis, have shown conspicuous marks of Oriental inspiration. Martha Graham has employed several non-Europeans both for the music and the decor of her remarkable productions. Insofar as the arts in the West are concerned, this simply marks the trend of the times.

The Only Jealousy of Emer is a slightly more ambitious work than *At the Hawk's Well*, almost equally indebted to influence of the Noh. It is also more melodramatic as theatre and less readily interpreted intellectually. The intricacies and envolvements of its imagery have much in common with the Noh. The Ghost of Cuchulain, the Figure of Cuchulain, and the Woman of the Sidhe wear masks; in the case of the two mortal women, Yeats' direction is indefinite: "masked, or their faces made up to resemble masks." The musicians, visible as always in Yeats' lyric plays, as in the Oriental, have "their faces made up to resemble masks." Like the shite in the Noh plays, the Figure of Cuchulain wears two masks. A curtain is drawn over the sick man's bed so that he may exchange his heroic mask for one showing the distorted face of a man in intense pain. With a duplicity of meaning typical of the Noh, another actor on the stage, performing the Ghost of Cuchulain, wears a mask identical with the heroic mask on the face of the enchanted, masquerading Figure. The Woman of the Sidhe, who both dances and speaks, is a second emanation of Aoife, Cuchulain's early love, by whom he has had his favorite son. This again mirrors the Japanese. Indeed, the present play, with its theme of jealousy, suggests in particular *Aoi-no-Ue;* the name Aoife itself may well contain a reminiscence of Aoi. Aoi, it will be remembered, is represented in Zeami's play only by a cloth, which quite accords with Yeats' use of stage-symbols driven to the limit of abstraction. The imposition of one level of meaning upon another in the instance of the Woman of the Sidhe, who is both natural and supernatural, once more agrees in spirit with the calculated and controlled ambiguity of the Noh. In the play's general scheme, however, it is Cuchulain, wearing the two masks, who is a divided personality, not the three women represented as having loved him. The psychological conception of one person being invaded by the soul of another accords with a familiar conception in the Noh. *The Only Jealousy of Emer,* the most elaborately stylized of all Yeats' plays, thus comes close to the Noh in a large number of its conventions. In fact, these are so many that they crowd and jostle one another on the stage so that their very multiplicity marks a departure from the simpler and more economical theatre of the Noh. As an enthusiastic convert to an aesthetic creed, Yeats has carried his zeal too far. His play is snared in the web of its own artifice ; it should probably be regarded as less subtle than the Japanese ; its intricacies lie conspicuously on its surface, making it hard to follow, especially when read by one unfamiliar with details of the Cuchulain myth. The subtlety of a Japanese play, on the contrary, lies well beneath the surface of its simplified action.

The comparative simplicity of *The Dreaming of the Bones*, then, by no means alienates it from strong likenesses to the Japanese. Here the story is of political rather than psychological significance. Ireland's destiny becomes the leading theme rather than the purification of passion, the attainment of the super-human, or the endless rotation of the wheels of history and of love, of the material and the spiritual worlds. Of its two outstanding likenesses to the Noh, one has already been mentioned, the singularly vivid nature-imagery, with the imagined climb to the summit of the holy mountain. The second likeness resides in the strict division between two periods of time and two classes of figures, namely, the living and the dead. The dead, two lovers in Ireland's heroic age who have sinned against her political destiny by introducing alien chieftains to her shores, wear masks and also costumes of the heroic age. The Young Man wears no mask and is in common modern dress. He is still alive, a soldier for Ireland escaped from the recent uprising in Dublin. The dead plead for unity and for self-dependence for Ireland. As ghostly shapes of the ancestors, they distinctly resemble heroes of the Noh. The chorus in this political play fulfills its functions admirably, compromising between the overstraining of the credulity and the underplaying of the imagination. Elements from the Noh prove fundamental, though in its total affect the play has considerably less magic and less mystery than the typical play either by Yeats or by Zeami. For this, the theme must in part account. A political ghost is as a rule less harrowing than a more distinctly personal apparition.

A Full Moon in March reflects one of the most extraordinary and artificial devices of the Noh, one figure speaking for another. Here there is no chorus as a group that speaks and sings in the person of one of the play's major characters. There is, in fact, no choral singing in the sense that two or more singers perform in unison. The two musical figures are no longer designated as choral figures but as First Attendant and Second Attendant. During the play's climax, the Queen's frenzied dance about the severed head, the First Attendant sings "as Queen," the Second "as Head." The former also laughs "as Queen," the Second laughs "as Head." The Second Attendant further speaks as Captain of the Guard. This technique belongs to the Noh and to scarcely any other type of play. Yeats' fondness for March as symbol, which to him denotes the turning-point of the year, at least suggests the Japanese fondness for using a season of the year as an important part of the play's imagery. Yet *A Full Moon in March* is by no means the closest of Yeats' works to the Japanese, as its use of masks indicates. The Queen apparently wears no mask at all, the Swineherd, only a half-mask. Here Yeats departs from the Oriental usage to the extent of using curtains ; there is both an inner curtain and an outer. The inner, however, may be regarded as equivalent to the curtain used in the entrance of the shite. It is employed solely to "discover" the Queen in attitudes of importance for the play's progress. She is twice unveiled, thus making two entrances, a treatment agreeing fully with the customary treatment of the Noh play's heroine.

In its general symbolism *The King of the Great Clock Tower* repeats the pattern of *A Full Moon in March*. Here it is "The Stroller" who plays the role of poet and lover, wearing, like the Swineherd, a mask covering only the upper part of his face. The Queen is described as wearing "a beautiful impassive mask ;" the jealous king, an eminently human figure, wears no mask whatsoever. Again there are two Attendants, one of whom speaks as Captain of the Guard and later sings as the Severed Head, the other singing as the Queen, who is once more a dancer at the play's climax. Much as in the Noh, at least two distinct dances are provided for the Queen, the first accompanied by a song, the second only by the instruments. The play is extremely powerful theatre yet its movement bears, perhaps, less resemblance to the Noh than to a Renaissance masque. The dancing in the end gains the upper hand of the words to an extent rarely encountered in the Noh, even though Yeats provides one of his fine lyrical passages sung by the Attendant for the play's closing moments.

The last group of Yeats' lyric plays with scenes laid in Ireland largely dispense with the Noh conventions. *The Cat and the Moon* stands nearer to the Koygen farces than to the tragic Noh, and the same may be said of the longer and more elaborate, *The Herne's Egg*. Here the bird-imagery, long cherished by Yeats, has a Japanese ring yet he has made it emphatically his own while his private metaphysics and mythology draw a fairly thick curtain between his play and whatever vestiges of the Oriental may remain. There is much humor and robust farcing, as in some of Yeats' early work, and, of course, alien to the Noh, which remains nothing if not serious. Those tragic verse-plays, *Purgatory*, and *The Death of Cuchulain*, mark still further departures. If .they resemble the Noh at all, it is in their bold liberties in dealing with time. The climax of *Purgatory* occurs in a vision superimposing a scene from many years before that of the brief play's enveloping action. *The Death of Cuchulain* summarizes the hero's life. The first play has no dance ; the second at least ends with a dance scene. Like most of Yeats' lyrical dramas and like the Noh, it also introduces a pipe or flute which becomes especially conspicuous in the climax. Nevertheless, the two works give the impression of romantic poetry and melodrama. The Irish scene and spirit carry great power, casting into the shade the world of more delicate artifice typifying the Noh.

In addition to the plays with a Celtic background, in two works Yeats experimented with a transposition of his lyrical dramas to biblical lands. Like a baroque composer, he uses similar technique for themes secular and divine. *Calvary* appeared in 1922, only a year after *The Only Jealousy of Emer*, and three years after *At the Hawk's Well*. This is also a play with musicians and masked faces, the three major actors representing Christ, Lazarus, and Judas. Again a symbolic cloth is wound and unwound. Three soldiers perform a sinister dance around the cross. Not even in the literature of the Noh is there a more cruel irony. *The Resurrection*, written eleven years later, is more philosophical and less lyrical and to this extent further from the Noh. Verse occurs only in the opening and closing songs, performed by three musicians as a trio. No dancing is seen, though a Dionysian dance is imagined off-stage and vividly described, while the musicians on-stage sing in impersonation of the female worshippers. The speaking characters are all anonymous, being a Greek, a Hebrew, and a Syrian. Their debate is chiefly theological, which at least to this extent by no means differs from a few Noh plays, though Yeats' tone, as befits his scene, is rather more Platonic. Christ, who has risen from the grave, does not speak. On the drawing of a curtain he is revealed in the play's climax as a hieratic figure with a "stylistic mask." The Greek idealistic philosopher, to his utter consternation, on touching Christ's wound feels the strong beating of his heart. Christ stalks silently across the stage into an inner room. A new and more turbulent age in history has begun. Only in the hieratical character and brilliantly contrived movement of this scene does Yeats' extraordinary play share any major features with the Noh. Yeats appropriately celebrates the last moments of an age of reason with a calculated coolness absent from his own "turbulent" Celtic plays.

On reviewing Yeats' discriminating and persistent use of the Noh through approximately a score of years, some generalizations are suggested. His remarkable achievement bears almost no relation to its popular reception in the theatre. The plays have been quite widely read and much admired but seldom seen. None of the plays in question has been given frequently and a few have been almost completely neglected as stage pieces. They were not intended for large audiences and have not been performed before them. Some were written with a particular actor or dancer in mind, whose availability determined much of the nature of the work. Yeats himself frankly viewed the plays as experimental, though he unquestionably believed in their aesthetic validity and the ideas contained in them. They have, then, flourished more as poems than as plays. Yet, like the Noh, they are both poems and plays, indeed, the harmony between the two media proves remarkable. Needless to say, they further combine, as does the Noh, verse, singing, instrumental music, spectacle, pantomime, dance. Brief as they are, such demands for production have generally discouraged the attempt. Original music must be found and music of a decidedly exceptional kind. The musicians must also be actors—no small demand upon modern instrumentalists. There must be at least one good woman dancer. The properties, masks, character-transformations, and general style of acting and reading of the lines make demands difficult today to meet. Yet production is by no means impossible. Any group of actors that has experimented with Noh plays will enjoy a pronounced advantage in approaching Yeats' works, as any group familiar with Yeats must enjoy a considerable advantage in approaching the Noh. The principles and practices controlling the Japanese plays are in varying measure present in Yeats' verse dramas. These comprise a treasure which must be increasingly opened up as the West itself becomes more at home with the East, from which so much of its inspiration springs.

Although probably no writer in English has gained as much as Yeats from the Noh tradition or fused its contributions so fully with his own creativity, a considerable number of poets and playwrights in both England and America attest to its force. With the greatly improved translating recently accomplished, this fertilizing power is certain to increase. In the America of our own century at least two poet-playwrights must be selected for comment here, Wallace Stevens and Kenneth Rexroth. Though it is often forgotten that Stevens wrote for the theatre, during the period of the First World War he composed two plays, the lesser of which was produced at approximately the time of its writing. *Carlos Among the Candles* is a monologue and dance. A middle-aged man in old-fashioned dress lights two dozen candles burning in different parts of a room and thereafter extinguishes them, reciting highly symbolic words as he does so. This is a play of dance and light. In no specific regard whatsoever does it suggest an Oriental stage. But its general affect is rococo and, of course, the rococo itself has strong ties with the East.

Three Travellers Watch a Sunrise, first published in *Poetry : a Magazine of Verse* (1916), and presented shortly thereafter is a radically different work with the one outstanding exception that each calls for imaginative use of light in the theatre. Like Yeats' lyric theatre, this play is eclectic : Oriental influence is powerful though by no means all-inclusive. Both Japanese and Chinese elements are present. Resemblance to the Noh appears chiefly in the extreme economy of expression and calculated acceleration of tempo and excitement from the dark and all but barren stage of the early moments to the grim tragedy of the conclusion. As usual in the Noh, little or nothing happens in our material world ; what action there is has taken place before the play begins. At first darkness is relieved only by a single lantern carried by the most sympathetic figure in the play, called only "the Second Chinese." At approximately the mid-point a candle is lit ; at length two lanterns are used ; finally, after considerable pantomime, embellished by periods of philosophic discourse, a slow dawn reveals the body of a suicide suspended from a tree. In the near-by shrubbery a girl is discovered, who declares herself the lover of the dead man, their union long thwarted by powers beyond their strength to resist. The pathos of the passive, briefly-speaking girl resembles that of many figures in Noh plays. The characters leave the stage, giving the girl their kindly aid. That is all. There is a total absence of dancing. If this be Noh at all, it is Noh in deep-freeze.

The phenomenal economy of the scene is both striking and affective. Beside the candle is placed a round jar of red porcelain, one judges, a specimen of Oriental ceramics. The reflections of the candle-light on the jar's surface symbolize the illuminations cast by art upon the world. The protracted debate between the three Chinese philosophers is completely typical of Stevens and in itself need not concern us here save that Stevens' work, like several Noh plays, is dedicated to the praise of poetry and the description of its qualities. The position of the three Chinese strictly as commentators on the situation at hand, conducting a philosophical debate only by indirection concerned with the girl and her lover, is far more in the tradition of the Western moralizing chorus than in that of the more active chorus of the Noh plays. Like the

Noh, this work centers upon a mental action but thought is not intimately tied to dramatic action. In this respect this didactic drama lacks the artistic integrity which the Noh invariably possesses. Stevens' brilliant but laboriously intellectual play may be described as abortive Noh. The mind chills the soul.

By virtue of its subject-matter, *Three Travellers Watch a Sunrise* strongly reminds its reader of the famous scene, already mentioned in these pages, of the two philosophical "go" players, or sages, in Chikamatsu's *Battles of Coxinga*. In this episode a hero, carrying with him a child rescued from threatened death, encounters high on the mountains of China (Stevens' scene is a hilltop in Pennsylvania) two sages bent over their board with its white and black figures. (Stevens is to Chikamatsu as the Alleghenies are to the Himalayas.) The game reflects the two elements in the universe, the *yin* and *yang*. It also affords an image of military strategy, foretelling the battles through which the hero is presently to pass unscathed. The Chinese sages are completely absorbed in their meditations. Obviously they are brothers to the unforgettable figures later to be imagined by Yeats in his *Lapis Lazuli* :

Two Chinamen, behind them a third,
Are carved in lapis lazuli,
Over them flies a long-legged bird,
A symbol of longevity.
The third, doubtless a serving-man,
Carries a musical instrument.
Every dislocation of the stone,
Every accidental crack or dent,
Seems a water-course or an avalanche,
Or lofty slope where it still snows
Though doubtless plum or cherry-branch
Sweetens the little half-way house
Those Chinamen climb towards, and I
Delight to imagine them seated there ;
There, on the mountain and the sky,
On all the tragic scene they stare.
One asks for mournful melodies ;
Accomplished fingers begin to play.

Their eyes mid many wrinkles, their eyes,
Their ancient, glittering eyes, are gay.

Many details in Yeats' extraordinary lines mirror the scene
as sketched in Stevens' play. In the play, for example, a
negro carries a basket containing a musical instrument played
later as accompaniment to a mournful song. Probably Yeats
was thinking of real objects of art, not of Stevens' play or
Chikamatsu's and probably, too, Stevens had never read a
translation of the great Japanese drama with its scenes in
China nor, even if he had done so, would have given it more
than a passing thought, if that, in the writing of his play.
Nevertheless, out of material of this nature many scenes in
the Noh are constructed. The meditative spirit praised by
Yeats and realized by both Stevens and Chikamatsu is also
of the Noh. This was part of the large heritage passed on by
China to ancient Japan.

One further detail in Stevens' play associating it with the
Noh calls for attention. This concerns a symbolical change of
costume, a device of much importance for the Noh. When the
three philosophical Chinese enter, they are described as dressed
in European clothes. These they wear only for the first few
moments of the action. Scarcely a hundred words are spoken,
when they begin, with the assistance of their two negro servants (mute throughout the entire action) to robe themselves
in ceremonial costumes of silk, designated as red, blue and
green. The feeling here is in the ceremonial spirit of the Noh.

Stevens' strangely neglected play is singularly beautiful.
The poet himself never included it in any collection of his
works, perhaps disappointed with it in that it had received
so little attention as a work for the theatre. It certainly
violated almost all prevailing principles of Western drama-
turgy. Nor was it strictly of the Noh, either, and far less of
the Chinese stage. Incidentally, that its three outstanding
figures are Chinese by no means alienates it from Japanese
theatrical tradition, for several Noh plays, as the famous
Kantan, have their scenes in China, as does Chikamatsu's
masterpiece. Stevens' work is much indebted both to the
current vogue of Orientalism in general and to the emerging
interest in the Noh in particular. He took keen interest

323

in Oriental art, as many allusions in his poems testify. He was familiar with the admirable scholarship of the contemporary American poet, Arthur Davidson Ficke, on the subject of the Japanese print. A wide and avid reader and an enthusiastic dilettante, he knew the early researches of Pound and Fenellosa and must have been familiar with the already superb collections from Japan in the Boston Museum of Fine Arts. Incitements from many sides converged to give his play its strong Oriental flavor and its curious parallels to technical and spiritual aspects of the Noh.

With at least one aspect of the Noh the urbane Stevens shows scant sympathy. This is the daemonic quality. The furtive negro mimists in *Three Travellers Watch a Sunrise* may have a bare touch of this, but no more. The romantic or even frenzied qualities in the Noh, on the contrary, are consciously suggested in *Beyond the Mountains,* a sequence of verse-plays by Kenneth Rexroth, himself a student of Oriental literature and translator from Oriental poetry and in his own art antithetical to Stevens' urbanity. His explosive plays have the frankness in sexual images in one respect typical of the Japanese. They likewise make effective use of theatrical dancing with symbolic intent. Their cloudy atmosphere of myth and mysticism at least approximates the world of the Noh. Although their subject-matter is from the Greek, the treatment is distinctly closer to the Oriental. With so many features resembling the Japanese poetic drama, the total effect would be considerably closer than actually the case were it not for a romantic turgidity entirely alien to both Wallace Stevens and to the clean-cut lines of the Japanese masterpieces. The conclusion is presumably that only poets of the stature of Yeats or Stevens can be expected to make really close approaches to the difficult art perfected by Zeami.

Stevens and Yeats wrote their verse dramas without the direct experience of seeing Noh productions in Japan and before the superior translations and accumulated researches of the last few years were at hand to aid them. Considerable familiarity with Japanese drama and art was obviously possible for them, though far less than is accessible today. It may confidently be expected that the plays themselves will henceforth be from time to time given outside Japan. With these developments in process it proves by no means difficult to foresee a steady increase in the influence of the Noh drama on the theatrical thought and activity of the West. The Noh plays may be expected to enter increasingly into the current of general culture both as masterpieces in themselves and as inspiration to the makers of new and increasingly imaginative dramatic forms.

9 / *The Future of the Noh*

THE WORDS, "the future of the Noh," may seem a contradiction in terms. The Noh resembles those characters in history whom we invariably think of as ripe in years. Perhaps of all art-forms this looks the most venerable. The time is not known when it was young. From what stately temple chants or dances, folk ceremonies or rituals of princes, its various aspects derived we have little or no precise knowledge. Its origins are veiled in conjecture, fascinating or baffling according to the temperament of the thinker. So far as history permits us to see, the form sprang fully mature from the creative mind of the older Zeami. His son and their numerous followers built for many years upon the well established foundations. Little or nothing appears to have altered less. How far this constancy can be literally understood is doubtless a matter for dispute. It is safe to presume that nothing can actually be as changeless as the Noh appears. As we have seen, there have been scholarly speculations as to the alterations in presentational style and in the style of playwriting. As far as known the evolution has been moderate and gradual. This is largely because the conservative practice has been willed. The literature and stage customs in the Noh correspond in this regard to the Episcopal Book of Common Prayer. No revolutionary changes have been made. Alterations at any given time have been minor and when they have occurred have encountered much resistance. The will to preserve has been considerably stronger than the will to reform. Beyond a doubt, what changes have occurred have insinuated themselves into the productions and have seldom, if ever, been deliberate.

There is a strong illusion of constancy. The Noh is the liturgy of a faith founded upon aesthetics. Against time's assaults it presents three imposing fronts : it is in itself supremely sound craftsmanship ; it is established upon mannered forms that are singularly precise and thus peculiarly easy to transmit intact, even though great labor is required to master the style ; and in its uniqueness it strongly appeals to a national pride. Nothing can be more preeminently Japanese. Hence it becomes a matter of patriotism that its ritual shall be retained. And preserved it has been, virtually as the rituals and secrets of Masonry and similar cults have been handed down from remote generations. To be sure, the Noh is a public art, a mystery openly performed. But from the viewpoint of its practitioners, concerned as they must be with the technical nuances of its production, it has virtually the tenacity of a secret guild the rigidities of whose practices resent serious modifications.

This acknowledged rigidity lends a piquancy to the term "modern noh." One instantly recognizes that from one point of view the Noh and modernity are wholly incompatible. In the strict sense of the words there can be no such thing as a modern noh. The conception is irreconcilable with the conditions. Figuratively speaking, the Noh is carved in the hardest stone, cast in the hardest bronze. It reminds one of the infant in the facetious rhymes of W. S. Gilbert. For it was born a classic. It was also born at a period when Japan was entering upon a long era of strength through conservatism, with the sternest possible insulation from contaminating change, a granite island surrounded by the weltering seas of history.

Making up for much time lost, Japan today unveils the story of one of the most rapid evolutions recorded by the historian. The flood-gates of change were, of course, opened a little more than a century ago. Is there a possibility that in some way even the Noh, the hard core of Japanese conservatism, may in time participate in its own fashion in the tide of evolution ? Can there be in some sense a new era or new incarnation for the Noh ? The question may well be answered in the affirmative. Certain forces by no means obscure are pressing in this direction. New types of music and dance are being inaugurated that may be wedded to the Noh with gratifying results. Even in Japan a fair possibility exists that there will be new graftings on the sturdy, ancient stem. For true works of art are never mechanical ; all are biological and subject to the laws of biological evolution. It is quite plausible that there will be important developments for the Noh in Japan and much more plausible that there will be such outside Japan. New translations and commentaries, above all, the translations into English of the major plays in the work of the Classical Translations Committee, may open up this area to the world as sensationally as the country of its origins was unveiled a century ago.

The plays themselves contain one of the happiest clues to the prospect that, the static past notwithstanding, a dynamic future lies ahead. According to Oriental habits of thought, a deity may manifest itself in any number of forms simply by virtue of being a deity. Similarly, it is in the very nature and definition of any presentational work of art rising to the dignity of a classic that it not only may but will be so manifest. There is no one way to perform Aeschylus, Aristophanes, Shakespeare, Bach, Mozart, or Beethoven. A core of mysterious yet highly potent vitality exists in works of such masters which brings it about that they will be successfully produced when translated into many different styles of performance. They will be variously understood and, what amounts to much the same, variously interpreted. They will also continually contribute new ideas of art affecting the taste of each succeeding generation. The universality is accompanied by a profound adaptability. If the Noh is as masterly in its art and as universal in its meaning as these studies have maintained, it follows that it cannot be indefinitely confined within a narrow presentational orbit. It will not only be variously produced but will exercise a pressure upon other art works in no way immediately related to itself.

Strict adherence to the classical Japanese idiom does not seem necessary to expression of the basic meaning of any one of the major Noh plays. Their remarkable abstract patterns can be covered with other flesh and sustained with transfusion from other blood. Modern Japan itself may well prove capable of maintaining their essence and rendering this all the more alive by presenting the plays with new inflections of speech, new styles of music, dance, mime, costume, acting, and decor. The very fact that "modern noh" have been written, fantastically unlike the old plays as these new works really are, indicates a bias for this hopeful direction.

Actually, the prospects for a new lease of life for the Noh hardly look greater or brighter in Japan than elsewhere in the civilized world. The world is now in possession of sensitive, elegant, and above all, reliable translations, especially into English, works well edited and critically described, with copious illustrations of a theatrical nature. Of course a translation can never be the equivalent of an original but it can be a work of great power and beauty notwithstanding its derivativeness. Also, if it is reliable, it may be so much the more useful, for minor variations in the interest of a purer expressiveness and a special audience may then be safely made. No translations remotely comparable to those of the Society for Classical Translations had been known during the long years between the rise of the Noh and the activity of this singularly well guided Society. When given abroad and with these texts as a basis there is certain to be much deviation from any possible production, new or old, in Japan.

The extremely exotic glamor of actual Noh performances in the land of their origin, the music so strange to Western ears, the exotic habits of speech and gesture, song and dance, need not conceal the warm heart within. Dressed in the most fantastic robes, the plays are almost naive in their essence. It is almost as though one of Wordsworth's poems of sentiment had been dressed in a learned Miltonic rhetoric—save that the simple core of the Noh play, unlike the romantic Wordsworthian lyric, is wholly free from suspicion of romantic sentimentality and the dramatic rhetoric not impossibly less bookish and more inspired than Milton's strained latinisms.

Of course not all Noh plays give promise of withstanding the long voyage out of the medieval past and into the modern idiom, either in or outside Japan. No foreigner will ever understand a Noh play quite as a Japanese scholar understands it nor will any foreign actors, dancers, singers, or, in particular, instrumentalists, perform quite as the Japanese do or feel as they do. The point of these remarks is not that a strict identity in production can be maintained but that some degree of diversity is inevitable if the plays are either to be read or produced outside Japan, or, for that matter, for an indefinite period of time in Japan itself. The question is simply one of relativity versus absolutism. Relativity is bound to catch up even with the Noh. If the plays are as fine art as many think them to be, they will not obstinately resist change but in various ways and degrees adapt themselves to it.

Many Noh plays are no longer performed. Although some of these unseen works actually deserve performance and would in all probability be successful if reasonably well given, undoubtedly a larger number have definitely become obsolete. They exist but they do not live. Plays of a narrowly feudalistic outlook, of a technically theological vision, or of insistently local reference have already faded from sight. Never again will they evoke the genuine enthusiasm which they once did evoke. A considerable number are congratulatory pieces, actually occasional pieces, written to celebrate local shrines and deities, lords and ecclesiastics. Like birthday odes, they have once served their purpose, gracefully or even brilliantly, but their survival is actually gratuitous. They have lived off the charity of time and not on the strength of their own deeper merits. Although some plays inspired by patriotism, as *Takasago*, have universal significance, many more in this category are current today, if at all, only in the country of their origin. Unquestionably, the editors representing the aforementioned translation committee knew well enough that some four or five of their selections have little more than historic significance. Such plays repay the attention of scholars. They occasionally represent dramatic types once flourishing in large quantity. But they belong to neither the living theatre nor the living literature of today. Clearly, only a part of the Noh literature withstands transportation. But in general the judgment of the committee translating the plays in the recent monumental collection promises to be authenticated by time. Their critical understanding appears in its field to be as classically sound as the creative mastery of the playwrights whom they admire. As a rule their own commentary indicates the rare occasions when they deli-

berately and knowingly consent to translate lesser works.
In this respect their judgment far surpasses that of Arthur
Waley or any other anthologist. There is a fair number of
great plays not among those in the already published volumes.
These volumes, however, give a remarkably convincing picture
not only of the best Noh literature but—which is saying much
the same—of that part of it which withstands not only the
inevitable violation of translation but the wrench also experienced when any such work is reborn in a new presentational idiom.

Something of the problems facing the believer in the universality of the Noh in its power to inspire the imagination
outside the cult now practicing the art of reading and producing
Noh plays in Japan may be indicated by a project undertaken
by the present writer. He has recently arranged a group of
nine Noh plays for possible production abroad, more specifically, in the academic theatres of the colleges and univer-
sities in the United States chiefly attended by negro students.
These institutions are ably represented by an organization,
The National Association of Dramatic and Speech Arts.
Leaders of this Association recognize no rigid demarcations
between the repertory which they favor and that of the American professional theatre, or the civic and community theatres, not to mention the academic theatres operated chiefly
by a personnel other than negroes. Yet on the whole they
lean more cordially and naturally than other groups toward
the non-European theatre. This means necessarily toward
the Asian theatre—Africa, for example, having in its tradition
little that in modern terms can be regarded as dramatic art.
Work in music and dance is not infrequently conducted in
the institutions represented in the National Association of
Dramatic and Speech Arts with much enthusiasm and some
success. Conditions are, then, favorable for the introduction
of Noh plays into this repertory. Clearly, when so introduced,
it is impossible to imagine them performed either strictly in
the manner in which they are now seen in Tokyo or in which
they were given six hundred years ago under Zeami's directing
eye. What plays will best bear such transportation and under
what terms? How favorable are the prospects for such an
enterprise? In facing these questions it is obvious that we are

331

dealing with the future. Very little has anywhere been done toward any productions of Noh plays outside Japan. On the few occasions when the experiment has been made, the philosophy of production has generally been a frank aspiration to come as close to the traditional, orthodox Japanese style as possible. Are other philosophies of production feasible ?

First for the type of Noh play that best withstands transplanting. Where a play is to be given outside Japan with a Japanese decor and in a style as close to the Japanese medieval tradition as possible, the distinction between one play and another may signify relatively little. The beauty of the costumes, the strangeness and possibly the elegance of the production will offer a stronger attraction than whatever truly literary, poetic, dramatic, emotional or spiritual values the play properly considered as a play may possess. One work may serve the purpose almost as well as another and a piece with little content may actually be preferable to one in which intellectual or emotional content obtrudes. The abstract beauty of the Noh style is indeed great and at least intimations of this may survive transportation onto a foreign stage. A few "congratulatory pieces", or a work such as *Takasago*, may be shown to good effect, though wide areas of meaning available to any educated Japanese audience will be lost on the greater part of even a well-instructed audience abroad. Production with such an effect, however, is divested of the greater part of the play's potential value as Japanese audiences know it and cannot well become a major event in dramatic experience. The values of the Noh for a cosmopolitan culture are of a more substantial character, closer by far to the value of *Hamlet* than to that of *The Mikado*. The plays have a cosmopolitan worth as plays quite beyond their worth as spectacles, dances, pantomimes, or superficial entertainments.

The first Noh plays to make a serious impression as stage productions upon the world outside Japan will presumably not be those of the most eminently philosophical, theological or religious character. There is small prospect, for example, for the warm reception of such an exquisite work as *Sanemori*, devoted to the celebration of a particular deity and shrine. They will be plays with a core of direct, simple and powerful emotional expression. Their focus will be on the emotional life as experienced far and wide throughout the human world. Their structure will exhibit the unsurpassed mastery of montage and other dramatic effects attained by the Noh playwrights. They will also be plays in which the dancing, though inevitably present, will not be the predominant feature. On the whole, the literary and strictly dramatic values are more readily transported than the choreographic values. Much of the former can be retained from the original; much of the latter will have to be laboriously recreated afresh in the foreign production.

The Sumida River and *Miidera* are ideal instances of Noh plays with potentially universal value. Each has for its simple situation the love of a mother for her lost son. In one of the plays the son, who has died, appears only for a few moments, visible in his ghostly body; in the other he is happily recovered. That one is to this extent a tragedy, the other a tragicomedy or dramatic romance, signifies little or nothing so far as their essential value is concerned, save that the pathos in the one and the ecstasy in the other afford unsurpassed dramatic experiences of different kinds. The values, both aesthetic and emotional, can be readily transported if a fair degree of imaginative power is expended. *The Stumbling Boy* instances another work based on the parent-child relation, in this case between a father and a son. It has unfailing, poignant power, a pure inspiration that nowhere can run dry.

With its conjunction of dramatic affects suggesting the most moving moments of *Oedipus at Colonus* and *Samson Agonistes*, *Kagekiyo* steps forth without a tremor of embarrassment out of the theatre of medieval Japan into the universal theatre of mankind. Although the professional Noh scholar will doubtless insist that only persons of his fraternity appreciate the multiplicity of its nuances, there is a sense in which the meaning of scarcely a syllable or a gesture need be lost upon any audience witnessing it creditably produced. The emotional relationship here is between father and daughter. Further deepening the play's value is the ironic or tragic treatment of time, the picture of the tragic change within a single soul between years of youthful power and triumph and declining years of misery and defeat. *Shunkan*, the supreme evocation of the pains of exile and loneliness, addresses itself to some of the most basic values and fears of mankind. To imagine it outmoded is to insult the breadth and depth of the human heart. Quietly and with complete assurance the play awaits its reincarnation in any time or place to which good fortune transports it.

There is a fairy-tale charm in plays such as *The Dwarf Trees* which gives them the elusive universality belonging to the best tales for children or the masterpieces of folklore. This play, too, can easily be imagined today as travelling from land to land.

Atsumori is widely ingratiating on both aesthetic and moral grounds. Admirably contrived as art, it proves no less affective in its image of reconciliation between enemies, its celebration of peace enforced by religious and imaginative vision. A successful warrior who has killed his foe broods with regret on his tempestuous, militant life. He becomes a monk. On his travels he meets a stranger who persuades him to pray for his soul. This stranger is finally revealed as the ghostly manifestation of his slain enemy. Man and ghost for a moment are suspended on the threat of renewed conflict but a higher wisdom conquers. The drama has great consoling and healing power wherever personal or public strife threatens to disturb mankind. It is one of the noblest of Asian religious dramas, comparable to justly celebrated pacifist and Buddhistic works in the Tibetan and the Tamil languages. The world today has more reason than ever to hold it in request.

Man's worldly, not his ideal or spiritual nature, is chiefly addressed in some of the most readily approachable of Noh plays, such as *Ataka* and *Settai* (Hospitality). Although these are in a sense melodramas of military life, stressing feudal and family loyalties which are far from being universally cherished, nothing alien to the basic qualities in human nature estranges an audience from participating whole-heartedly in them. Given human nature as it is, the universal is not always the profound. Though lacking the spiritual depths of the dramas recently cited, they have the simplest and most direct appeal and present the most vivid theatrical situations. Scarcely any plays in the entire classical literature for the stage can rely more safely on broad popularity. *Ataka* is possibly the less serious but presumably the more thrilling as theatre.

Its mastery of dramatic suspense and exciting pantomime long ago made it one of the most successful scenes in the Kabuki theatre. Although it makes great demands upon the actors, there is nothing of an esoteric nature in these demands. It is almost certain to be to some degree effective whenever, wherever, and in whatever idiom it is produced, with the further distinction that there is no end of the nuances that superior skill may contribute to its presentation.

From the foregoing survey it may be seen not only wherein the seeds of universal drama lie in the Noh but how varied are the affects which the plays offer. Especially in translation, the text, it must be confessed, is likely to appear almost oversimple in its rhetoric. As preceding chapters have illustrated, the high artistry of the plays derives from structural and symbolic rather than from strictly linguistic refinements. But these circumstances give encouragement to a wide purveyance of the plays. Translation generally signifies a serious loss in strictly linguistic refinements but no such loss in structural and symbolical elements, which readily survive transportation. The presentational problem hangs largely on the use of a highly stylized theatre, without absolute demands as to the type of stylization. The essence of a Noh play can hardly be translated into a naturalistic theatre—one of the obstinate facts forbidding certain forms of "modern Noh." But there are many mansions in the world of style, to almost all of which the Noh plays are potentially welcome guests.

Many aspects of the Noh suggest that their areas of conquest lie in a strongly musical theatre. To begin with, from its inception the Noh plays have themselves always been a musical form of theatre. But their music as it has survived constitutes on the whole a less attractive contribution to modern taste than their poetry or spectacle and probably a less gratifying element than their dance or mime. Its vocal line is by no means universally attractive; its instruments and their sounds to most ears appear somewhat archaic. The world as a whole, including Japan, has developed musically during the intervening centuries at a remarkable pace. Especially outside Japan the plays invite a new type of musical setting, indeed they must receive such a setting if they are really to flourish widely across the map of the world. To

335

hold that the Noh should be or can be converted into opera constitutes, perhaps, a mere quibble in words. There is little in the form of opera, peculiar to the West, which specifically suggests the Noh. But music-drama in a variety of idioms it certainly may become, while its texts promise a substantial improvement on the familiar *opera libretto*. The large amount of dancing further encourages musical arrangements. The dispositions of the parts, with the regular chorus, the semi-chorus supplied by the attendants, the duet and frequent antiphonal singing, and the lyric quotations all invite or even demand musical settings. This is further enhanced by the mood of the plays, their pronounced emotional tone, their dramatic "paragraphs", their studied phrasing and unsurpassed achievement of montage. In most cases the range of the parts is favorable. In the cast are old persons and children, as a rule both men and women, though three of the nine plays just reviewed—a representative group—are without women. Use of Noh plays in the Western repertory of music drama well might contribute materially to the advance of the musical stage. A composer in any land in search of inspiring examples of skill in the writing of music drama can do no better than consult the classical theatre of Japan.

Are these developments for the Noh probable or even possible ? Is the Noh stage, notwithstanding its unquestionable brilliance so far as the arena of its native country is concerned, too insular or too medieval in temper to withstand transplanting in any form ? Is it destined to be known abroad only as written drama and as a secondary inspiration for plays, such as those by Yeats, Stevens and Rexroth, only vaguely like the Eastern works ? These studies began with a statement that the species is in a special sense unique. Does this indicate that they must remain isolated from the pre-sentational point of view and largely infertile in creating mixed forms ? The obstacles to their intercourse with the world theatre are only too clear. The Noh is a cult of almost incredible virtuosity, with a spirit of such an uncompromising purism among its performers that to them, probably above all, such developments as suggested in this chapter appear not only fantastically unreal but positively distasteful. Their outlook argues in behalf of all or nothing. As too often the case, those knowing an art best trust its circulation the least. The premises of the purists are that thus far little or no change has occurred and that as far as possible none should be encouraged. According to this outlook, the play is the style and the traditional style, no matter how imaginative in itself it is, is to be followed literally and unquestioningly. It can easily be pointed out that there have been really no additions to the accepted canon of the plays since the rise of the Japanese puppet theatre and the Kabuki at about the beginning of the seventeenth century. According to this view, the books of the Noh are closed yet long live the books according to the tradition in which they were first deposited! This reading of history erects in the domain of art a closed state comparable to the conception of the closed society as described by sociology. But be it ever remembered, Benkei and his lord got past the barrier.

The strong arguments supporting this position nevertheless leave a modern thinker with latent dissatisfaction. Such absolutism ill accords with our conceptions of a world in continual evolution. The rapid turn towards cosmopolitanism in both society and the arts accelerated to so pronounced a degree even within the present generation suggests another and less drastic outlook. We are loath to witness Japan as an insular culture burying her treasures without setting them out to loan. The relatively recent reception of other Japanese arts by the world suggests a totally different course. Japanese architecture, sculpture, painting, and the decorative arts today enjoy world currency to a remarkable degree. Why not also the most synthetic and by no means the least powerful of Japanese arts, the theatrical? There is something unwieldy in the Kabuki. It flies heavily, pelican-wise. The Noh is swallow-like and may in the end girdle the world on a swifter wing. It has already gained impressive advocates and enlisted the minds of superior scholars and dilettantes, both of the East and West. A still larger reading public and a new theatrical audience may shortly be found. Our culture is opening up our heritage from past centuries with surprising success. History offers possible analogies, one of which cannot easily be overlooked.

At approximately the time when growth was arrested in

the Noh, or early in the seventeenth century, another theatrical form of local origin was about to wing its way over all Europe though at that time the barriers of communication denied a flight around the world. The *comedia dell' arte* bore an Italian name ; seldom has a type of art been so strongly marked by the place of its birth. Its characters came from Naples, Bergamo, Venice, Milan and several ancient cities of the Italian peninsula. It developed primarily as a theatrical, certainly not as a literary, art, which in itself might have been supposed to have discouraged its wider provenance. Insofar as it relied on language, its speech tended to the broadest use of dialect. All these delimiting features notwithstanding, within a generation its vogue swept through virtually all nations of the Western world, large and small, from Spain to Sweden and from England to Russia. Can it be that in our twentieth-century perspectives, so much ampler than those of the seventeenth century, the Noh will correspond to the *comedia dell' arte* and the world to Europe ? The suggestion is possibly over-sanguine and yet the analogy may have elements of truth not cavalierly to be dismissed.

Our world grows apace and nothing in it at so rapid a rate as our communications. Since the developments in modern art and in our spiritual life are almost certain to be rapid and astonishing, even the seemingly impossible cannot well be lightly regarded. The claims of the Noh to the serious attention of the modern aesthetic world are certainly strong. Here is undeniably a pinnacle in both poetic and theatrical achievement long overlooked. The Noh is now entering into the consciousness of the modern world. One can hardly believe that it can so enter without consequences impossible to predict with certainty but difficult to conceive as of minor importance. Even if one dismisses a clear prophecy or a specific prognostication, this quarter of the horizon is worth watching to note what forms emerge.

It may even be profitable to speculate regarding another great area of the world that is neither East nor West, namely, Africa. Today Africa possesses arts of immense theatrical potency but really no theatre. What types of theatre, it may be asked, will attract Africans in aiding them to create a theatre of their own ? The answer is in part, no doubt, not one type but several. Yet the essential humanity of the Noh theatre, its remarkable conjunction and harmonizing of primitivism and sophistication, myth and refined artistry, simplicity and intricacy, may well please African taste and gratify African imagination. One can easily imagine Zeami as more attractive to Africans than, say, Molière, Ibsen, Brecht, Pirandello, or Shaw. If concerning the entire future of the Noh throughout the world one conclusion is sure, it is that the unexpected is to be expected, whatever this reality may be. In the case of the Noh reflective thinkers best acquainted with it will presumably best trust it to leave a deep impression on men's minds. With confidence they may repeat Emily Dickinson's aphoristic words: "trust in the unexpected." The Noh is not a brittle, rigid, dry and unnegotiable commodity, a book from the past enclosed in jewelled clasps. It is rapidly becoming an open book to the worldof imaginatively thinking men. Even now its wider influences seem just beginning to be felt. Classical in more senses of the word than one though it may be, like all valid art, it is not ancient but young. Despite what was said in other connections in the first words of this chapter, the time is actually not imaginable when the Noh will become old.

Index

Index

Index

346

Index